CONVICT
WOMEN

Kay Daniels

ALLEN & UNWIN

First published in 1998 by
Allen & Unwin Pty Ltd
9 Atchison Street, St Leonards 1590 Australia
Phone: (61 2) 8425 0100
Fax: (61 2) 9906 2218
E-mail: frontdesk@allen-unwin.com.au
Web: http://www.allen-unwin.com.au

National Library of Australia
Cataloguing-in-Publication entry:

Daniels, Kay, 1941–   .
Convict women: rough culture and reformation.

Includes index.
ISBN 1 86448 677 5.

1. Women convicts—Australia. 2. Women convicts—
Australia—Social aspects—History. 3. Women convicts—
Australia—Social conditions. 4. Australia—Social conditions—
1788–1851. I. Title.

364.3740994

Set in 11/13pt Bembo by DOCUPRO, Sydney

Printed by South Wind Productions, Singapore

10 9 8 7 6 5 4 3

CONTENTS

————————————

ACKNOWLEDGEMENTS

M y interest in convict women and research in the area began while I was teaching at the University of Tasmania, but this book has been written since I joined the Australian Public Service. While I have missed the advantages an academic environment provides—not least the time and the advice of colleagues—there are benefits for a historian in gaining a familiarity with the complexities of government policy making and administration and these have, I trust, been of value here.

Convict Women has taken a long time to write and I am grateful to my publishers for their patience; in particular I thank John Iremonger for his encouragement and Colette Vella for her assistance. I am grateful to Venetia Somerset, who has been both a demanding and a sympathetic editor. My thanks also go to Annie Bickford and Sharon Sullivan who have discussed ideas about heritage with me; to Sylvia Carr and Jane Hyden who helped me locate information about the Rajah quilt; and to past students who have shared an enthusiasm for Tasmanian history, especially Audrey Hudspeth, Lindy Scripps and Tony Rayner, whose work in the area of public history I have drawn on here, and Kim Pearce, who helped me track down the elusive Dr Irvine. I owe a particular debt of gratitude to the

Archives Office of Tasmania and the Archivist, Ian Pearce. Ian and Vicki Pearce and Liz Fell have been generous friends and I thank them for their support. My special thanks goes to Mary Murnane who believed that I could write this book and encouraged me to think so too.

Convict Women is dedicated to my mother, Jean Daniels.

KAY DANIELS
CANBERRA

INTRODUCTION

This book is an attempt to retrieve and wrest some meaning from fragmentary and unsatisfactory records of past lives and places. It is not an analysis of the quantifiable data available in convict records nor the application of feminist theory to a body of information about female convicts. It is concerned with the social, cultural and economic world convict women inhabited and their experiences of that world. Just as a singular phrase used about routine everyday events alerts us to a cultural difference between groups of people, in history a single act or event can reveal an essential element in a relationship or in perceptions—or between our time and past time. The book moves, therefore, between the minor narratives that make up the experiences of individual women and an interpretation of the broader, changing landscape of convictism and its management.

Central to the argument is the idea that the interaction between policy and administration on the one hand and the actions and experience of convict women on the other was complex and significant. The behaviour of convict women, their responses to assignment and incarceration, all posed problems to which government and administration were forced to respond; they provided a context within which the agenda of reform was pursued.

Over the period of transportation the experience of convict women was different from that of convict men, and their management was reshaped in distinct ways. Influencing that reshaping were changing and gender-based perceptions of respectability (and of what it was to be feminine) and the ongoing debate, in Britain and Australia, about criminality and punishment. Both had particular, intersecting resonances for female convicts, for whom incarceration became the common experience and who were subject, to a greater extent than male convicts, to a regime which increasingly focused on individual reformation. Although they were never subject to the same degree of physical pain inflicted on male convicts, the shift from punishments intended to hurt and humiliate to discipline designed to reform was of great consequence for convict women. Moreover, their reformation was thought to be especially difficult, in part because higher standards were expected of them but also because the path to reformation seemed so uncertain. Confidence in the capacity of institutionalised discipline to reform the individual was weaker in the penal settlements than in Britain, and the argument for assignment (in various forms) and marriage as an alternative to incarceration continued to be persuasive. Furthermore, although establishments holding convict women were rearranged in accordance with the new prescriptions, their success as places of reform was not striking, and characteristics of the older factories continued to be clearly discernible in the new.

Convict women's experiences took place within this environment, but were not determined solely by these forces. This book explores the ways that female convicts, whose lives were dominated by two unequal relationships—with the state and with men—helped to shape the culture in which they lived. To have influence at the margins often serves only to demonstrate ultimate powerlessness, and I am not suggesting that convict women created their own world. But they did attempt to reshape the world that was offered to them, in the female factories and when assigned, and it is that contested space and the impact of their actions to which I have paid attention.

The relationships between convict women and the state (in the shape of the penal administration) are central to this exploration and take a number of forms. The opportunities male convicts gained through transportation and the convict system were not to the same extent available to women. At best, male convicts were able to establish themselves in the marketplace, their labour valued and rewarded, even before they received their freedom. The emphasis on female convicts as sexual partners, wives or mothers rather than as workers, and the slender chance they had for achieving independence distinguished them from their male counterparts. The need for a protector (the government or an individual) rather than the opportunity for independence characterised the female convict experience and marked out its difference from that of the male convict. If the ambitions of convict women and convict men converged it was not around employment (which offered fewer opportunities and in many ways replicated for women the restraints they experienced within the convict system) but around the home: the possibility of family life, of children, of 'doing better' than in Britain. This was their most tangible opportunity. At the same time family life was not built on equality between the sexes, and domestic inequality was re-inforced by the inequities of the law and the economy. As convicts, women had learned to deal with the state and, on occasion, to use its (public) patriarchal authority to advantage in their (private) domestic lives. There is irony in this and that will be explored. Consigned to domestic patriarchy—hidden, unregulated, often brutal, but still the most likely chance of happiness and opportunity—women continued to experience the intimate but uneven interventions of the state in their lives.

The book begins with the story of one convict woman, Maria Lord, whose history introduces many of the themes examined later. The next two chapters provide a framework for the rest of the book by examining the way historians have written about convict women (Chapter 2) and by giving a context (Chapter 3) to the more intensive discussion of convict experience that is the subject of following chapters. Both chapters pay particular attention to the work of other historians and their contributions to the major questions about convicts which have so far dominated the debate. Many of these questions are taken up in later chapters through an examination of the experience of convict women within the changing context of their management.

While a major focus of these chapters is on the experience of convict women themselves, I have been particularly concerned to place this in a historical framework, to try to suggest how and why that experience changed (or remained the same) and to move away from the idea that the key relationships of convictism were static and can be analysed without reference to period or place. Where possible I have also tried to use this study to illuminate the older questions asked by historians about female convicts, without being trapped by them. While deciding, for instance, whether convicts were 'good' or 'bad' women seems to be a fruitless enterprise for a historian, looking at why women were commonly thought to be bad or to be prostitutes and at whether convict women so named faced a future different from those of other women is relevant to the female convict experience. Relevant too are questions about the harshness of their lives as assigned servants and inmates of institutions, whether female convicts were passive victims of convictism, whether they had only a 'degraded' future in the penal settlements, and whether their opportunities were more circumscribed than those of men. Two contemporary views of convict women have influenced much historical analysis. The view of many observers that all convict women were whores— immoral, degraded, 'worse than the men'—underpinned the report of the Molesworth Committee and early historical writing about convict women. A second contemporary view has become influential in more recent historical writing: that while the majority of convict women 'reformed' and became ordinary wives and mothers, some were 'incorrigible' and remained of 'bad character'—a stereotype of the 'incorrigible' woman thus replacing that of the 'whore'. I suggest here that many convict women who were so designated at various times (on board ship, in the factories, while assigned) came to live ordinary lives. Moreover, not all colonial observers (or penal administrators) were insensitive to these moral subtleties and to the fact that circumstance rather than character was a powerful factor in determining the fate of convict women in the new environment.

I have not looked in detail at the experience of convict women before they arrived in Australia, although there is some discussion of the debate about origins and the voyage out. The book concentrates on major issues that relate to their experience after arrival during assignment, confinement and release. Particular attention is paid to Van Diemen's Land because of its importance in the history of convict women in the nineteenth century, the richness of its records, and its relative neglect. Of particular significance is the inquiry into female convict discipline established by Sir John Franklin, Lieutenant-Governor, and carried out in Van Diemen's Land between 1841 and 1843. This is not only a remarkable source of information about convict women but a strongly argued response to the ideas put forward in the Molesworth Report and to the views on assignment and reformation which underpinned the shift to the probation system. The inquiry's findings were too controversial and politically inconvenient to be published, but they show that by the 1840s, at least in Van Diemen's Land, colonial officials had developed a more complex understanding of the consequences of transportation for women than other reports suggest.

Most of the book deals with experiences and ideas. An epilogue (Chapter 10) looks at the material remains of female convict society.

1

MARIA LORD

Maria Lord was a convict woman who was sent to New South Wales in the early period before Macquarie became governor. Her shipboard companions were among the first women to be housed in the Female Factory at Parramatta and she was said to have been chosen there to become the mistress of an officer. She arrived in Hobart at a time when there were very few female convicts in the settlement, became one of its richest and most successful women and lived through the whole period of direct transportation to Van Diemen's Land, dying just after its cessation in 1856.

My first glimpse of Maria Lord in the historical records was as an early entrepreneur, a 'Vandemonian Mary Reibey', who had married a trader, a rich man in his own right, and had gone on to manage the business.[1] A fleeting reference in *Historical Records of Australia* added another dimension. She was an 'infamous' convict woman who, unlike Mrs Reibey, was not reclaimed for respectability nor given ultimate national recognition on the face on an Australian banknote. Notoriety exists in the eye of the beholder, and the beholder in this case was William Bligh: the description was one abusive phrase among many, and directed at her husband Edward rather than at Maria herself.[2] Was this by itself so damning? More research revealed a complex story. Mrs Lord was the mother of a large family, accepted in Hobart's best society, but her marriage did not last and Edward Lord's repudiation of her was highly public. She continued independently in business and announced her intention to provide for herself and those of her children not removed from her by her husband.

The female entrepreneur, the convict whore, the happy family woman and the abandoned wife represent four major narratives in the debate about the nature and fate of women in colonial society. Too much time has been spent choosing between them. Maria Lord's story demonstrates that not all women were destined for the single fate suggested by these stark categories.

What we know about Maria Lord is so little that it would be rash to call what follows biography. There are no diaries or personal letters. No text reveals her inner life or her daily experiences. There is no portrait or sketch. What is known about the first twenty years of her life fills half a page, and little more is known about the last thirty. The press provides some information in the form of advertisements, notices and shipping lists. Her own writing consists of copies of business letters, signatures on receipts and on some documents which mark public rites of passage—marriage, birth. Because she was a convict and came before the law we might expect those records to disclose most, even if from an impersonal and partial perspective. In her case, however, the criminal record of her early life is scant, and when the intimate details of her personal life came before the courts and the press in a most unusual way, what is remarkable about the occasion is the deliberate silence of the public record. There is, however, a certain appropriateness about the absence of documentary evidence. One of the more bizarre acts of her husband, Edward Lord, was to burn the archives of Van Diemen's Land on the death of the man he succeeded for a short time—Lieutenant-Governor Collins.

This historical invisibility Maria Lord shares with other convict women. The prominence of her husband allows us to reconstruct much more of her life than would have been possible had he been less important. If we begin with the story of Mrs Lord, successful entrepreneur, 1820 is an appropriate starting point. This is the height of her economic power and influence in Van Diemen's Land and the best documented period in the history of the Lord enterprise. In 1820 Edward Lord, by now said to be the richest man in Van Diemen's Land, had gone to England to pursue another land grant from Lord Bathurst and to challenge Macquarie's assertion that he was 'vindictive and implacable', leaving Maria in charge of the business.[3] During 1819–20 Maria's dealings attracted the attention of the colonial authorities, and she was accused of attempting to create a monopoly in wheat and meat. She was said to be trying to inflate prices and use her influence over other large suppliers to ensure that they did the same. To Commissioner Bigge she was described as 'the person possessing the greatest local influence in the colony', with her control extending to over a third of the local resources of the island. It was anticipated that within a year the commissariat stores would be 'at the mercy of Mrs Lord and one or two others'.[4]

Mrs Lord's monopoly did not stop at wheat and meat. In the same year, 1820, she was said to share with Kemp & Co. almost total control over the best-quality rum in Van Diemen's Land. She was also in business with partners other than her husband. She and her brother John Riseley, who had come out as a free settler in the previous year, acquired at that time eighteen merino rams, more than any other buyer in the colony.[5] When Bigge came to Hobart, regardless of the repute in which he held her, he stayed in Mrs Lord's house in Macquarie Street. He was, she wrote, 'to be accommodated with my House, which has been put in a state for his reception'.[6] It was the best house in town and the setting for some of its grand balls and dinners. Maria, as usual, made a good profit from the arrangement.

Whether we see her at this time as one of the most powerful people in Van Diemen's Land or as the wife of its richest man, Maria Lord's success in the fifteen years since her arrival was remarkable.

Maria's husband, Edward Lord, was born in Pembroke, Wales, on 15 June 1781.[7] His father had been mayor of the town and his mother was the daughter of Lieutenant-General John Owen, brother of Sir William Owen, fourth baronet, of Orielton. He was also connected to the Barlows of Lawrenny, another wealthy Pembrokeshire family. His elder brother inherited the Orielton estate, took the name Sir John Owen and went on to serve as a Member of the House of Commons for over fifty years. Edward joined the Royal Marines as a second lieutenant, accompanied Lieutenant-Colonel David Collins to the aborted settlement at Port Phillip and subsequently to Van Diemen's Land in February 1804 when Collins took over from Lieutenant Bowen at the Derwent. There he was quick to see the opportunities the new settlement offered. His family connections (publicly proclaimed in the names he gave to his two substantial colonial properties) and his colonial contacts were both to serve him well.

In Van Diemen's Land, with his friend Adolorius Humphrey, a mineralogist, Lord quickly got into the meat trade.[8] The form their infant enterprise took—providing the kangaroo carcasses which sustained the hungry settlers—was an indication of the primitive and desperate state of the camp at Hobart Town in its first years. Acquiring five dogs for £25, they provided (according to Humphrey) 1000 pounds of kangaroo meat to the settlement a week at sixpence a pound, as well as selling the skins for shoe leather. Kangaroo formed an essential part of the diet of the settlement. The Revd Robert Knopwood recorded its first killing 'by any of the gentlemen in the camp' on 13 March 1804, and thereafter (when not listing his own bag of quail, ducks, pigeons, black swans, 'horks', and 'emews') records occasions when he ventured out with Mr Lord and his 'doggs' after kangaroo or sent his servant and his own dogs out for the same. Giving evidence before a committee of the House of Commons in 1812, Lord testified to the hardship of the early years: 'During eight or nine years we entirely depended on the woods. We had 2lbs. of biscuit weekly for thirteen months ... I have often myself been glad to go to bed for want of bread.'[9] Lord bought and sold flour and livestock, and like his fellow officers in the New South Wales Corps, bought and smuggled rum. While he was involved in supplying the resource-starved settlement with goods he began to build up extensive landholdings stocked with cattle and sheep.

He and Humphrey together built a small house, the first in Hobart. Knopwood dined there with him for the first time on 19 June 1804. Building at the settlement was slow and haphazard, and much of what was built was insubstantial. The wattle-and-daub cottage consisted of four rooms, one of which accommodated Humphrey and his equipment, one Lieutenant Lord, and a third was lent to fellow officer William Sladden and his wife. As John West said, 'That it was the first, constituted its chief claim to distinction'. An early drawing of the house exists and a sketch of Hobart at this time shows it as 'Sladden's cottage'.[10]

After a year in the southern settlement Lord asked for sick leave to return to England. He and Humphrey left Hobart on 4 March 1805 on the return trip to Sydney of the *Sophia*, which had arrived in the estuary a month before with a small group of female convicts on board, but instead of going to England he spent six months in New South Wales, returning to Van Diemen's Land on the *Sydney* on 28 November.[11] He brought back with him some cattle and sheep, including a gift from Governor King—a ram 'near the Spanish breed', probably from the flock of the man with whom he has been compared, John Macarthur. Promoted to first lieutenant at the end of the year, early in 1806 he received his first land grant (apart from the land on which he built his house): 100 acres. By late 1806 he was the colony's largest stock-owner and the second most senior officer in the settlement.[12]

The 1805 trip was auspicious for more than the gift of the merino. John Pascoe Fawkner describes the subsequent arrival in Hobart of Lord's 'Paramour', 'notorious Maria Risley of

Sydney', bringing with her a quantity of trading goods for what became her shop.[13] According to Fawkner she quickly became involved in the rum trade, making huge profits. Allegations about Lord's involvement were made but never substantiated (though Knopwood recorded in his diary in 1807 that Lieutenant Lord had landed a cask of spirits without a permit—'His men came past my house with it in a barrow', he wrote).[14] One of Lord's accusers was the splenetic Governor Bligh, who alleged that he traded through his wife while he was still an officer and barred from commercial dealings. If he did, and it seems certain that it was so, he followed the pattern established by some of his fellow officers in Sydney who used assigned convicts as middlemen in their trading ventures.

For this part of Maria Risley's (or Riseley) career we are dependent on hearsay, and Maria herself formally dated her business activities from 1813 (when they were clearly legal), not 1805.[15]

When Collins died in 1810 Lord took over the control of the settlement until relieved by Captain Murray. It was he who burnt the records of the colony and organised the elaborate and expensive funeral for his dead commander. He went to England in 1812 and, disappointed when he failed to be appointed lieutenant-governor, he resigned his commission. Before this he had received land grants of about 600 acres. Through the influence of his brother, Sir John Owen MP, he received a further grant of 3000 acres, half of it in New South Wales, and he returned to Van Diemen's Land in March 1813 with £30 000 worth of goods on his own ship, the *James Hay*. Lord's fully fledged and legitimate entry into trading began at that time and coincided with the opening of the ports of Hobart and Port Dalrymple to general trading and to trade in spirits. Maria, it seems, was his partner in 'the shop'—the trading establishment which grew so greatly after 1813.[16]

How involved was Maria Lord in the Lord enterprise? One must assume that she played an active enough role during Lord's presence in the colony for him to place quite happily with her the entire running of his Van Diemen's Land ventures during his absences, which from 1819 became longer and more frequent. Advertisements in the *Hobart Town Gazette* in 1818 when Edward Lord was in Van Diemen's Land carried her name. On one occasion during that period she advertised for sawyers, labourers and seamen to join the brig *Jupiter* on a trip to the Gordon River, in pursuit, no doubt, of Huon pine. When he was absent in 1819–20 she acted as his agent. On Christmas Day 1819 it was Mrs Lord's festive greeting which appeared in the *Gazette*: 'Mrs Lord calls upon the numerous Persons who stand indebted to her, as Agent to Edward Lord, Esq, to come forward and settle their respective Accounts at the close of the present Month and Year.'

She was always very involved in the running of the store in Hobart. It was usually referred to as her store. Whether Lord was in Hobart or not, notes for goods went to his wife. When Lieutenant-Governor Davey wanted a pound of green paint or a quantity of salt the note went to Mrs Lord, as did this note from his daughter: 'Miss Davey will thank Mrs Lord to send her by the bearer one ounce of white bugles [beads].'[17] On Christmas Day 1814 William Morgan sent an order from Hollow Tree: 'Mrs Lord please to let the Blackman Cazzar have two Gallons of Rum for me and place the same on my account.'[18] Knopwood placed his orders for tea, sugar, butter, tobacco and gallons of rum with Mrs Lord and, when in Bagdad in March 1814 he saw a party going to Port Dalrymple with a cartload of goods, he identified them as hers.[19] Each of these last references came from a year when Maria was not engaged in child-bearing, although in 1812, with a newborn baby and Edward in England, she seems to have been in charge of the business.

It is tempting to characterise Maria as the shopkeeper, the partner who stays at home and minds the business, and Edward as the peripatetic adventurer, constantly adding to his empire, fighting rivals both in the marketplace and in the courts. He travelled to England in 1812 and stayed there some months, again during 1819 and 1822 returning only briefly between October 1824 and early January 1825. Although he returned to Van Diemen's Land three more times in 1827, 1838 and 1846, from May 1822 he was a visitor to the colony rather than a resident. While he was in Van Diemen's Land he visited Sydney, sometimes for lengthy periods, travelled to Port Dalrymple and took frequent short sea voyages to relieve his asthma.[20]

No serious attention has been paid to his wife's role in the accumulation of the wealth of 'the richest man in Van Diemen's Land'. The assumption usually made is that the business brain behind the building of the Lord enterprise is that of the well-connected Welsh lieutenant and not that of the convict woman. Mable Hookey, for instance, described Maria Lord this way:

> Mrs Lord, an unlettered woman, was left behind [when Lord returned to Britain] though as the settlement was well aware, she and the Lt were legally married. She opened a store and traded with the whalers that came to the port of Hobart Town. She could not read or write but employed a sort of sign language in keeping her accounts—a circle represented a cheese and so on.[21]

A closer look at the period when Maria was creating her monopolies within the Van Diemen's Land economy does not suggest that she was either illiterate or that she was merely 'minding the shop' while her entrepreneur husband initiated bolder ventures.

Her letters of this period are those of an astute woman, 'assiduous in Business' as she described herself later; a woman, too, with broader ideas about the economic development of the colony.[22] They reveal that she was acutely aware of what later came to be seen as the central problem in the infant economies of the penal settlements. In the absence of an export staple, the large sums of money which flooded out to pay for goods imported by overseas traders were not balanced by export earnings. What Hainsworth said of New South Wales in the early period was true of Van Diemen's Land: the major export of the new colony was not goods but money.[23] In these letters Maria Lord comments on the effect on trade of the numbers of British ships which arrive in the colony 'laden with merchandise', glutting the market and pulling down profits. The key issue, she suggests, is the shortage of money which results from the repatriation of profits and cash to Britain with the departure of each of these trading ships. Local men of property, such as her husband, have wealth but not money. As she says of Edward, 'extensive as his property here is the unconvertible shape of the great bulk, together with the uncertainty of Markets for produce, and the little Money on the Island, frequently leave us with little more Cash than local demand requires'.[24] Elsewhere she comments on how much can be done with money in the colony, what 'the opportunity [is] of turning it here'.[25]

While the Lord enterprise was largely based on selling imported goods and on their internal trade in meat and grain, like his New South Wales counterparts Edward Lord ventured early into the export trade, with dealings in timber, seal skins and whale oil. The search for an export staple which dominated the early economic history of the elder colony was simplified in Van Diemen's Land because in the early days export in Hobart terms included the Sydney market, to which the Lords sent meat and grain. Maria had a good eye for trading opportunities. Early in 1820 she suggested that her husband's English associates should not send out European goods for some time, as 'everybody here is a dealer now'. At the same time she advised the firm's Calcutta connections that there would always be a market for staples of good quality at good prices: rum, tea, and especially sugar from India. Later she sent a message to Lord that there was a market available for all materials and goods appropriate for use by convicts and in convict works. Of the colony she comments: 'the Town is improving fast [and the settlement] likely to be of consequence'; wool in particular is, she suggests, of growing importance (this just before her acquisition, with her brother, of the merinos).[26]

Maria's role in building up particularly the trading side of the business, in putting to use the capital and the land, was quite crucial in the acquisition of wealth. Here she seems to have been both careful and ruthless. If Maria Lord emerges as an astute business person who can converse on the shape of the market or the implications of the Bigge Report, Edward appears more erratic, less organised, more rash in his behaviour. Fawkner, who regarded Maria as shrewd, described Edward as a gambler who lost much of the money she made for them both.[27] In his words,

> she was a worldly wise woman and set herself to make a home, and to provide means for herself, her children and her master. She foresaw that much money was to be made and how. She by the credit of her master, and her own tact and shrewdness obtained a quantity of goods and proceeded with these under her own control to Hobart Town set up a shop almost the first there, and continued for years trading successfully. He, rambling about and fooling away the money she made for the family.

The first of the business letters written in late August 1819 to Lord's New South Wales business associates shows Maria's attempts to untangle the mess left by his departure from Sydney a month earlier, when he left no records or accounts of what he took to Sydney with him or of the sales he made there.[28] (Maria's last child, Emma, was born just a month after this letter, in late September.)

Lord's interest in trading and shopkeeping was intermittent. His wife remained a trader throughout her career. After her marriage to Lord broke up in 1824 she continued her business ventures, doing what she did very well, though now on a smaller scale: she set up in Hobart a store which dealt in imported provisions—wines and spirits, pickles and cheeses, 'gowns of the newest fashions', muslins, flowers and feathers. The store also contained a butcher's shop in which she bought meat and accepted meat as payment for other goods. In 1829 she thanked her friends and 'the Public' for the kind assistance they had given her in her 'Endeavours to obtain a future support for herself and her Children' and she pointed out that for the last sixteen years the whole colony had known her for her 'integrity and assiduity in Business'. This dating locates the origins of the Lords' legitimate trading ventures in 1813, the time of Edward's return on the *James Hay*. Twenty years on from the 1829 announcement Maria Lord was still involved in trading. Police reports mention a theft at the store owned by her in Bothwell, the town in which she died.[29]

Edward was an adventurer, whose great successes lay in two areas: his ability, particularly through his family connections and also through contacts with brother officers, to get land grants (and the free labour to work them). Just as important was his ability to raise capital. In pursuit of the latter he entered into a tangled web of financial deals and partnerships and was frequently, and often unsuccessfully, engaged in litigation. While he accumulated vast wealth and land, he lost much of it, and the property he retained was heavily mortgaged. At the time at which he was said to be the richest man in the colony, around 1821, he owned 35 000 acres, 13 000 head of sheep and cattle, three ships, warehouses, and a number of other properties, including the house in Macquarie Street, Hobart, built by his friend John Ingle and known as Ingle Hall. He also owned two large estates, Lawrenny on the Clyde and Orielton Park, on which he had built a 35-room mansion. His holdings grew rapidly in this period, with Maria in charge and Edward abroad, and much of this growth seems to have been due to her.[30]

Regardless of her skill and acumen, it was Edward who could get land and Edward who could raise capital. Even in his earliest ventures this was crucial. The house he built in 1805 cost the not insubstantial sum of £50 and also depended, as Humphrey said, on 'the help we have had', which consisted of an acre of town land, nails, locks, glass, paint, a fire stove, pitch and tar for the roof, and, not the least, 'men to help'—all from the Governor.[31] Humphrey himself regarded the capital cost as great, particularly given the assistance they had, but pointed out that they had already been offered money for the house and within a year's time it would be worth five times what they had spent. Lord's family connections gave him access to much greater sums of money and much larger grants, thus privileging him above most other men. In these activities women were restricted in their dealings. It has been suggested that, as the raising of capital became more important in colonial business, women were increasingly restrained in the roles they could play in the economy. Clearly Maria Lord was hampered in these ways, as most women were even in the earliest days of the settlements, when access to cash, land and labour made vast fortunes.

Whatever responsibility Maria had for the growth of her husband's fortune, historians have been more concerned with Edward Lord than with his wife. Lloyd Robson follows Manning Clark in seeing Lord as one of the 'wolves' who brought ruin to the small settlers in the country districts of Van Diemen's Land. In the paragraph in which Robson lists Lord's good connections, his family's association with Lord Bathurst, his colonial mansion, his vast landholdings, he also mentions 'Maria Risley, his mistress, transported evidently in 1804 for stealing in a dwelling house'.[32] Robson is no more sympathetic to Lord than the land commissioners he quotes:

> Edward Lord they saw as one of the greatest destroyers of the prosperity of the colony because by corruption he secured lucrative tenders for meat and wheat for the commissariat, and being in possession of some 30,000 acres he kept it only as stock runs, occupied by ruffians of storekeepers under no control, galloping after wild cattle in every direction.[33]

This 'crypto-magnate', as Robson calls him, the 'ruthless' Edward Lord, epitomises for him the rapaciousness and dishonesty of many of the early landowners. But there is another inference: among all Lord's possessions (his name, his wealth, his land, his houses), the one possession not to be envied was his wife.

For those who wish to see Lord more sympathetically, the figure of Maria presents some difficulty. E. R. Henry has been Edward Lord's most appreciative biographer, and his article is the most substantial work on him. There he shows Lord as an entrepreneur, 'the John Macarthur of Van Diemen's Land', concluding:

> There is no doubt that with his astuteness, determination and ability to think and act in a big way, he had played a notable part in the development of Van Diemen's Land in the first 20 years. He also had the benefit of ample convict labour and freely available capital and knowing the right people in the right places he was able to exploit all these advantages with benefit to both himself and the settlement which in its first years seemed doomed to failure.[34]

On the other hand, while emphasising Edward Lord's role in building the economy and in accumulating wealth, Henry underplays Maria's role (although he does quote Bligh's comment that through her Lord traded contrary to regulations). Robson, too, only mentions her economic activities briefly: he refers to the attempt of 'Edward Lord's wife Maria' to create at one time a 'complete monopoly in wheat'.[35]

If Edward Lord is to be remembered for his part in crushing the small settlers, Maria Lord's major contribution to this process should not be forgotten. Yet the part she played has only been taken seriously by historians looking specifically at the role of women. Her role as an entrepreneur comes out, for instance, in Diane Snowden's thesis on women and work in Van Diemen's Land, where Maria Lord appears as one of the most successful of a number of female entrepreneurs active in the first twenty years of the new colony.[36]

In fact neither Maria nor Edward Lord have received much attention in the major histories of Australia or Tasmania, although both were substantial and significant figures in the first two decades of European settlement in Van Diemen's Land. While it is true to say that Edward Lord has usually been looked at alone, the focus has also moved to his wife when the aim has been to illuminate something about Edward himself. At its most general, the 'something' that Maria tells us about Edward is that he is 'a man of his time'—an officer who took a convict mistress. Marriage did not always follow, however, as it did in Lord's case after he obtained a pardon for her from Lieutenant-Colonel Foveaux in 1808. More precisely, references to Maria are used as a way of denigrating Lord. The knowledge of his wife's convict past was exploited in the same way by Lord's contemporaries. The person who demonstrates this well is Bligh. He had no liking for Lord, who had backed the rebels against him in New South Wales (and with whom Lord had much in common); Lord also opposed Bligh in Van Diemen's Land. When Bligh called Maria 'a Convict Woman of infamous character', his words need to be read in the context of his relationship with Lord rather than as an accurate account of Maria's virtue.

Bligh and the historians who echoed him were not alone in seeing Maria Lord, at more than one time in her career, as no more than a convict whore.

Born Maria Risley in 1780, she was sentenced at the Surrey assizes in August 1802 to seven years' transportation for stealing from a dwelling house. She arrived in New South Wales on the *Experiment* in June 1804. Women from this ship were among the first to be accommodated in the two rooms above the prison at Parramatta which became the Female Factory. Some were indented, others worked on manufacturing cloth. Some of her shipboard companions from that voyage arrived in Van Diemen's Land on the *Sophia* on 5 February 1805, a matter which must have caused her some embarrassment. Her own journey to Van Diemen's Land is undocumented, and the first mention of her in Hobart Town is in Knopwood's diary entry for Sunday, 22 December 1805: 'Lt. Lord drank tea with me and his friend.' In January the three spent the day together, going by boat to Risdon and dining there. Knopwood continued to see Lord regularly but seldom mentions Maria. On those few occasions (before her marriage) he refers to her in the same discreet way.[37]

Fawkner's story suggests that Maria returned from New South Wales with Edward Lord on the *Sydney* on 28 November 1805 or came separately before him. Three days before their meeting with Knopwood there is a reference in the Tasmanian public records to the inoculation of a child,

Caroline Maria Risaley, who is undoubtedly hers. And almost exactly nine months after Lord's return to Hobart Town, Maria's second daughter was born (26 August 1806). This time the child was Edward's, but it did not live. In May 1823 at the age of seventeen Maria's oldest child, Caroline, married Hobart solicitor Frederic Dawes, by special licence.[38] By not publishing the banns Caroline's name was concealed. She was, however, always known as Miss Lord and treated as Edward's child, although that was not the case. Edward Lord was in New South Wales only between April and October 1805, sailing there on the return voyage of the *Sophia*, which brought from Sydney many of the women of the *Experiment*. Caroline's birth is recorded in the New South Wales records as 25 June 1805, a year and a day after Maria arrived at Port Jackson. She is recorded as the daughter of John Thompson and Maria Risley and her name is given as Carolina Mary Risley.[39]

Given that evidence, it is likely that John Pascoe Fawkner's version of their meeting is accurate in outline, if not without embellishment. He described the impetuous young officer setting out for Sydney with his friend Adolorius Humphrey, both with the intention of 'finding wives'. Lord, he said, found his companion at the Female Factory at Parramatta. Chosen by Lord from a parade of all the women, Maria Risley was asked if she would go with him to Van Diemen's Land, to which she—'learning he was an Officer'—agreed: 'She was at once let out, and he took possession of her, as truly a slave to do his behests, or suffer for neglect or refusal.'[40] Maria was either pregnant at the time or had recently given birth; pregnant convict women were confined in the factory and Maria's pregnancy may have been the reason she did not accompany her shipmates from the *Experiment* on their voyage to Hobart earlier in the year. Whatever the story of Maria's previous relationships and Caroline's paternity, the records do not show her as being treated differently from Edward's other children during his lifetime.

Maria was, it seems, assigned to Edward Lord as his convict servant. She kept this status until he obtained her pardon in

1808 and married her on 8 October of that year. She had by
then served six of her seven years' sentence. One of the few
occasions when she is mentioned in Knopwood's diary before
their marriage was New Year's Day 1808, when Knopwood,
having taken some wine with the Lieutenant-Governor and
Lieutenant Lord, records going to Lord's and naming his child.
On 10 January he performed Divine Service, 'churched' 'Lt
Lord's friend', and dined with them in the afternoon. Later in
the month he records that he dined with Lt Lord and 'X'tianed
the little girl'.[41] Maria, still a convict and unmarried, is invisible
in these records, though the ceremonies have the trappings of
legitimacy.

Maria Lord's two eldest daughters were illegitimate and
fathered by different men. Whatever chance Edward had of
disguising her status (had he wished to do so) would most
likely have been undermined by the coincidence that the first
boatload of convict women who came to Hobart bore some
of her shipmates from the *Experiment*. Two of those women
were subsequently charged with offences against Edward Lord's
friends, one for stealing from Mr Humphrey and another for
abusing Mr Ingle and striking his wife.[42] Edward Lord is said
to have had a woman convict flogged for insulting his wife.[43]

There is an impression given in much of the writing about
women in the early colonial period that there are two sorts of
women. Some, through the circumstances of British society,
had been led into crime, but, confronted by the opportunities
presented in the colonies, became good and virtuous women,
the founding mothers. Others, a minority, were incorrigible.
They became the 'damned whores' who have been seen as
typical of all women. Had the historical record ceased for Maria
Lord with her marriage and the birth of her seven children,
she could have been remembered as one of those women who
'reformed'—a founding mother in the new colony. Instead,
the records document her return, in 1824, to 'ill-repute' and
thus she remains in the historical narrative as the mistress she
was when she entered it.

The occasion which served to confirm Maria's earlier status was the case which Edward Lord brought against Charles Rowcroft for 'criminal conversation' with his wife. When Edward Lord dragged Rowcroft through the Hobart Supreme Court for two weeks of sittings often extending into the early morning hours, his intention was to prove his wife's adultery and to protect his property.

From 1816 Edward Lord was, increasingly, absent from Van Diemen's Land, travelling regularly to England and often taking one or more of his children with him, to leave with relatives or in educational establishments. On 7 June 1819 he left on the *Hibernia* for Sydney *en route* for England, returning on the 28 November 1820 on his own ship the *Caroline* with Miss Lord and his sister-in-law Mrs Riseley. Maria had been left in charge of the business and her brother John given charge of Orielton Park.[44] On 30 April 1822 he left again for England via the Cape on the *Royal George*, this time taking with him their children William and Corbetta. Knopwood dined with him twice in the week before his departure and on each occasion met Charles Rowcroft, a young ex-Etonian who had recently been made a magistrate.[45] From that time on Rowcroft was frequently in the company of Mrs Lord. He was often at her house for dinner when Knopwood went there and was one of the guests at Caroline's birthday dinner (in June 1822) and at the tea, ball and supper which followed. The entry for 22 August 1822 reads: 'Mrs Lord went to Port Dalrymple & Mr Rowcroft.' Dinners with Mrs Lord did not resume for three months, nor was Rowcroft mentioned during this time.

Just at this time (at the end of October 1822), news came of the wrecking of the *Royal George* off Cape Town. Not only Edward was on board but two of their children and a substantial cargo including 40 000 pounds of the island's wool and 6000 bushels of wheat.[46] Maria may not have known for some time that her husband and children had survived.

With Mrs Lord and others, Rowcroft visited Revd Knopwood, or they met casually, as they did on this warm summer's day: '... went to the river garden; met Mrs & Miss Lord,

Mr Rowcroft by the church; they went with us into the garden and eat fruit, currents, raspberries, and apples.'[47]

Often Miss Lord and other young people formed part of the group, and it would seem that the liveliness of Maria's social life at that time was at least in part the result of having her eldest daughter at home with her again after three years. Perhaps Charles Rowcroft was one of the eligible young men to whom Miss Lord was introduced. The conviviality bore fruit. On 20 May 1823 Knopwood dined with Mrs Lord and a party including Mr Rowcroft, and on the next day Miss Lord married Frederic Dawes at St David's. Mr Dawes, aged twenty-five, was a little younger than Mr Rowcroft, who was one of the witnesses. The wedding party breakfasted and dined together. The following day Knopwood breakfasted with Mrs Lord and dined with her the next evening. Rowcroft was present on each occasion and a day later accompanied Mrs Lord and Mr Lawrence to Orielton. They were there again on 8 June.[48] If Rowcroft's attendance at the Lord household had been to court Caroline or if there had ever been any pretence to that effect, the marriage ended such speculation.

On 9 August 1823 a notice appeared in the *Hobart Town Gazette* withdrawing Mrs Lord's authority over the Lord business. On 18 October 1823 Knopwood recorded in his diary that Mrs Lord left her residence in Hobart Town and went to New Plains to live there. Her marriage was over. Her name is not mentioned again in his diary for more than a year and then in connection with the trial about to commence in the Supreme Court.

Rowcroft was newly arrived in Van Diemen's Land when he met Maria Lord; he was a magistrate, and at twenty-six, fourteen years younger than she.[49] His novels about colonial life lay in the future. He was not rich. When the judge awarded Edward Lord only one-tenth of the £1000 he claimed, it was on the grounds that Rowcroft was at that time penniless. Maria was not. The trial, therefore, was as much a matter of business as it was of morality.

Knopwood again records some of what little is known about the trial (apart from the protagonists, their lawyers and the verdict, all of which are documented in the court records which remain).[50] The trial opened on 6 December 1824. Edward had arrived in Hobart a few weeks before and Revd Knopwood, no doubt nervous about the numerous social occasions he had enjoyed in the company of Mrs Lord and Rowcroft, lost no time in assuring Lord of his friendship, dining with him and staying with him at Lawrenny. Knopwood himself did not appear in court until 15 December when he was examined by Hone (for Rowcroft) for nearly an hour and by the Attorney-General for Mr Lord. He was examined for a second time two days later. He was anxious about the trial and the length of its sittings. On the first day the court sat until midnight. On the second day he recorded that John Drummond, servant to Edward Lord, 'was in the box from 9 in the morn to 1/2 pas 2 the following', repeating the performance the following day with only an hour's break. It was not until half-past eleven on the night of Saturday 18 December that a verdict in favour of Mr Lord was given. Early in the trial the *Gazette* had promised the people of Hobart Town the details of the trial 'handsomely printed & published *in Sheets*, on or about 1st of Jan', exciting the fury of local schoolmaster James Thomson, who wrote immediately to Governor Arthur:

> If it is unfortunate for the interests of Morality that such a business should ever have been the subject of public enquiry, and consequently curiosity, it will be much more so if the evidence adduced, filthy and disgusting as it is, be put into such a form, as will enable it to reach the domestic circle, and give to the young and the thoughtless, already beset with too many allurements to evil, a means of gratifying a perverted curiosity and of reviewing scenes full of guilt and infamy. What will be the consequences of statements so obscene meeting the Public eye, in a community formed of such ingredients as this is, what, but a renewal of such gross scenes? ... Enough of evil is already done, that one who ought to have been not only the guardian of the public safety, but of public

morals should have been guilty of such an outrage on domestic peace is bad enough, but if the particulars are made public the effect will be incalculably more injurious.[51]

The press in the colony, as Thomson pointed out, was 'subject to a censorship', and he advised the Governor, 'if ever there was the occasion for this control being exerted it is now'. Neither the promised sheets nor an account in the press was to appear.

Rowcroft was young, educated and articulate. He was certainly an adventurer and was seen by others as a 'sponger'. A poem of that name written about him was circulated on an earlier occasion when he had an altercation with Maria Lord's brother. One verse reads:

> Who, when all other Trade were found to fail
> Became (Reader I see your Cheeks grow pale)
> Petticoat pensioner!! O Wretched Tale
> The Spunger [52]

The author was Edward Lord's friend R. L. Murray. The other verses are as damning. They allege a series of borrowings and misrepresentations about money involving a number of prominent citizens. Rowcroft and his brother had come to the colony representing themselves as men of substance and had been treated as such.

The trial not only confirmed that Maria had committed adultery but demonstrated that her civil status was now such that her sexual behaviour was a matter of legal consequence in a way it was not before her marriage to Edward. She had moved from being a convict whore to a mistress to a lawful wife, but the trial which branded her again 'a whore' took place not only because of sexual morality and marital status but because of property.

The trial was as much about money as it was about the changed standards of sexual behaviour and the increased emphasis on respectability that accompanied the Arthur period. The first public act Edward took against Maria was to send someone else to take over from her as his agent (Dr Hood) and to place advertisements in the press removing her authority over the business.[53] After the trial, Lord's agents sought confirmation that Mrs Lord, having in effect been convicted of adultery, no longer had legal rights of inheritance over her husband's property even though she had not been divorced by him. The question was debated between the Crown Solicitor and the Attorney-General in relation to the transfer of land near the Domain from Lord to the Crown.[54] Under these circumstances it is likely that while Maria ceased to have any claim on Edward's estate, he retained legal rights to her property and wealth. This was to be a matter of relevance some years later when she died a few months before her husband and her property at Bothwell (including her striking Gothic house, The Priory) became part of his estate.[55]

In bringing the charge of criminal conversation against Rowcroft, Lord showed that, in his social circumstances, the fidelity of a wife and the 'misuse' of her body by another man was of legal consequence. The compensation he was awarded demonstrated not only the importance of property in early Van Diemen's Land society but also the 'property' rights of husband over wife before the law. The Lord–Rowcroft case is less well known than another case of this kind in the 1820s. In 1828 James Bowman, Principal Surgeon of New South Wales and son-in-law to John Macarthur, was sued in the Sydney Supreme Court by ex-convict Thomas Hart. Hart's wife (a convict) had become pregnant to Bowman, who had contrived to send her to Van Diemen's Land. Bowman (unlike Rowcroft) was not a pauper and Hart was awarded the very considerable sum of £2000.[56]

Once he had secured his control over the property they had acquired together and made a settlement on her, Edward took no further legal action though strenuously urged to do so by his friends and relatives. R. L. Murray wrote to D'Arcy Wentworth that Sir John Owen and his other friends had 'set their Hearts' on Edward obtaining a divorce and that no interest or expense would be spared to achieve this. He added: 'I heartily hope that he may yet enjoy the Society of an honourable and virtuous woman, who may know how to appreciate his value and be deserving of his affection.'[57]

Lord's own life was not exactly above reproach. Later in 1828, he was named as the father of the child of a convict woman in proceedings seeking maintenance of such children (unsuccessfully in Edward's case).[58] Such behaviour on his part would not have prevented him from obtaining a divorce should he have chosen to pursue the matter through the British Parliament. Perhaps he was in 1825 no more sentimental about marriage than he had been twenty years earlier when he first met Maria. The trial had ensured his control over his property and his rights to hers. It may have achieved as much as he wanted and prevented his wealth from finding its way into the pockets of a penniless adventurer. It also involved the humiliation of his wife and the demise of Rowcroft's colonial hopes, and this may have been satisfying to someone who was often irascible and who used litigation tirelessly against his enemies.

More, however, might have been at stake. The trial followed a period in which Maria had effectively run the Lord business, during which time it had grown substantially. Moreover she had begun to go into business with others, including her brother John. She had begun to collect her kin around her, bringing her brother to Hobart. She had married her daughter to a young solicitor. She was, in fact, rebuilding her own family. If one of the main reasons women were so vulnerable in the early days of the settlement was the absence of the protection afforded by kin, the reconstruction of these ties increased Maria's independence. And whether she was guilty of adultery as alleged, or merely of an indiscreet friendship, such a relationship was another sign of her growing independence. Lord's friends recognised that she was no longer his appendage when they urged him to find someone who would put him in his rightful place.

When before the trial Maria left the Macquarie Street house to live at New Plains, the partnership as well as the marriage was over. Edward gave her a separate allowance from the estate and made the new arrangements public in mid–1824 by having his agent announce it in the *Gazette*, along with the notice that he was not responsible for her debts.[59] Lord spent little time after this in Van Diemen's Land. His future, if not the source of his wealth, lay in Britain, where he established a second family, without the benefit of legal sanction. She remained married, supported in part by her absent husband but not legally free of him.

What we make of Maria Lord depends on whether we treat her as an individual or as Edward's wife. As an individual she has been mostly ignored, except as the somewhat scandalous wife of a prominent man and as a minor figure in the history of entrepreneurial women.[60] While her economic role in the early history of colonial Australia deserves more emphasis, the problem of looking at her as one representative of a small group of successful women is that in this picture Edward Lord tends to be left out, just as in the earlier version there was little room for Maria. In these historical narratives the view of Edward determines the representation of Maria. Simply a 'convict mistress' to his critic, Robson, she presents greater difficulties for his admirer, Henry, anxious as he is to reinstate Lord as the Macarthur of Van Diemen's Land. To Henry, both Maria's background and her subsequent fall from respectability is an embarrassment. In Henry's romantic version of Edward's life, Maria is deprived not only of the entrepreneurial role but also of the supporting roles usually attributed to such women in the realist accounts of colonial society. She emerges as neither a 'helpmeet' nor a pioneer woman, though clearly she was both of these. Instead she is made to bear at least part of the blame for the physical and emotional decline of her husband. The combination of factors which stop Henry from offering her the usual accolades are these: she is a convicted felon and her first children were born out of wedlock; her pardon is dubious and casts a shadow over the legality of her marriage. Furthermore she is unfaithful to Edward, and her infidelity (which is also seen as the ingratitude of a social inferior) is partly the cause, in Henry's view, of Edward's decision to leave the colony.

Henry treats Maria differently from Robson because he wishes to enhance rather than attack Lord's reputation. Consequently her reputation becomes of some account and anything which undermines it is painful to him. (There are no asides here about convict mistresses). Deprived of all title to respectability, she can only be accommodated in the story in one way—as predator, with Edward as her victim.

Feminist historians would propose an alternative image. Surely Maria was the victim, first through Edward's possession and then his repudiation of her—both acts culminating in the trial. Yet, persuasive as this image is, it is also legitimate to look at them not as predator and victim but as partners—partners in money-making in a new colony ripe for every form of commercial enterprise and exploitation; domestic partners and parents, creating a distinctive form of domesticity in a raw, uncivilised environment.

If we go back briefly to mid-1813 this is what we see. Lieutenant Lord of the Marines has just been succeeded by Mr Lord, trader of Hobart Town, shipowner, proprietor of vast acres, husband, father. He is thirty-two years old. Maria, a year older, is the mother of four children under seven: Caroline, born in 1805, Eliza in 1808, John in 1810 and Edward Robert, born in Sydney in March 1812, just before his father's departure for England. Maria's second child, Elizabeth, had been born in 1806 but had not survived. (Maria was to have two more daughters, Corbetta and Emma, in 1815 and 1819 and another son, William, in 1817.) Together they made up an early colonial family.[61]

Not only has the role of women in nineteenth-century Tasmanian society been neglected—in fact almost omitted from most general histories of the period—and the role of women in business for the most part overlooked, but domestic life in general, the various forms of domesticity which developed in the earliest days of the settlement, has not received serious attention. The dominant impression given of the early settlement in Robson's history is of disorder and violence. In the 1830s a respectable society began to emerge, more provincially urban, more apparently ordered than what had preceded it. But earlier, amid the apparent anarchy, the beginning of a European society was established, transplanted to the new environment. An attempt was made from the very beginning to create a 'civilised' society. Households, forms of ordered social and domestic life were established, forms which are in many ways interesting and distinct because they involve relationships between people not regarded as social equals.

Convicts allowed the development of particular forms of domestic life. In large country houses such as Edward Lord's property Orielton, which was said to employ directly and indirectly 1000 people, a version of life based on that enjoyed by the English landed gentry was recreated. In Hobart servants made possible the dinners at Mrs Lord's at which Knopwood was such a regular guest, and the balls, dances and picnics. The records reveal the difficulties Mrs Lord, like other mistresses, had with convict servants and the charges she brought against them. Other forms of order were built up too, through the transplanting of a set of structures which related to law, punishment, religion, welfare, education and the socialisation of children and the lower classes. Edward and Maria Lord participated in this process, christening the newborn children, taking the family pew at St David's and giving prizes to hard-working labourers through the Agricultural Society and the Mechanics' Institute.[62] Other glimpses of this process—and the increasing importance of 'respectability' and family life— can be gained by looking at the relationship between Edward and Maria Lord and at their children.

Some care and considerable expense was taken with the education of both the girls and boys in the family, and all the children spent some time in Britain. The eldest son, John, was sent away to England at the age of six in 1816. In 1817

Caroline, aged twelve, seems to have been sent abroad too, to be educated by a governess, returning in 1820. Eliza and Edward Robert sailed together in about 1820, the boy to be educated at Mr Wallace's Academy in Hertfordshire with his older brother. Corbetta and William accompanied their father in 1822. Like Emma, the youngest child who Edward took to Britain in 1824, references to William cease with the child's departure. It seems possible that Maria Lord never saw some of her children again after Edward bore them off to be educated 'at home'.[63] One who did return was the eldest son, John, who drowned shortly after his arrival in 1829 while swimming in the river at Lawrenny.[64] The concern that both parents felt for their children is apparent, though the evidence is fragmentary. There are frequent references to the Lord children in Knopwood's diary and to their accompanying their mother on visits. One of Edward's intentions in returning to Hobart in October 1824, apart from formally ending his marriage and sorting out his business affairs, was to take his youngest child away with him, though she was five and must have barely known him. Caroline (by then Mrs Dawes) was present at a large party which farewelled the travellers, even though a little more than a week before Edward had destroyed her mother's reputation before the court and the people of Hobart.[65]

Two pieces of correspondence tell us something about the relationship between parents and children. Among Maria Lord's business papers is a letter to Eyre Coote Lord written in 1820 sending him part of the annual sum remitted to Sir John Owen, Edward's brother and business partner, 'earnestly requesting' that any needs of her children should be met from this. She goes on to say:

> I beg to assure you of my grateful impression of your constant goodness in attention to my dear children, and I would request you to take a favourable opportunity of acquainting me in what manner they landed as to equipment, clothes etc; a very large sum having been expended to fit them for the voyage in provisions and for their appearing before Mr Lord's friends.[66]

Here we see the mingling of her concern for her children with her concern for money and expense and, as well, her anxiety that her children should make a good impression on her husband's important relatives and friends in Britain—in a social world she threatened to enter but never did.

Any idea that discipline and the proprieties had little place in such a household or that domestic orderliness awaited the arrival of a new era with Governor Arthur is dispelled by the letters written by Eliza Lord to the Revd Hassall from Pembroke in 1821. (Hassall, later the son-in-law of Samuel Marsden, had been a shipboard companion to Eliza and her brother on the voyage to England.) She wrote:

> I have so many relations here who are very kind to me, and I trust when placed at a distance from them that I shall at all times remember their goodness to me, and when I return to my beloved Papa and Mamma I hope to prove, that during my absence I have not been unmindful of the parental advice they so lavishly bestowed [upon] me, when I left them; and that I have learned to be [what they] so much wished, a good and useful member of Society, as I hope to make it the study of my life, to promote their comfort and happiness, as a trifling return for what they daily do for me.[67]

Not long after this the partnership and the marriage ended, with Maria's public humiliation and abandonment. But for all that, contact remained. Early in 1828 when Lord became very ill during a visit to the colony, it was at Maria's house that he sought and found refuge, and where Knopwood met him, thereby visiting Maria, with whom he had once dined so regularly, for the first time since the trial.[68] It was the beginning of the resumption of their acquaintance. Similarly, when the two eldest sons returned to Hobart in 1829 they returned to their mother. And when John drowned in the Derwent not long afterwards, the local press reported her presence at the Lord property, Lawrenny, 'where the unhappy mother of the late promising youth has been since the first news of this melancholy occurrence reached her'.[69] Maria Lord was not irretrievably banished from either Hobart society or from contact with her family after the trial. Nor did she take her humiliation meekly by retreating from the public eye to live in obscurity on her allowance. Instead she publicly announced herself to be a woman working to support her children. And she continued to play a prominent if reduced role in the commercial activity of Hobart.

There is an epilogue to the family history of Edward and Maria Lord which continues the convict story. In 1841 allegations were made about the sexual behaviour of the master of the Queen's Orphan School, Revd Thomas Ewing. Among the graphic testimony was evidence from a young boy at the school who said that all the boys talked about Ewing committing adultery with one of the girls, and he himself had seen the master with the girl 'buttoning up one side of his breeches'. Many of the inmates of the school were the children of convicts and the boy in question, named as 'Edward Lord Fry', was most likely the son of assigned convict woman Ann Fry who had in 1828 named Edward Lord as the father of her child.[70] Edward Lord had refused to pay anything to maintain the child, and while his other children prospered, this boy, aged about thirteen, was in 1841 still caught up within the convict system as Maria had been nearly forty years before.

In looking at Maria and Edward Lord we see two people who together played an important part in the development of the early colonial economy—who in some ways helped to shape it. The story of the one makes little sense without the other. The omission of Maria from early narratives deprived us of an important part of the picture. But it is not useful, in restoring her, to call Edward 'cunning' and 'rapacious' and Maria a 'successful female entrepreneur'; that is to replace one double standard with another. Nor is it sufficient to see them as mistress and marine, a saga of seduction and scandal, a revelation of the pre-Arthur morality. Both played a more complex part in Van Diemen's Land society than that, helping to create forms of order, of civilisation, and of domesticity in the new colony.

In 1983 I wrote about Maria Lord in the press and a little later gave a paper about her to the Tasmanian Historical Research Association in the appropriate surroundings of the museum. The public rooms, furnished with colonial furniture and stuffed marsupials, stood across the road from Maria Lord's old home, Ingle Hall, a colonial Georgian building on the corner of Macquarie and Argyle Streets, a block from Constitution Dock. I sensed that Maria Lord was still a little notorious in Hobart (180 years after her arrival there) and I was sensitive to the fact that in referring to her first child's paternity I may have been a cause of disappointment to any descendant in the audience who hoped that Maria's eldest daughter was like her other children, the offspring of her well-connected Welsh husband. My intention, however, was not to indulge in historical gossip but to reveal her as a character around whom much more complex narratives could cluster, and to show her as a figure capable of bearing such complexity.

At present Maria Lord is a minor character who has barely entered Australian history. Her life, however, illuminates a number of narratives which together make up the female convict experience in Australia. The form of her eventual portrayal will depend on the ideas the historian wishes to mobilise around her. It is unlikely that she will continue to be seen merely as a mistress or a whore, but she may be used to suggest a society in which woman were sexually exploited and subject to a double standard of morality, where they were economically and legally vulnerable and denied full participation except through men. Or she may be used to demonstrate how colonial society opened up new opportunities for women, how it was a society of upward mobility through both marriage and employment, a society which moved quickly towards establishing 'civilised' social structures and domestic arrangements which worked to the advantage of women. Her experience is rich enough to illuminate either perspective, but neither alone is enough to express the complexity of her life. Moreover, the narratives her story reveals are the major narratives in the history of convict women in Australia.

2

WRITING ABOUT CONVICT WOMEN

It is more than twenty years since Miriam Dixson and Anne Summers, in books written for a wide audience, challenged thinking about both the position of women in contemporary society and the way Australian historians wrote about women.[1] In both studies, an exploration of the female convict experience introduced and underpinned the central thesis. Over the intervening period women's history, women's studies and gender studies have become established areas of research and teaching, with a growing academic literature attached. The Australian women's movement of the 1970s has started the enterprise of writing its own history and feminist theorists and historians of the 1990s have begun distinguishing themselves from their recent predecessors. Intergenerational debate thrives on claims of disjuncture and novelty, and feminist history, in portraying earlier writing as insensitive to the differences between women and to the construction of femininity, has been no exception. Without wanting to be too distracted by that debate, I am conscious that this book contributes to it and that it provides some of its background, and that now is a particularly opportune time to be reviewing the way the history of women has been written in this country.

How have convict women been treated in the general histories of convictism and in the specialist writings of the last two decades where they have increasingly received separate attention? Women have not been ignored in the general histories of the convict period, but while there is a tendency to see the position of women as different enough to require special treatment, female convicts have traditionally been incorporated into frameworks developed by reference to the male convict experience. The less well they fit into that structure of analysis, the more marginal they have tended to be. Their relative neglect in a number of general histories reflects not only a lack of interest in female convicts as a subject of historical discussion but also the difficulty of accommodating women convicts within structures devised primarily for men. While the history of convict women has consequently been developed much more effectively in studies devoted exclusively to women than in general studies of convictism, these studies too are often derivative in both framework and questioning. At the same time important new works on the convict experience have drawn less on the experiences of convict women than could be expected from the wealth of information which has become available over the last twenty years. John Hirst's major work of reinterpretation, *Convict Society and its Enemies*, for instance, is less conspicuous for its investigation of convict women than for the effect of its conclusions on later interpretations of female convict history.[2]

Some examples illustrate this tendency to incorporate women into a pattern designed initially to accommodate men. The more 'heroic' the male convict, or the more political, the less evident is the female convict. Where male convicts have been primarily characterised as the detritus of British society, members of a 'criminal class', convict women are most likely to be portrayed as 'prostitutes'. This image in particular has been a difficult obstacle for all subsequent historians concerned with women's history.

In the 1960s A. G. L. Shaw, Manning Clark and Lloyd Robson set out to demonstrate the inaccuracy of the earlier image of the male convict as a victim of an unjust political system. Robson, looking back, commented: 'I think I had utterly demolished the poacher theory. The convicts, I had found, were, to put it simply, largely crooks who had been caught stealing. There was little evidence of nobility à la Wood and the Hammonds.'[3] These historians, convinced of the idea of male convicts as habitual criminals, echoed nineteenth-century British commentators in seeing the convicted woman as the classic female companion and criminal counterpart of the underworld criminal—the street or bawdy-house whore. (There was ample evidence that this had also been the view of nineteenth-century male observers in New South Wales and Van Diemen's Land.) The effect of this has been to compel historians examining the history of female convicts to ask, with varying degrees of sophistication, how many of the female convicts transported to Australia were prostitutes. And to ask, as if a moral conclusion can be easily drawn from these 'facts', how many of the convicts transported to Australia were 'good' women ('family women') and how many were 'bad' ('prostitutes')?

Historians writing specifically about female convicts have usually grappled with the issues that have arisen from their conceptualisation as members of a criminal class by debating the question of prostitution. Early feminist historians such as Summers and Dixson tended to accept the views, if not the moral judgments, of Clark, Shaw and Robson as demonstrating that convict women were the victims of sexual exploitation not only in Britain but more importantly also in the penal colonies. Revisionist historians, especially Portia Robinson, accepted the negative picture of British society but substituted a more benign view of the antipodean settlements.[4] The argument about prostitution is therefore intimately interwoven with judgments not only about Britain and criminality but about the colonial experience. Late twentieth-century historians, not burdened with biological determinism or ideas about inherited criminal characteristics, could accept that these 'unfortunate creatures' could be transformed into respectable family women. Only an outcast minority failed to grasp the opportunities offered in the colonies for social advancement through work and marriage.

In 1984 I attempted to move the debate about prostitution away from what must inevitably be a thankless and absurd historiographical task of sorting and counting the women in each moral category. I suggested that Australian historical writing which absorbed the nineteenth-century, middle-class male vision of women has deformed the way Australian historians have perceived women in the colonial period by making the moral question pre-eminent: from the existence of prostitution is extrapolated an image of two kinds of women, totally alien and distinct in experience and character. This may have been the mythology of the Victorian period, but real life is less easily confined by such simplistic characterisation. The first steps towards exorcising these old myths lie, I suggested, not in shifting the emphasis from one group of women to another (from 'damned whores' to 'colonial wives', or from professional whores to ordinary lower-class women) but in doing away with the categories of 'good' and 'bad' women altogether and in exploring the key conceptual problem: the meaning of prostitution.[5]

Historians of female convict history have continued to feel trapped by these questions. As Marilyn Lake pointed out in 1988 (echoed by Joy Damousi in 1996), these moral dichotomies still pervade the discussion of women convicts.[6] Some of the consequences for Australian historical studies of the popularisation of the convict woman as prostitute are explored in Chapter 7.

Challenges to the view of male convicts as members of a criminal class have also served to reconceptualise the female convict woman, but from a different perspective and again within a framework whose key features are derived from the male convict experience. An illustration of this is *Convict Workers: Reinterpreting Australia's Past*, edited by Stephen Nicholas in 1988 and containing an essay on female convicts by Deborah Oxley.[7] In its own words it 'offers a new and dramatic reinterpretation of the convict system' by challenging the 'received interpretation' which emphasised male convicts as 'hardened and professional criminals, females as prostitutes and convictism as a brutal and inefficient system of forced labour'. The crux of the argument in this book is that although Clark, Shaw, Robson and others clung tenaciously to the nineteenth-century idea of a separate criminal class, there was in actuality no such thing, and that far from the statistics showing that convicts transported to Australia were habitual criminals, they reveal them to have the employment profile of ordinary working-class men and women.

The book concludes that many of the convicts were 'experienced migrants', having moved within the British Isles before transportation, that they brought with them a cross-section of useful skills (including, among an elite, the skills of the labour aristocracy), that they were on the whole better educated than their working-class compatriots, and as healthy.

Was this robust 'human capital' squandered or employed efficiently in the new environment? The second part of the argument in *Convict Workers* is that this labour force was effectively used in the penal colonies. Only domestic workers and unskilled urban workers had skills which could not be fully utilised in the early settlements, and these tended to be assigned to useful public work. In general the organisation of labour and its allocation, the system of rewards and incentives and the general treatment of the convicts (punishment, working hours, accommodation, food and care) were all conducive to productivity. The exception to this pattern was women, who brought immediately useful skills to the settlements which were under-valued and squandered, to the detriment of the economy.

Valuable 'human capital', on the one hand well used and on the other wasted. Why? Deborah Oxley argues that women too brought significant skills with them.[8] Far from being prostitutes, habitual criminals or 'the dregs' of society, most of the women were from the semi-skilled or skilled working class. Three occupations dominated: general servant, housemaid and kitchen hand. But women's labour was undervalued and they remained underemployed in the colonies. The explanation of this situation is tenuous at best. According to Oxley, in Australia women became the victims of a 'recasting of the sexual division of labour' which contracted the demand for their work and ensured that they were, as workers, undervalued and underpaid. 'So few, they were valued less—a violation of the classical law of supply and demand determining price.'[9]

In a full-length study, *Convict Maids: The Forced Migration of Women to Australia*, Oxley adjusts her argument to take greater account of the neglected contribution of convict women to colonial development.[10] To say that convict women were a wasted resource is to go close to committing the feminist sin of undervaluing unpaid domestic work, and Oxley makes it clear in the later volume that she is aware of this. She points out that historians have tended to deny women a productive role in colonial history because they believed them to be without skills or without skills which were useful in the colonial economy, or because they believed that they were a wasted asset. A fourth option exists, she suggests: that women had contributed to economic growth but that this contribution had been undervalued. The argument is not new, as the title of Katrina Alford's 1984 volume suggests: *Production or Reproduction? An Economic History of Women in Australia*.[11]

It is clear from what I have said above that much of the historical discussion about female convicts has been structured by the more general debate about convict origins: were convicts habitual criminals and the women among them prostitutes, or were they ordinary working-class people, with skills that were useful in the new colonies? Historians of women's history have tended to position themselves within that discussion, accepting its fundamental assumptions but challenging aspects of the debate where it affected women. The same pattern is evident in the second major area of debate in convict history which looks at the experience of convicts in the penal settlements and the nature of colonial society. How harsh and exploitative was the convict experience? Were conditions worse in the Australian colonies than they were in Britain and

Ireland? Were there greater opportunities in New South Wales and Van Diemen's Land than had been available to convicts in their home countries? This debate carries more significance for women's history in Australia than the debate about origins. Whatever women were in the old world, what were they able to become in the new?

While the idea that convict society was excessively exploitative and degrading received an enormous fillip from Robert Hughes' *The Fatal Shore*,[12] the repudiation of this view and its corollary, that later Australian society continues to bear the warped imprint of its convict origins, has been at the heart of the recent academic rewriting of Australian history—in the work of John Hirst in particular. But unlike Nicholas, Hirst does not repudiate the idea of the 'criminal class'. Here, for example, is Hirst describing the background of transported convicts:

> In the largest towns, living amongst the most disorderly, was the true underworld of professional pickpockets, thieves and prostitutes … Fewer than half of the convicts sent to New South Wales came from the country. Nearly all of these were used to regular work and they were less likely to have been regularly involved in crime … But most of the convicts had not been bred as proper servants. They came from the loose disorderly sort, chiefly from the towns; they were unused to regular hours, regular employment or hard manual labour; large numbers of them were professional thieves.[13]

But Hirst is more careful than his predecessors to avoid moralising and to differentiate actual from alleged behaviour. He does not brand convict women as necessarily 'worse' than their male counterparts, although he is aware that they were often seen that way. He acknowledges that it was more difficult for women than for men to meet the standards expected of them. This, in his view (which derives from earlier feminist work), was less the result of their sexual behaviour than of their employment as servants, which brought them into a special intimacy with the master's household.

Female convicts play a minor part in Hirst's book, but the most important element of his argument does carry significant implications for women: that our view of the excesses of the penal period is coloured by the picture of corrupt and exploitative masters, brutalised and exploited convicts that was put about by the opponents of transportation to discredit the system. The image of New South Wales as a giant brothel derives from this argument. Hirst, whose book deals largely with the male convict experience, concludes that while it is impossible to establish the extent to which women were exploited, the view that the penal settlement allowed only a 'degraded role' for women is 'untenable'.[14]

Central to this argument is the idea that the convict colonies did not brutalise 'slaves' and deprave 'masters' but allowed the growth within the penal framework of a free society which was law-abiding and as normal in its patterns of social intercourse as the society from which it had sprung. Those who argued to the contrary were led to do so by other motives—from the Molesworth Committee and James Mudie through to the anti-transportation movement. And just as Australian society did not continue to carry the distorting imprint of its convict origins, nor was criminality indelibly imprinted on individual convicts. Whatever the reasons for their original fall from grace, convicts were offered in the penal colonies the chance to rehabilitate themselves. Transportation reformed convicts more effectively than the rigours and moralisation of the penitentiary ever could. Changed social circumstances—particularly the availability of employment—created the conditions that made rehabilitation possible. Only the 'incorrigibles' remained untransformed. Moreover, these convicts—by now reduced to a deviant minority among the larger transported group—were those who attracted the most brutal treatment and gave the 'enemies' of convict society their most damning evidence of the effects of transportation. They were the ones who were whipped, chained and brutalised by the system. As Hirst comments, in reference to the convict memorial in The Rocks: "'The Convict'" is put in chains though, as the plaque on this modern sculpture explains, only incorrigibles suffered this fate.'[15] In the views of both Hirst and the colonial opponents of Molesworth, to the limited extent that the 'depraved' convict world existed, it was a world built out of the experience of a minority.

Hirst and Robinson have been critical of the way some historians became captive to particular contemporary views of convict society. There is some irony, therefore, in the fact that they have come to depend so much on the contemporary concept of 'the incorrigible' without paying too much attention to its construction. Much analysis has taken place of the manufacture of social divisions within the nineteenth-century working class, such as those between the deserving and the undeserving poor, the respectable and the rough, the criminal and the working class, and the role of the working class itself in internalising and sanctioning those divisions. In the context of convict society the 'incorrigible' gathered into itself all those negative categories. By exploring what was meant by the incorrigible, we are able to explore the boundaries penal society drew around acceptable and deviant behaviour, and what, in relation to women, it defined as feminine.

The construct of 'the incorrigible' convict has come to assume something of the same mythic importance in recent convict history as the concept of the criminal class did in earlier work. In women's history Portia Robinson has been one of the vocal exponents of the view that only they remained 'degraded'. In her study of the first generation of native-born, *The Hatch and Brood of Time*, Robinson 'rejects entirely' what she describes as 'the feminist excuse-explanation interpretation of the forced degradation of the colonial lives of convict women' during the first four decades of European settlement, pointing to the 'completely different opportunities which were available to women in the colony'.[16] While some women continued with their criminal or 'immoral' activities, their behaviour in the colonies was a matter of 'choice and inclination' rather than 'economic necessity' (as it commonly had been in Britain).

While Robinson has made the most explicit attack on the ideas of mid–1970s feminist history, Hirst's book contains a powerful but implicit rejection of both its method and its conclusions. In Summers and Dixson (and most explicitly in the work of the latter) the particular inheritance of British society is irrevocably imprinted on the new colonies through the convict experience. To Summers, women who had been exploited in the old society were even more vulnerable to exploitation in the colonial environment—'colonised' as a group by men and disciplined through their acceptance of the 'good' and 'bad' woman stereotype. The continuing oppression of women in Australian society, originating in the convict period, is the central theme in *Damned Whores and God's Police*, and to illustrate it Summers drew on the views of male ruling-class observers who were unsympathetic to and ignorant of working-class culture and morality but also intent on using their observations to brand the penal system itself as barbaric. As evidence of their sexual exploitation Summers used the same historical material that her predecessors had used to demonstrate the immorality of convict women. Dixson's emphasis is less on the oppression of women than on their low status and self-esteem (the internalising of the ugliness seen in them by others) and that she ascribes to the inheritance of the formative convict period. In *The Real Matilda* the convict woman is the 'victim of victims' and 'slave of slaves'.[17]

The 'degraded role' of women, originating in the convict period (and repudiated by Hirst), is central to the argument of both Summers and Dixson and of much feminist writing which followed them, but it is quite apparent, even from Summers' title, that feminist writers for the most part do not see only a degraded role for women in colonial society. (The 'whore' required its opposite.) The historian who is closest to that position is Robert Hughes, whose picture of a cruel and sexually exploitative system, while brilliantly reinforcing many of the arguments of the feminists, implies that the exploited are completely brutalised and allows little room to explore other aspects of their response (or their humanity).

The striking contrast between the early historiography of convict Australia and the writing that came out of 1970s feminism was the emphasis placed on the sexual use of convict women. While historians like Clark, Shaw and Robson emphasised the sexual histories of convict women as evidence of their moral failure and their membership of a criminal underclass, the first wave of women historians drew attention to their sexual exploitation in the colonies as an indication of the patriarchal nature of penal society. Prostitution was less important as an element in the criminal profile of transported convicts than as a description of the fate that awaited them in the penal settlements, where they were treated as 'whores' and where, in Anne Summers' vivid phrase, the government played out the role of 'Imperial whoremaster'.

Michael Sturma's influential early essay on feminist history 'Through the eye of the beholder' explored the way middle-class perceptions of convict women's behaviour misconstrued working-class cultural practices but were absorbed uncritically into feminist texts. Feminist historians were not alone in their unsophisticated use of evidence. They were, however, unusual in constructing an account of convict history which took gender as a determining structure.[18]

Sexual and reproductive exploitation are twin themes in early feminist history. Always interlinked, the dominance of one over the other is continually debated. Were women sent to the penal settlements for sexual or reproductive reasons—to be whores or mothers? What other choices did women have? To what extent were they able to survive independently, outside marriage? What occupations were open to them? What other contributions could and did women make to the economy? Historians taking an optimistic view have tended increasingly to reduce the issue of prostitution to a question relating to a deviant and incorrigible minority rather than a theme which illuminates more generally the position of women in the penal colonies. Reproduction, on the other hand, became an emblem of the opportunity held out to all women to embrace a 'normal' domestic life and a sign of their 'valued' contribution to the community.

Within the extensive discussion of women's reproductive role in colonial history, reproduction has been seen as a significant factor influencing the British authorities to send women to the penal settlements and as the most valued contribution made by women to the economy of the new settlements. In general histories women's contribution to colonial development as 'mothers' is seen as relatively non-problematic. The centrality of this role for women is assumed rather than questioned, although a number of subsidiary issues arise from the assumption. For example, were convict women as mothers of the first generation 'good mothers'? Within women's history the issue of motherhood is much more contentious. The work of Alford and, more recently, of Jan Kociumbas fits within this framework. Kociumbas argues that, in a period in which demographic concerns were being given a new priority and there was a growing demand for industrial labour, women were sent to the penal settlements largely because of their child-bearing capacities. 'Women's bodies', it was increasingly assumed, 'existed merely to reproduce'.[19] At the same time new views of male sexuality emphasised male aggression and the need for men to express their sexual drives. A distinction was made between those women who were reserved for reproduction and those with whom sexual encounters were pursued: 'Thus for the women in New South Wales this new definition of women in terms of their reproductivity was not only one of the reasons they had been sent to the colony but was also one of the reasons why they were being treated with such contempt.'[20]

Like Summers before her, Kociumbas sees colonial administrators as planning the reproductive future of the settlement as well as officially sanctioning the exploitation of women's sexuality. Women from the Pacific Islands would serve the sexual needs of the marines, while the more virtuous of the convict women could be expected to become wives for convicts, who would be encouraged to marry them by the provision of plots of land. The sexual needs of convicts would also be served by a form of convict prostitution, although native women might also be induced to play this role. These arrangements were to be backed up by heavy sanctions against 'unnatural' sexual behaviour, with heavy punishment for sodomy and for the violation of young girls.

Why were female convicts sent to the new penal colonies? Are the reasons advanced for the sending of male convicts sufficient to explain the sending of women too? Were they sent because they made up part of the criminal population and there was as much need to find a new place to send female criminals as there was to send males? Or did the colonial administrators take a broader view, looking beyond exile and punishment and mindful of what was necessary to sustain life and civilised society in a colonial outpost? How much thought, or how little, went into this part of the grand project? There is no doubt that penal administrators were ill prepared to deal with the complexity of the issues relating to women which were to emerge early in the history or New South Wales and Van Diemen's Land.

That this is so is not surprising, given the range of matters which confronted the colonial authorities. Instead of having to deal solely with questions relating to punishment, confinement and reform, they were drawn early into uncharted realms of social policy as it related to women, to children and to family formation. Behind each seemingly minor issue were substantial questions about women's role in society and the role of government in structuring that role. Were freed convict women, for instance, to be workers, and if so was this to be something that would be confined to the period before marriage, or would women continue to work as part of a family unit? Should the colonial administration provide or try to find work for women or other means to help them to be self-supporting, or should it rely on the marriage market rather than the labour market, and the support of a husband? And if a marriage failed, would it be better for the supporting mother to be assisted or for the children to be removed from her care?

If women were to provide sexual partners for men, would this not be more appropriately pursued (at least in the longer term) in the context of marriage rather than of prostitution or concubinage? At least that would go part of the way towards ensuring that the children of these relationships did not become encumbrances on the state. On the other hand, might not the state, in some circumstances at least, provide a better upbringing for a child?

It would be odd if the responses of colonial administrators were completely coherent in the light of such complexities, and odder still if, confronted with these issues, they had decided to strike out into new territory rather than relying on inherited policy and dominant prejudice.

Kociumbas attributes more intent and coherence to the views of colonial administrators than is perhaps warranted. While she talks of 'the officials' blueprint for the exploitation of female bodies' and later of some women being able (through work) 'to subvert the reproductive aims of the system', there seems to have been little sustained attempt to engineer a distinctive future for the settlement in reproductive or sexual terms.[21] Rather, colonial administrators appear to have either tried to recreate English patterns of civilisation (as they believed them to be) or to have made no plans at all. The early debate about finding partners for convict men and the marines is less an imperial or penal blueprint than a fragmentary set of responses to what might become a difficult issue: if convict men were to stay at the far end of the world as exiles and other men were to guard them and administer the settlement, with whom should they have sexual relations? The conclusion that they should find partners among their own class and kind (but not their own gender) seems to have been reached by default after more imaginative alternatives had been contemplated. They were obviously unprepared for what must have been the most startling demographic result of settlement: the increased fertility of convict women in the new environment.[22] Nor were they able to cope effectively with the tendency among confined groups to seek sexual relationships with members of their own sex.

Kociumbas and Alford develop, with the benefit of much greater research, some of the arguments suggested in Summers' work. While Robinson's moral scorn for 'prostitutes' and 'incorrigibles' puts her with Manning Clark, the emphasis on the benign and progressive elements of early colonial society in her work places it (and that of her colleague Monica Perrott) squarely with that of historians like Hirst.

Where has recent women's history taken the discussion of convict women? Both *Creating a Nation*, edited by Marian Quartly with Patricia Grimshaw, Marilyn Lake and Ann McGrath, and *Freedom Bound*, a two-volume collection of documents whose five editors include Quartly, Lake and Grimshaw, have been described by their authors as reflecting different concerns and approaches from work which preceded them.[23] *Creating a Nation* starts with the proposition that gender is a central category of historical analysis and that history is constituted in gendered terms, taking as its central theme the relationship between 'domestic government', as exercised by the male head of the household, and state government, which has 'also institutionalised male rule'. *Freedom Bound* exaggerates its difference from prior feminist historical studies by ignoring the consideration in earlier work of differences between women, particularly those of class and race. At the same time it reflects a new preoccupation with differences of ethnicity and sexual preference, a greater emphasis on the pursuit of independence and desire, and a relative lack of interest in some earlier preoccupations of women's history, such as poverty and the institutionalisation of women and children, including early work on 'the stolen generation' of Aboriginal children.

Within these volumes, which define themselves as representing a new feminist history, Marian Quartly writes about convict women. Quartly's recent work has also appeared in *Gender Relations in Australia: Domination and Negotiation*, edited by Kay Saunders and Raymond Evans (and dedicated to Miriam Dixson, Beverly Kingston and Anne Summers).[24] Her studies of convict women sit oddly in these volumes, tending, in their conclusions at least, to lend support to the views of John Hirst rather than those of more radical feminist studies. In her contribution to *Gender Relations in Australia* she suggests that 'the effects of patriarchy within the penal system sometimes advantaged convict women over convict men, and even over poor women in Britain'.[25] Struggling with the view that convict women were both 'trapped and enabled' by the contradictions of the penal settlements, Quartly observes that historians long 'beguiled by the refractory prostitute' have only just begun to 'imagine the loyal wife'.[26] In restoring the emphasis on the latter, she is not as sanguine about the happiness of married life as Robinson. Her married couples marry for 'prudent' reasons rather than from affection, and husbands are frequently brutal and violent.

It is the subtext of Quartly's work that fits best into this historiography, as Miriam Dixson points out when she suggests of convictism that Quartly has

> smoothed over its tragic, violent side. Yet to an important degree, her argument gathered into a 'normalisation' case data that, if not undermining this case, sat with it so awkwardly as to suggest an alternative emphasis … Taken together, Quartly's discrete incidents of actual violence add up to a fairly extreme and pervasive relational harshness.[27]

In Dixson's view, 'what emerges between the lines' in Quartly's work 'is a ubiquitous violence, inside and outside the home'. The ambivalence is seen in *Creating a Nation,* where Quartly comments that 'the system was easier on women and trapped them more securely'.[28]

If Quartly's work on convicts sits somewhat unconfidently within the new agenda, in *Depraved and Disorderly* Joy Damousi positions herself quite clearly within it by setting out to ask 'different questions' about female convict history and to focus on 'unravelling the cultural meaning' of key actions and gendered relationships.[29] Like the editors of *Freedom Bound,* Damousi creates something of a mythical past of feminist historiography in which her predecessors neglect the varieties of female convict experience, ignore the construction of femininity and remain trapped by a series of traditional questions and assumptions. In stating that a central purpose of her book is to make gender and sexual difference the basis of analysis 'rather than simply "adding" women to the narrative', Damousi restates rather than challenges the aim of feminist historians from the 1970s. And while she brings new tools and language to the task of deciphering the meaning of key relationships in convict society, and a refreshing focus on sexuality and cultural anxieties, the waters she traverses are not quite as uncharted as she suggests (Marian Aveling's [Quartly] work on marriage, Paula Byrne's on women and the colonial law, my own work on prostitution and convict resistance).[30] Nor does Damousi sit right outside the traditional debates. In *Depraved and Disorderly* convict women are construed as having 'agency' (they resist authority in multiple ways) and the state is perceived to be exploitative and intent on degrading and humiliating their charges. Ultimately, however, there is no real bringing together of the micro-environment of convict experience with the larger world of policy and historic change. While women make a space for themselves, they have no impact on the system, which remains unresponsive to them and intent on its purpose of humiliation and control. Both sides exist in a static world, in which policy is determined elsewhere and an individual's laughter is as effective a form of resistance as a mass riot.

Writing the history of convict women has indeed been dominated by a series of questions which emerged from convict history generally about the origins of convicts transported to Australia and their fate in the penal colonies. Many of these questions, which deal with the comparative treatment of convict men and women, the differing relationships between them and the state, the changing forms of convict management, questions of sexual, economic and legal exploitation and vulnerability, are of considerable importance if we are to understand the history of convict society and the position of women within it. At the same time, disentangling these questions from the moralising that has so frequently clouded them—part of the nineteenth-century inheritance—has meant that historians have felt compelled as well to deal with questions about the 'typical' female convict (prostitutes or wives) and about the most appropriate arena for investigating the effects of convictism (the factory or the family). One consequence has been that sophisticated versions of family history (like Babette Smith's study of her ancestor Susannah Watson in *A Cargo of Women*) have sometimes been more successful than broader studies in suggesting the complexity of convict women's lives.[31]

This book does not seek to ignore the questions that have dominated discussion of convict women in past historical writing. But it does set out to extricate the important ones from the thickets that have entangled them and, by reconstructing those questions and focusing on the experiences of convict women and their response to the economic, social and cultural world they inhabited, attempts to approach them in ways that allow us to penetrate more deeply into the history of convict society.

3

TRANSPORTATION
AND ITS MANAGEMENT

While the focus of this book is on the experiences of convict women in the colonies, there are some broader aspects of transportation which need to be explored to place this experience in context. This chapter looks at aspects of the debate about the origins of convict women, the pattern of their dispersal within the colonies, and some key factors in the chronology of their management.

The profile of convict women themselves is important: some of the major work on convict women has been statistical, with the interests of historians directed primarily towards establishing the pattern of movement to the penal settlement and towards questions of origins, criminal profile, age and marriage data and more recently, with Deborah Oxley's work, skills and employment background. Oxley provides a much sharper focus on female convicts than earlier statistical studies, and her work is much less distorted by moral distractions. While the pattern of direct transportation from Britain and Ireland is well established, and is summarised here, the less formal movements of convict women between convict settlements is more elusive, particularly (as Maria Lord's story suggested) in the case of the arrival of convict women in Van Diemen's Land before direct transportation. Historians of convict history, most significantly

A. G. L. Shaw, have analysed the changing structure and objectives of convict administration in the penal settlements, providing a framework within which the experience of convicts can be interpreted. The pattern of administrative change as it relates specifically to women has, however, received less attention. In part this reflects the dominance in convict women's history of the New South Wales experience. Yet half the female convicts transported to Australia went to Van Diemen's Land and as Lyndall Ryan has pointed out, only that colony experienced the three phases of female convict transportation: exile, assignment and probation.[1] Some consideration is given in this chapter to the general framework within which female convict history can be explored and to the probation period more particularly, as well as to the Inquiry into Female Convict Discipline, carried out in Van Diemen's Land between 1841 and 1843, which in the history of convict women is as significant as the better known Bigge and Molesworth reports are in the broader history of transportation.[2]

One of the consequences of the Sydney-centred view of female convict history has been to concentrate attention on the pre-Macquarie period before the more formal and systematic elements of assignment were put in place. Women who went to New South Wales in the first twenty years and those who went to Norfolk Island and to Van Diemen's Land in the first decade of those settlements undoubtedly experienced the convict system very differently from those who were transported later. In numerical terms this was predominantly a New South Wales experience, although many of the same concerns and problems arose in the southern settlement. The introduction of the probation system changed the way male convicts were managed and is a significant stage in the history of convict administration generally. For women this change was less dramatic, and it is likely that the progressive implementation of reform of the system and the increasing emphasis on reformation and respectability was of greater significance for women than any abrupt change in policy. In that sense the history of convict women in Van Diemen's Land is of interest not mainly because it allows us to consider three distinct phases of administrative history but because it gives the opportunity to scrutinise incremental change over a longer period after 1820 when dilemmas of management had intensified.

For more than sixty years from 1788 when convict women landed with the First Fleet, female convicts were transported to New South Wales and Van Diemen's Land—24 960 in all. Until the early 1820s almost all of the women sent from Britain went to New South Wales, although a number arrived indirectly at settlements on the southern island or were transshipped to other settlements, at first to Norfolk Island and then to settlements of secondary punishment such as Moreton Bay. The *Maria*, which embarked in 1818 with 126 female convicts, brought thirty of them to Hobart. It was not until the *Morley* arrived in 1820 (by which time about 500 convict women had arrived indirectly in Van Diemen's Land) that a female convict transport came direct to Hobart. In 1840 transportation of convicts to New South Wales stopped and Van Diemen's Land became the sole destination for transported women. The *Duchess of Northumberland*, which arrived in 1853 in Hobart with all but three of the 219 women who had embarked on her, was the last ship to carry female convicts. Although transportation to Australia did not cease until 1868 when the last convict ship docked at Fremantle, none of the nearly 10 000 convicts sent to Western Australia were women. In all, over 132 000 convicts were transported, with women making up about 15 per cent of the total.

The twenty-year period from 1830 was the time in which the transportation of female convicts was greatest, with approximately half of the women transported during this time. But the ending of transportation to New South Wales in 1840 meant that for half this period Van Diemen's Land carried a disproportionate burden. From that year 8673 women disembarked in Van Diemen's Land, averaging 667 a year, compared with 223 a year between 1826 and 1840 and seventy-four a year from 1820 to 1825.[3]

According to Robson's figures, of the nearly 25 000 women who were sent to the penal colonies, 55 per cent were tried in England and Wales, 33 per cent in Ireland.[4] Irish-born made up 47 per cent, while 43 per cent of the women were born in England and 9 per cent in Scotland; the difference in the figures is testimony to the number of Irish women who had already experienced migration and relocation. While many Irish women had been sentenced in Britain—most commonly in Lancashire and London—46 per cent of all the female convicts were sentenced in a county other than where they were born. Deborah Oxley has calculated that of the Irish women 80 per cent committed offences in towns, even though most had been born in the country.[5] Young women (with greater frequency than young men) moved to towns and cities, in search of work, entertainment, better marriage prospects and away from what could be the suffocating demands of kin and community. Domestic service offered a home as well as a job and made migration easier, so that servants from rural areas were among the most mobile.

The average age of transported women was twenty-seven, and though women selected for transportation were meant to be under forty-five there was no strict regulation to that effect and the range of ages stretched, according to Robson, from eleven to seventy.[6] In the cluster of women Oxley looked at who were sent out to New South Wales between 1826 and 1840, the oldest woman was Catherine Finn, a first offender aged eighty, who died in the Female Factory at Parramatta in 1826, six months after her arrival.[7] Of the 3859 Irish-born and 2320 English-born convicts transported during this period only eight women were seventy or over, all Irishwomen. On Oxley's calculation 70 per cent of convict women were between fifteen and thirty (compared with 35 per cent of Ireland's and 28 per cent of England's female population). Young girls below the age of fourteen, though present in British gaols, were seldom sent, and girls of that age were the exception. One 13-year-old, charged with her mother and sisters in 1828 for stealing prints from a stall near Shrewsbury

Market, was given a sentence greater than her age. Her first colonial charge (there were few) was to be found in the groom's bedroom at her master's house—a youthful adventure rather than a serious misdemeanour.[8] Oxley suggests that the 'relative shortfall caused by not exporting children' was made up by sending out greater numbers of women in their twenties.[9] Her figures show that of 6758 women, only forty-two were fourteen and under (0.6 per cent of the whole).[10] From fifteen on the numbers begin to increase rapidly, so that 17 per cent fall into the 15–19 age-group, 32.1 per cent are aged 20–24, 20.7 per cent 25–29. The remainder (approximately 30 per cent) were aged thirty and over.

About two-thirds of the women transported were unmarried, and in Robson's calculation one-third of the 34 per cent who had been married described themselves as widows. Oxley's figures are 62 per cent single with 14 per cent widowed; on her estimate a quarter of those married were 'effectively divorced by the distance'.[11] Many of the women who said they had left husbands at home later married in the colonies, perhaps because they had been widowed or because the marriages had not taken a legal form, or because time severed the relationship and they were able to convince the authorities that they were free to marry again. Certainly some women were refused permission to marry because the authorities were not convinced of their status, but in the early period there appears to have been a degree of carelessness (and pragmatism) on both sides and later a more considered flexibility. Phillip Tardif concluded that of the women in his study of 1675 convicts sent to Van Diemen's Land between 1803 and 1829, 57 per cent were known to have married in the colony, a figure he found very high.[12]

Women left children behind but also brought them with them, probably in lesser numbers. Both circumstances were of consequence. In the former case the pain remained; in the latter the presence of children posed from the beginning certain obligations on the colonial administrators.

The records are full of references to families that were broken up by transportation and exile. Elizabeth Disney, a laundress from Cork, brought all her three boys with her on the *Harmony* in 1828, but many of her shipmates made other arrangements: Ann Dunlop from Scotland left her children with her father; Elizabeth Fairham left her children in Sheffield with her husband's relatives; Ann Garret had her small son with her, but four others remained behind with their father on the Isle of Man; Margaret Harley, whose husband was in the army, left her 3-year-old with her mother-in-law; Mary Kirkland was a widow with six children, two of whom lived with her sister and two in Tralee; Rosannah Macdowell from York had one child with her, perhaps from lack of any alternative because her father, mother, brother, sisters and two husbands had all been transported.[13]

If transportation broke up families it could serve to reunite them. Also on the *Harmony* were Dorothy and Mary McWilliams, sisters aged seventeen and nineteen who had been transported for uttering forged notes. Originally from Belfast, they were convicted in Glasgow. Both stated that they 'wished to get out to our mother', Jean Jarvis. Jarvis had been convicted in 1821 and transported to Hobart Town where she married a free man, Archibald Campbell. She was aged forty. Both her daughters married not long after arriving and though a new start seemed likely, by 1833 Mary, who had been assigned to her mother, had died and a year later her sister was widowed. The system—both transportation and assignment—was used by the sisters for their own ends. Efforts were taken by the authorities to reunite the families of convicts, perhaps to ensure that women and children were supported within a family unit rather than become a burden to the state, whether that was to happen in Britain or in the colonies.

Robson saw the transported women as an almost undifferentiated mass, 'almost all' domestic servants or prostitutes who occasionally 'may have acted' as domestic servants.[14] Although a few were 'more skilled' (such as bonnet-makers and needle-women) some of these callings were, according to Robson, 'probably invented on the spur of the moment'. As an example of this he gave Phyllis Perry, a prostitute, who, though recorded as a domestic servant, warned 'I have never been brought up to housework'—a statement which appears to confirm that Perry was one of those women with a less than serious attitude to work. Going back to the records it is clear that Phyllis Perry was in fact from Staffordshire, and the reference to her lack of domestic skills was an indication of her work experience rather than her attitude: she was not a servant but a nailer. This was 1829, about which time nail-making was one of the main trades employing women in the Black Country's metal industry. It was wretched, hard physical work, beset by fluctuations in employment and, in the words of a parliamentary report, one of the 'unfit occupations for women': certainly not a training ground for domestic service.[15] Nor was it a trade in demand in the colonial labour market. In saying that she had not been brought up to do housework Perry was responding to the attempts of the authorities to find out not whether she had skills but whether she had that limited range of (mostly domestic) skills that could be put to good use in Van Diemen's Land.

While women mainly fall into a narrow range of skill categories, it is their diversity rather than homogeneity of occupation that is striking. In *Convict Maids* Oxley sets out to show that what was true of convict men was also true of convict women: that they were ordinary British and Irish working-class people, who far from being 'unskilled in all but vice' brought with them a representative range of skills which made them well equipped to contribute to the economic prosperity of the new colonies.[16] Oxley places the women from her cluster in five categories: professional occupations (none); intermediate occupations such as publican, schoolmistress and fruit dealers; skilled occupations, a vast range which include artisan trades (needlewoman, straw bonnet-maker, upholsterer, mantua-maker, milliner), traditional occupations (butter-maker, midwife), specialist servants (cook, housekeeper, housemaid), industrial occupations (weaver, potter, nailer, wool-spinner), institutional workers (nurse, asylum attendant); semi-skilled occupations (various indoor and outdoor servant categories, stage dancer, reaper, governess, charwoman, washerwoman); and unskilled occupations (servants of all work, pedlar, hawker).

There seems to be much that is arbitrary in these classifications which link occupations with skills, and Oxley is not completely happy with the categorisation, particularly in relation to the occupations designated as 'unskilled', a description which she doubts can be 'justifiably applied to many jobs'. Her view, which appears to be that most women's work is by definition either skilled or semi-skilled, further reduces the usefulness of this classification system and her conclusions. If few female occupations are unskilled and all convict women listed occupations on their records (regardless of whether they were employed or unemployed, when they last worked, for how long they worked or how proficient they were in their trade) it is unlikely that the evidence could demonstrate anything other than the conclusion that most convict women were skilled or semi-skilled. Nor is it likely that evidence of criminal association will appear as significant, although many female convicts, if not members of a 'professional criminal class', had been transported because of their involvement in a criminal subculture. More useful is Oxley's conclusion that they were 'surprisingly' literate and numerate and that in comparison with women generally, convict women from England came disproportionately from domestic service occupations, while factory workers were underrepresented.

Oxley not only examines the employment backgrounds of the convict women but dismisses the conceptual framework which underpinned much of the earlier work—the concept of a 'criminal class' itself, which she sees as a powerful myth created by moral entrepreneurs such as Patrick Colquhoun, Edwin Chadwick and, most influential in the context of Australian convict history, Henry Mayhew.

The criminal backgrounds of women transported to Australia have long been the subject of historical inquiry, but it would be hard to say that the picture that emerges from the largely statistical studies is completely satisfying. Whether or not women were prostitutes—not an activity for which women were transported—was given some emphasis by Robson in his early study, and this, along with the particular attention paid to London, supports his general view that the convict women were 'an indifferent' class or batch of women.[17]

Robson concluded that it was probable that about 60 per cent of women transported had been punished previously, and that if the number of former offences is taken as the criterion of criminality, Scottish women were 'the most abandoned', followed by the English and then the Irish; at least one woman in five was a prostitute.[18] Eighty-three per cent of the women in Robson's sample were transported for 'offences against property', largely larceny and theft of wearing apparel. Robson's women are remarkable largely for their homogeneity, committing similar offences whether in the large towns or the provinces. Crimes that diverge from this pattern are 'man robbery' (of interest because of its association with prostitution), animal-stealing (mainly an Irish crime) and arson.

Oxley's study looks in much more detail at a larger number of convict women.[19] She has regrouped the crimes into new categories which make analysis simpler: breaking, picking pockets, receiving, robbery, shoplifting, stealing, vagrancy, violent crime and other crimes. Goods stolen are also classified into eight categories. She calculates that 58.9 per cent of convict women were transported for stealing and another 19.6 per cent for robbery. These figures change somewhat according to country of origin and location, so that 66 per cent of Irish convicts were transported for stealing and only 51.4 per cent of English convicts for the same offence. Robbery, shoplifting and picking pockets were ranked next. The striking difference between English and Irish convicts is vagrancy, for which 4.6 per cent of Irish convict women were transported and no English women. The theft of clothing was by far the most likely among thefts of property. London women were less likely to steal money, food or animals than other women and more likely to steal jewellery and homeware, related to the fact that, Oxley suggests, they most often stole from employers and lodging keepers. A greater proportion of convict first offenders from London—both male and female—were transported, in the case of women over 80 per cent (compared with less than 60 per cent of other convicts).

Oxley's main concern is to establish that convict women were not habitual criminals and were not drawn from a criminal class. Consequently London, where criminals were thought to congregate, is the subject of some attention. By showing that crime in London did not fluctuate according to the season (as suggested by Mayhew and others who talked of the rogues leaving town in the summer) while rural crime fluctuated in relation to the seasons, she suggests that crime was driven by economic need rather than the opportunistic behaviour of professional criminals.

The transport of women to the penal settlements is not looked at in detail here, but its history provides a microcosm of the general history of convict management. In the minds of contemporaries and later historians the ships carrying convict women were linked to images of sexually aggressive women and promiscuous relationships formed on board. This view is coloured by descriptions of early voyages such as that of the Second Fleet vessel *Lady Juliana*, which arrived at Port Jackson in June 1790 with an exclusively female cargo of convicts who had been on board for nearly fifteen months. In the words of ship's steward John Nichol, 'when we were fairly out to sea, every man on board took a wife from among the convicts, they nothing loath'.[20] The enclosed world of the ship allowed investigations into sexual relationships to be more conclusive than similar inquiries conducted in the penal institutions, so that when, for instance, the *Janus* arrived in 1820 carrying a number of pregnant female convicts, blame was attached to individual seamen, including the captain, to whom one convict woman was pregnant.[21]

A similar situation involved the captain and crew of the *Duke of Cornwall*, in which women said to be in relationships with the first mate and surgeon-superintendent became pregnant while on board.[22] Strong evidence suggested that numerous liaisons between captain, mates, sailors and convict women had taken place, and although no specific claims were substantiated, an inquiry concluded that there had been such 'great irregularities' that those in charge had showed themselves 'unfit for so important a charge'. Hatch doors were said to have been left unlocked to allow women to spend the nights in officers' cabins. A convict woman 'pimped' for the crew, enlisting young girls and hiding them in the water closet until it was safe to send them below—a profitable practice until they 'got in with' the officers and did not need her help any longer. Gifts of rings, money and silk handkerchiefs changed hands. Moreover, relations between officers and women appear in other ways to have been informal, with the first mate in the habit of pulling the bedclothes off women in the wards to make them get up and the captain saying to another, 'If the black cook took a fancy to you, you would go with him'.

These incidents are all the more striking because they took place well after a stricter regime had been introduced. Just as there were attempts from the 1820s to ensure that assignment was administered more efficiently and that there was less opportunity for masters to sexually exploit convict servants, regulations were also progressively introduced on ships requiring the separation of crew and prisoners, preventing the transport of male and female convicts on the same ships, and introducing greater supervision of convict prisoners. As in the convict institutions, female prisoners found that they were under greater surveillance, more subject to the disciplines of work, daily routine and instruction. The surgeon–superintendent took on a supervisory role, becoming responsible for both the moral and physical well-being of convict women.

In the case of the *Duke of Cornwall*, which left Dublin with 200 convict women and arrived in Hobart on 27 October 1850 (thirty years after the *Janus* and sixty years after the *Lady Juliana*), not only were strict regulations in place but the ship also carried free settlers (one of whom said he had never told what he saw for fear of 'becoming a marked man among the sailors') and a matron.

While attention has tended to focus on the progressive enforcement of more effective regulation on board convict ships and on the increasingly significant role of the surgeon-superintendent, these changes and the employment of women supervisors did not eliminate the practices noted on earlier vessels. In the 1840s English prison reformer and Quaker, Elizabeth Fry, had convinced the authorities of the efficacy of sending out matrons on convict vessels to assist surgeon-superintendents (usually women who were to work in one or other of the colonial institutions), but the task of changing the male culture on board ship was a daunting one.[23] As matron, Mary Anne Downing had tried to intervene on the *Duke of Cornwall*, only to be abused by the captain and told by the surgeon that the reports she had heard were false. In the relative safety of the Bishop's Residence in Hobart, where she gave evidence, she said she considered she had not been supported enough by the surgeon–superintendent and the officers during the voyage.[24]

The journey to Australia carried certain hazards, including sexual exploitation, but disasters at sea were infrequent, and in all the years of transportation shipwrecks claimed fewer than 550 lives, of which nearly half were convict women on two ships.[25] The first of the convict ships to be lost on the journey to Australia carried a female convict cargo, 106 women accompanied by twelve children. In 1833 the *Amphitrite* ran aground during a storm near Boulogne on the French coast. With thousands watching on the shore (and a nervous surgeon-superintendent preoccupied with the fear that his charges, mustered on the deck, would escape), the ship broke up. None of the women and only three of the crew survived.

About 145 convicts were lost when the *Neva* was wrecked on rocks off King Island in Bass Strait. A female convict transport carrying 150 women, the ship sailed from Cork for Sydney early in 1835. Nine free women and fifty-five children

were also on board. Attempts to launch the boats were unsuccessful and many of the women died on board the ship when
it broke up. About twenty survivors, including twelve of the
convict women, clung to wreckage and found their way ashore,
where more died of exposure before some were found two
weeks later.

Apart from these major disasters, some perished on the
journey to Australia through illness and misadventure, and
some found the journey unbearable, following as it did the
separation from family and friends. The voyage of the *Duke of
Cornwall* was striking not only because of the sexual behaviour
of convict women and crew but for the mass hysteria that
swept the ship as it crossed the line, with twenty women at a
time 'taken ill with fits' so severe that they required four
women to hold down one (and which persisted for some even
after arrival).

The arrival of ships carrying convict women direct from
Britain and Ireland is well documented, but women were also
transshipped between settlements and arrived as individuals in
less formal ways. Moreover the major settlements spawned
penal outposts to which convicts were sent for secondary
punishment, and female convicts were dispatched to some of
those.

Van Diemen's Land initally received female convicts in a
haphazard way. Among Lieutenant Bowen's party, which
established the first European settlement in Van Diemen's Land
in 1803, were three convict women. One of them was Mary
Hayes who had been convicted in 1801 at the age of thirty-four
for receiving stolen goods. She was accompanied at Risdon
Cove by her husband, who had been convicted with her, and
her 14-year-old daughter Martha who became Bowen's
mistress and bore his two daughters. Mary Hayes became
the proprietor of the Derwent Hotel and remarried after
her husband's death. Mary Lawler, from Ireland, also came
with Bowen's expedition, remained dependent on the government when his party left, and died in 1814. Other convict
women were among the second expeditionary party to land in

Van Diemen's Land, that of Lieutenant-Colonel Patterson whose settlement was established at Port Dalrymple in 1804. And as we have seen, in 1805 a group of women who had been transported to Sydney on the *Experiment* came down to Hobart on the *Sophia*. By 1810, with a population of 1321, there were twenty-three female convicts, and a ratio within the convict population of ten men to every woman.[26]

Increasingly women began to arrive in Van Diemen's Land in larger groups. After Colonel Davey became governor in 1813, 200 female convicts were brought from Sydney, many on the brig *Kangaroo*. Disposal was chaotic rather than systematic and appears to have replicated the early experience of New South Wales. Of one such arrival John West commented:

> Proclamation was made, and the settlers were invited to receive them. There was little delicacy of choice: they landed and vanished; and some carried into the bush, changed their destination before they reached their homes. Yet such is the power of social affections, that several of these unions yielded all the ordinary consolations of domestic life![27]

It has been suggested that from 1814 a more orderly regime was established in Van Diemen's Land as the demand for convict labour, including female convict labour, steadily increased,[28] but while convict women came in greater numbers from that time, there is little order in the process, at least as West describes it. A substantial number of these women arrived late in 1814 when the *Kangaroo* brought nearly sixty women to Hobart from the ship *Catherine*, which had earlier arrived in Sydney with 97 female convicts on board. These women were Irish convicts, and many were married soon after arrival, a number to free men. Most did not vanish (at least not from the convict records, which document their marriages and their continued brushes with authority). One, however, literally disappeared. Lost in 'the Woods' (can any experience have been more alien for a servant at home in Dublin's streets?), Ann McDermott's body was found after three days.[29]

Knopwood's diaries record the regular cargoes of female

convicts which arrived during this period on ships plying between Sydney and Hobart. He gives no details and ventures no opinions of the women, but he does record the way Hobart society celebrated the arrival of such vessels. In October 1814 Knopwood's own dinner party included the master of the *Kangaroo* and his wife and the Lieutenant-Governor, and was followed in the space of a few days by a ball and supper on the ship (which had by then relinquished its cargo), a ball at Government House and then 'the greatest dinner given in the colony': a dinner, ball and supper for all the ladies and gentlemen in the colony, given by Mr Lord and his ex-convict wife.[30] The batches of convict women who arrived from this time were entering a society intent on recreating some of the familiar forms of civilised behaviour. They were unlikely to have the same, exceptional opportunities that Mrs Lord herself had experienced.

The main early convict settlement established from Sydney was Norfolk Island, to which a considerable number of women from the Second Fleet were dispatched. Convict women were also sent to the more remote settlements established in New South Wales as places of secondary punishment: Newcastle in 1804 and Port Macquarie in 1821. Dispatch to assignment in 'the interior' (in Van Diemen's Land) and to confinement in outer settlements became a way of dealing with refractory women and continued well after secure places were available to hold them in the main centres. 'Exile' thus remained a strategy in the administrative repertoire of convict administrators, and women, like male convicts, could be doubly banished as a form of secondary punishment. Consequently some women were sent from Sydney and Hobart to the settlements established for the worst offenders, although none went to Port Arthur, the last and most sophisticated of these.

Female convicts were sent to Moreton Bay, which became a place of secondary punishment in 1824, and to its adjunct Eagle Farm after its establishment in 1829. In 1831 thirty-three women from the 'crime class' at the Parramatta Female Factory (the class to which women were sent for committing offences) were sent to Moreton Bay for three years for rioting.[31] By 1836 more women were working in the fields at Eagle Farm than were employed in the usual institutional tasks in the Female Factory in Brisbane, and a year later all the female convicts were removed there. The number of female convicts at Moreton Bay varied from an average of under 50 in the early period to between 60 and 70 when the establishment was closed in 1839.[32]

Convict women in Van Diemen's Land were also sent for a short period to one of the places of secondary punishment more usually seen as the destination of 'the worst description' of male convicts: Macquarie Harbour. Eight females were among the group of about 120 convicts initially sent to the settlement. They were not the only women there, as the settlement also included some military wives. Agreement was given for convicts' wives to accompany them (if 'of good character'), although one female convict sentenced with her convict husband to secondary punishment there was prevented by Arthur from accompanying him (this man had previously been convicted for brutally beating his wife).[33] The convict women occupied what was described as 'the penitentiary' built on the small island in Macquarie Harbour. Some of the women gathered shells for limeburning; others were employed as servants. It was not long before disciplinary problems arose, with three soldiers being court-martialled for visiting the women. As a result of 'numerous cases of immorality' the women were moved back to Hobart.[34]

Lyndall Ryan has suggested that historians have tended to treat convict history as if all women had the same experiences, when in fact three clearly discernible phases of transportation took place over a period in which there was also considerable change in economic and social conditions.[35] Writing of Tasmanian history, Ryan describes the early years between 1803 and 1813 as a period of 'exile' ('the open prison'). The period from 1815 to 1843 she suggests was the time in which systematic transportation of convict women from Britain began and their treatment was transformed into 'a coherent system of forced labour'. This coincided with a move to settle retired defence force officers and their families in the colony and to encourage the creation of a gentry. Transported female convicts were assigned to become their servants and, according to Ryan, they lost the opportunities they had previously possessed: to work for themselves and earn money after hours, to contract marriages with the officer class, and to gain access to land grants on becoming free: 'Their social and economic opportunities were more clearly directed as members of the working class.' The last period from 1844 to 1853 she describes as the period of 'probation/incarceration' in which women were withdrawn from society for long periods and subjected to a regime of silence and instruction.

Ryan's argument is a timely reminder that women experienced convictism differently in different periods and that the tendency to merge these experiences into one timeless set of relationships can be risky. How useful her periodisation is will be tested here. Convict women's experiences clearly differed not only according to time but according to place. While the extensive use of incarceration signals a major shift in the management of convict women, the idea that in the early period female convicts enjoyed greater benefits is difficult to assess, especially as the greater the freedom women experienced the less protected they were. Moreover the nature of the benefits varied from place to place. The unusual features of early penal settlements which encouraged relationships between people of different social status and which led on occasions to advantageous marriages (Esther Abrahams to George Johnston and Maria Risley to Edward Lord) were largely confined to New South Wales, where there had been substantial numbers of convict women from the beginning of European settlement. While Maria Risley enjoyed some of those advantages, which stemmed from her meeting with Edward Lord in New South Wales and her arrival in Van Diemen's Land as his companion, her shipmates from the *Experiment* who came to Van Diemen's Land on the *Sophia* and were assigned as servants did not. The only administration that seems to have encouraged the economic independence of women on the same terms as men was Norfolk Island under Major Ross, who, in contrast to Phillip at Sydney, not only fostered the economic self-sufficiency of convicts by giving them land to work full-time but seems not to have structured these arrangements on gender terms, so that women as individuals, in sexual relationships or in groups with male convicts, all received the same land and assistance.[36] While in many ways the features of the early period are distinct, differences between settlements are also evident.

The extent to which assignment ceased to be of such significance in the last years of transportation is problematic as it persists in new forms, reflecting colonial scepticism about institutional reformation and the belief that women were destined for a domestic future. Regardless of the attack on assignment as a 'lottery' in official inquiries and support from Britain for that view, in the colonies faith in the policy of assignment for women was never completely abandoned. To place this in context requires some attention to the report and evidence of the 1841–43 Inquiry. This unpublished inquiry is a substantial and sometimes acute investigation of both assignment and incarceration, and deserves a place in history alongside the Bigge Report and the report of the Molesworth Committee. Its conclusion, that in assignment lay the best chance of reform for women, came after the Molesworth Report had condemned assignment generally and as the British Government acted to end assignment for women in the penal colonies.

The Select Committee on Transportation (the Molesworth Committee) was appointed in April 1837 and reported in August 1838. It was against the background of this debate that Glenelg wrote to both Bourke in New South Wales and Franklin in Van Diemen's Land in May 1837, asking them for any suggestions they might have 'with a view to the discontinuance, at the earliest practical period, of the Assignment of Convicts to individual settlers'. Convinced that 'the great improvements which have of late years been adopted in our

system of Prison discipline in England' should also be introduced in the colonies, Glenelg also asked Franklin to examine
what means he had at his disposal for ensuring that 'any
portion' of the convicts were subjected to a 'more efficient
system of prison discipline'.[37] Bourke was responsive, but it was
not until he received further instructions in July 1838 to stop
assignment immediately that Franklin announced its abandonment. In the following month the Molesworth Committee's
report, critical of transportation in general, condemned assignment in particular. Witnesses were particularly scathing about
assignment as it applied to female convicts, suggesting that they
were 'retained in the service of the lower description of settlers,
by whom ... they are not uncommonly employed as public
prostitutes'.[38]

In 1840 transportation to New South Wales ceased, and
in the following year the assignment of convict women in New
South Wales ended. The census showed 1838 convict women
under assignment, 979 in government employment (most of
these women were in the Parramatta Female Factory) and 316
ticket-of-leave holders. In 1842 the women remaining in the
factory petitioned the Governor, asking for assignment to be
revived. They had been sentenced to transportation, they said,
not to transportation and imprisonment. By 1846 there were
only 250 women in the factory, and its declining role was
apparent. In the same year female inmates from the insane
asylum were moved there. By 1848 the administrative positions, including that of matron, had been abolished.[39]

The cessation of transportation to New South Wales created more difficulties for the southern settlement struggling to
introduce the new probation system. From 1839 female convicts were only to be assigned after they got their tickets of
leave, but in 1842 Stanley urged the absolute end to the system
of assignment for women convicts. No newly arrived female
convict was to be assigned, nor were they to be allowed to
mix with the old hands at the Female Factory, but to be
confined separately. In Stanley's words: 'This is a system which
it is necessary altogether to remodel; while it continues, the

evil it engenders is constantly perpetuating and increasing itself.'[40] Over the remaining period a number of changes were made, but forms of assignment continued to play a part in the system of female convict management. By the end of transportation women were being assigned on arrival in Van Diemen's Land, much as they had been thirty years before.

The 1841–43 Inquiry could not reverse official opinion on assignment, but it did indicate that attitudes to assignment for female convicts were far from negative. It also dramatised the need for reform of the female factories. Exile could not remain the only form of punishment for convicts in the infant penal settlements. Secondary offences and misdemeanours committed in the colony gave rise to the need to confine or punish those offenders in some other way. Once the state adopted the role of moral custodian, a place of confinement became a necessary element in the effective functioning of both the assignment system and secondary punishment for women. The more chaotic arrangements of the earlier period were transformed into a system in which labour (mainly through assignment) and punishment (through a network of female factories) became the twin concepts underpinning female convict management.

The practical need to create places of confinement for women (constrained by the cost of doing so) intersected with the British and American debates about punishment and prisons. In Britain the Molesworth Committee (which was critical of immediate, physical punishments as well as assignment, for similar reasons) followed two other inquiries into punishment and prisons which formed part of a move to reform and create a more uniform prison system in Britain and give the central government considerably more power over penal institutions.[41] Central to these reforms was the debate between the advocates of 'separate confinement' (in which cellular isolation played a major part) and the silent system in which prisoners worked in groups. Separation was designed to remove the most abandoned from contact with the well behaved, and reformers saw it as a solution to many of the problems which had been insufficiently addressed by other measures such as the classification of prisoners. But it was costly, requiring expensive renovation of existing prison accommodation or the building of new structures.

The reshaping of the institutions holding convict women was influenced both by these debates and by local concerns and considerations. While the ideas of Elizabeth Fry were influential in the 1820s through Darling and Arthur, by the late 1830s in New South Wales and early 1840s in Van Diemen's Land (following the inquiry) ideas based on cellular separation and silence became influential. It is this rather than the introduction of 'probation' that makes incarceration in the later period different.

Ryan sees two successive phases of institutionalisation under the probation system in Van Diemen's Land, culminating in the effective silencing of women. Women continued to be confined in a number of institutions through the probation period, but the capacity of the authorities to restrain them seems to have varied considerably between institutions.

How distinctive the probation period was generally for convict women is difficult to establish, especially since implementation of policy fell so far short of intention. While it is possible to describe fairly clearly both the aims and the impact of the probation system on male convicts, its effect on female convicts is less easy to define. What perhaps it showed best was the intractability of the problems which faced the managers of female convicts and the problematic nature of their continual search to find a surer path to reformation for women convicts than that provided by their simple release into marriage or the labour market.

The policies and methods of female convict management manifested themselves differently in different places and changed substantially over the period of transportation, with considerable impact on the way women experienced convictism. This took place, however, in a colonial setting in which there was a strong strand of scepticism about reform through institutionalisation and an alternative endorsement of marriage and assignment as the best means of reforming the individual. And convict women were never totally compliant or passive, either as assigned or incarcerated convicts; the shape of convict management bore their imprint as well as the effect of wider debates in Britain and the penal colonies about transportation, punishment and reform.

4

ASSIGNMENT

Assignment was at once the most criticised element of the penal system and the most lauded. Its critics saw it as a form of slavery and as a lottery. Masters not only freely received the benefits of the convict's labour and controlled their lives beyond the gaze of the authorities, but for the assigned man or woman the burden of punishment could be heavy or light depending on the character or whim of the master. Both punishment and reward could be excessive. At a time when reformers came to believe that the best way to manage criminals was to subject them to the discipline of daily routine, measured tasks and standardised punishments—as well as constant observation—the unpredictability and private nature of assignment increasingly became a source of difficulty. On the other hand assignment allowed convicts to live in society, not to be shut away from it. It held out the possibility of reform, if not the likelihood of deterrence. It provided both a transition to freedom and a foretaste of it.

From the early period of settlement a form of assignment took place and convicts worked as servants to the military and to free settlers. As well, female convicts were assigned to their husbands and male convicts to their wives. But assignment as

a systematic element within the architecture of penal administration did not develop immediately.

In the beginning of European settlement the management
of female convicts was haphazard. Their disposal was largely
resolved in two ways: by encouraging the formation of relationships of varying kinds with the male population of the
colonies and by allowing those men who wanted servants to
select women for domestic work. The two strategies were
interlinked. It was to the nature of that connection that some
initial attention was paid, rather than to the issues of public
policy and administration which would later become significant. The Select Committee on Transportation reported in
1812 that women convicts had been 'indiscriminately given to
such of the inhabitants as demanded them, and were in general
received rather as prostitutes than as servants; and so far from
being induced to reform themselves, the disgraceful manner in
which they were disposed of operated as an encouragement to
general depravity of manners.'[1]

The relationship between assignment and sexual behaviour
continued in the case of women and this, along with the lower
value that was attached to female labour and the particular
intimacy of domestic work, meant that the female experience
of assignment was very different from that of their male
counterparts.

Convict women were employed in domestic tasks as soon
as the ships arrived, in the tents of the early settlements, in
work such as cleaning and laundry, and they continued to work
as government servants on various tasks as the settlements grew:
in the hospitals, orphan institutions and the female factories
(sometimes working on the manufacture of cloth), doing
needlework and laundry. Women are recorded as assisting in
the building of the first settlement by making pegs for tiles
and collecting shells from the beaches and Aboriginal middens
to be burnt to make mortar[2]—work that was later taken over
by the male 'shell gang'. But to observers such as Tench the
first months of the settlement at Sydney Cove were remarkable
for the 'total idleness' of most of the female convicts[3] (in

marked contrast to the heavy work being undertaken by the men). From the start, the decision that women would not do heavy manual work structured the workforce around gender. Their employment as field labourers later at Moreton Bay was unusual since essential work for the government such as farming, clearing bush, building roads and public buildings, which continued to be a large employer of male convicts, provided only marginal employment for women. And though women convicts on arrival were either assigned into private service or kept to work for the government, public labour never played the part in their employment that it did for male convicts.

In August 1789 assignment into private service began, and from this time convicts worked for officers and officials, and increasingly for free and freed settlers. Land was granted to serving officers, and large-scale farming increased after Phillip's departure at the end of 1792; officers were given convict labour to clear and cultivate the land and to erect buildings. Phillip had believed that granting convicts to officers and settlers would decrease those labouring for the public good, but Grose and Hunter allowed them ten convicts at public expense, although they were after 1797 expected to maintain them.

Governor Hunter, who was less comfortable than his predecessors with the idea of female convicts being assigned to individuals, wrote in 1796 that there was 'scarcely any way of employing' convict women, and even if employment was available many women were taken up with nursing infants ('the charming children with which they have filled the Colony'). King, in 1802, described those female convicts engaged in public labour as 'generally the refuse of London', with few capable of doing useful work such as spinning.[4]

In 1798 Hunter had tried to bring some order into assignment by requesting that officers and other householders notify the Judge Advocate's Office of the names of their female convict servants and report when they discharged them (along with a 'character'). Women were not to be withheld from public labour or retained for purposes other than those permitted by the authorities. From an examination of the records of the eighty-seven women on Hunter's assignment report, Portia Robinson has argued that 'all women were not necessarily treated as prostitutes by their masters'.[5] She also concluded that while some of these women were 'without doubt' assigned to respectable families, fourteen were described as wives to their masters and many others were assigned to men they would eventually cohabit with or marry. This suggests that assignment in the early period operated as an effective means of enabling men (and convict women) to find sexual and domestic partners.

Governor King—to whom convict Ann Inett had borne two children while he was in command of Norfolk Island—wrote in 1806 that 1216 of the 1412 convict women in the colony did no government work but were self-supporting or living with men, with a small minority, 'mostly incorrigible' women, confined within the Parramatta Female Factory. He reported that 'the well-behaved' were 'selected and applied for by settlers and others to become their housekeepers or servants'.[6] After selection by the 'industrious part of the settlers, with whom they either marry or co-habit', they proved themselves to be very useful, 'not only in domestic concerns and rearing stock, but also in agriculture'.

The distinction that King made between the 'well-behaved' and the 'incorrigible' and his assessment of the suitability of convict women for domestic work (preferably within a household economic unit) rather than for public work defined the boundaries of appropriate female behaviour and continued to underpin the administration's thinking about female convicts and their disposal. Rather than challenging these assumptions, later debate focused more sharply on the process of disposal and relationships within the household.

As private servants women did both indoor domestic work and outdoor work, providing some of the essential farm labour (especially milking and butter-making). Phillip had female convict servants, one of them becoming his housekeeper.[7] Convict women were later assigned to small employers such as shopkeepers. Often they did the heavier, less skilled domestic chores such as washing and cleaning, and lived as members of the household. But in the first two decades of the settlement in New South Wales the majority of convict and ex-convict women lived in legal or de facto marriage relationships, and their work as servants was indistinguishable from their responsibilities as wives.

For assignment to operate effectively as a system of domestic labour, women needed to be housed before and between assignment periods, but at first, both in New South Wales and Van Diemen's Land, there were no institutions for that purpose. Women were left to find their own lodgings and shelter and it was commonly believed that, 'let loose upon the Inhabitants to find a lodging where they can', many were forced into cohabitation and prostitution.[8] Describing the building of the main street of the new town at Rose Hill in 1788, Watkin Tench mentions nine houses for unmarried women, as well as a number of small huts for 'convict families of good character'.[9] From early in the settlement single women like Esther Abrahams and Mary Johnson, who had the protection of officers, had their own huts.[10] After the establishment of the first female factory at Parramatta this continued, since the building was inadequate for housing the numbers of women in need of accommodation. Even those women working for the government were not assured of shelter: evidence given to Bigge in 1819 showed that nurses employed at the General Hospital in Sydney still lived at lodgings in the town.[11]

Similarly in Van Diemen's Land there were no attempts either to house or systematically dispose of women convicts who started to arrive in the colony in greater numbers from 1814. Those who came from Sydney as individuals in the early years were often already assigned and accompanied their masters (such as Ann Ward, who arrived in 1813 as the servant of a married couple, and, less formally, Maria Lord). But increasingly women convicts came in larger groups. In 1820, the year in which direct transportation from Great Britain to the colony began, Lieutenant-Governor Sorell advised Macquarie that without suitable accommodation for the women in

Hobart there would be no alternative but to allow them on arrival 'to go at once at large'.[12] Dispersed at the dock or from the deck of the arriving transport as West described, they were easily exploited by masters who wanted a 'concubine' rather than a servant.

Some evidence that this was the case is suggested in the Tasmanian convict records, which show that women arriving at this time in Van Diemen's Land sometimes married the men to whom they were assigned, as they had done in New South Wales—a practice that ceased as assignment became formalised. Mary Moore, who arrived at George Town in 1820 and at the 1823 muster is listed as servant to J. Luffman in Launceston, is listed in 1827 as 'Now Luffman'. Ellen Kennedy and Mary Doyle also married their masters. All were transported to Sydney on the *Janus* and were in a group of women transferred to Van Diemen's Land on the *Princess Charlotte*. Also on board was Mary Funnell, aged 51, who was listed as a servant to Mr Willson at the 1823 muster. She married Willson three years later and in 1831 they were joined in his Harrington Street house by her son, who had been transported to Sydney. Of the women who arrived on the *Princess Charlotte* these seem to be a small minority; many married convicts and some became servants to well-established Hobart households (Mrs Lord had considerable difficulty with some of the convict women assigned to her from this vessel in 1820). How many were taken as sexual partners is not disclosed in the records.[13]

Little concern was paid by the authorities to either the intentions or the behaviour of a master with an assigned female convict servant in the early period of settlement. While concern with the sexual balance of the small population of the penal colonies was paramount, what was tacitly acknowledged was that a variety of relationships involving women included a sexual transaction. Work was not completely separate from sexual exchange, and many relationships involved both labour and some element of sexual service. While in reality this continued, greater concern with respectability and evangelical morality demanded that work be redefined as separate from sexual service except in the case of prostitution, leading to the idea of 'the prostitute' as a worker quite different from other workers.

But condoning the sexual relationship which assignment frequently became began to give way to concern about its practical and moral implications. The temporary nature of domestic arrangements added to the numbers of women and children being left for the government to support. And as greater attention was paid to the reformation of convict women, more emphasis was placed on marriage and on redefining the assignment relationship as formally that of master and servant. Marsden's observations on the condition of female convicts drew attention to the moral issue and to the absence in the first twenty years of settlement of any 'serious Attempts for the Reformation of the Female Convicts'.[14] First Bligh and then Macquarie were urged to attend both to the reformation of convict women and to the question of marriage.

These new concerns led to the reshaping of assignment as an instrument of public policy. In 1810 Macquarie advised the Secretary of State for the Colonies that he had prohibited the 'shameful practice' of the indiscriminate disposal of convict women which King had outlined, and from 1812 on he tried to ensure that female convicts were assigned only to married settlers. De facto relationships ceased to be publicly condoned and were no longer encouraged by practices which allowed women in such relationships special rights of inheritance. Stricter and more rigorously enforced rules about assignment were calculated to reduce sexual exploitation. But the unwelcome sexual demands of masters, male members of the household and other male employees and servants continued to be a hazard for assigned women.

In the early period penal administrators structured both work and dependence around gender. Assumptions about work and the family meant that women were for the most part thought of as sexual partners and mothers, while men were thought of as workers. The labour market as it developed in New South Wales had distinct advantages for male convicts.

Because male labour was in the early period in short supply, convict men could earn extra wages for additional work. Those working for the government were required to earn enough for their lodgings and worked a short day. Tickets of leave were given to encourage convicts to work for themselves and to spare the government the expense of supporting them. This reduced the effectiveness of convict control. Just as the management of female convicts could not be efficient without the provision of institutions to hold them, male convicts could not be controlled unless there was a place to accommodate them. In the case of women, lack of government accommodation made them more vulnerable to the demands of individual men, and the lack of employment forced them into prostitution and dependence.

In 1814 Macquarie recast the system of convict administration by forbidding masters to let their servants work for themselves. He built the Barracks to house male convicts (completed 1819) and the new Female Factory (completed 1821) to house women. The assignment of servants was formalised, with magistrates supervising their employment and punishment. The final element in the system was the provision of appropriate and respectable masters, which was helped by the increased number of settlers with capital emigrating to New South Wales after 1816.[15] Even so, by 1819, with greater numbers of convicts sent to New South Wales, it was impossible for private assignment to absorb them, and substantial numbers of convict men continued in government employ on Macquarie's building program.

The assignment of women as servants to private households became the experience of the majority of convict women in Macquarie's time, and after 1818 in Van Diemen's Land. Macquarie introduced a certificate of indenture in 1815 which bound masters to providing for their female convict servants for a term of three years (although the impracticality of such a measure suggests it was seldom implemented). In 1818 in Van Diemen's Land wages for assigned servants were set at £10 a year for men and £7 for women, including rations of

£7 and £5 10s if slops were supplied. Assigned servants had no right to their own time, since they were not allowed to work for themselves or others without the master's permission. Further regulations in the same year stipulated what rations should be given, what was to be left to the discretion of the master (tea and tobacco were included in this category), what clothing and bedding should be made available and under what circumstances, and that suitable lodgings and medicine should be provided. Other regulations defined the boundaries governing the convict's freedom; they included the provisions that convicts must not be allowed out at night, should not labour for themselves, and should have no set working hours.[16]

The female factories enabled the development of assignment as a systematic element in the management of convict women. They operated as holding depots for newly arrived women and those awaiting assignment, and were essential to the disciplinary process, as it was through these institutions that women were punished for their behaviour while assigned. The classification system at the new Parramatta factory allowed women to pass through to assignment as a reward. Women in the first class—the only class from which women were to be assigned—were treated with greater leniency, and women progressed to this class if they had been guilty of colonial crimes or misdemeanours. Assigned women who committed minor misdemeanours could be committed to the second class, while more serious offences might lead to incarceration in the third (or penal) class. The numbers of women in the first class fluctuated in relation to the numbers of new arrivals and the demand for female servants. As free female immigrants began to compete with convict domestic labour, numbers increased. While the condition of the labour market lay outside the government's control, various governors (e.g. Bourke in 1832 and Gipps in 1840) sought to control numbers in the factories by introducing penalties for masters who returned servants who were not guilty of an offence.

The early patterns of employment in the penal colonies seem to have advantaged male convict workers, but tighter regulations restricted their capacity to earn extra wages and brought them under greater supervision. These restrictions affected women's independence less. Female convicts received fewer benefits from the earlier practices and gained some comfort from the provision of what could be a refuge (harsh though conditions in the female factories were). On the other hand they lost some of the opportunities for forming partnerships which the laxity of the earlier period provided.

Assigned work, as it became more regulated, continued to provide different experiences and opportunities for male and female convicts. As well as the hazards of sexual exploitation and the difficulties of the labour market, female convicts were faced with other conditions which structured the way they experienced assignment and made their experience quite different from that of men. Male convicts often worked outside without supervision and frequently enjoyed the companionship of fellow convicts. Women were more likely to work indoors and tended to be more closely supervised. Like domestic servants, female convict servants lived in close contact with the master and other members of the household. They had less contact with fellow convict women, and their opportunities for mixing with their fellows was constrained by their lack of control over their working hours. Domestic work was not, like task work, measurable and discrete. As Paula Byrne suggests, the domestic work of female convicts 'did not result in a quantifiable amount of free time which the female servant could sell to her employer or another person'.[17] It flowed into the whole day, so that when the routine tasks were completed other activities (like minding property and children), continued. In response, the most common offences tended to involve absences and neglect of work. Women were charged with taking children with them to public houses. Hannah Clewlow, a Staffordshire potter found in a house of ill fame, evaded the consequences of such a charge only because her master said he had 'given her liberty to take a walk out with the children' (1830).[18] Because no time was their own and masters were increasingly responsible for the reformation of convict servants and therefore for their moral welfare, all aspects of their behaviour became legitimate objects of concern.

The double moral standard which existed in nineteenth-century middle-class society meant that greater demands were made on women than on men. This distortion in expectations was compounded for female convicts because of the greater intimacy of their living arrangements. Consequently the reformatory process was, for women, more demanding. Behaviour which was acceptable in a man working out of doors was not acceptable in a woman living as part of the household and caring for small children. It is not, as John Hirst suggests, that contemporaries were oblivious to the fact that they expected much more of women as servants than they did of men.[19] While the Molesworth Committee internalised the double standard (and this underpinned their view of convict women and their assignment), colonial administrators by the 1840s were sensitive to this distinction and its implications and were less willing to condemn the assignment of convict women merely because complaints about them were so clamorous. In the words of the final report of the committee inquiring into female convict discipline in 1841–43:

> Neither were we ignorant that a degree of coarseness of character which might not unfit a man for labouring in the field would completely disqualify a female for being attendant upon a family, that Society had fixed the standard of the average moral excellence required of women much higher than that which it had erected for men, and that crime was regarded with less allowance when committed by a woman than if perpetrated by a man, not because the absolute amount of guilt was supposed to be greater in the one case than in the other, but because the offender was deemed to have receded further from the average proprieties of her sex ...
>
> ... a higher degree of reformation is required in the case of a female, before society will concede to her that she has reformed at all ...[20]

Because so much was expected of female convict servants

and so little private space was given them, complaints were frequent. Many were concerned with sexuality, ranging from sexual acts to behaviour that was lewd, improper or provocative (such as being 'saucy' or 'pert'). 'Coarseness of character' encompassed both appearance (dirty or unkempt) and behaviour which fell outside the accepted boundaries of what was 'feminine'—foul and abusive language, outrageous conduct, drunkenness, raucousness and insolence. While male convicts were commonly charged with acts such as theft, convict women were frequently charged with transgressing norms of feminine behaviour.

Complaints were also made about the capacity of assigned convicts to perform the duties of servants. Although the vast majority of women who were transported gave their occupation as 'servant' or some similar category (housemaid, nurserymaid, cook, 'country service'), many women did not possess the skills expected of domestic servants. Nor did they meet the exacting standards of their masters. Some women were returned because they were 'useless'. Free servants were often unsatisfactory too, and were charged with similar offences under legislation which regulated both convict and free, but convicts had additional disadvantages. As convicted felons, they came without what was called a 'good character' in a free servant; as convicts, they could easily be returned from domestic to government service should they prove unsatisfactory. These factors encouraged complaints about assigned servants and reduced the likelihood that charges against mistresses and masters would be taken seriously.

The existence of female factories helped in the transfer of assigned servants between masters, as Paula Byrne has noted of Parramatta, and the factory acted as a pool of labour for dissatisfied employers. Her figures suggest a rapid turnover: in the half-year for 1829, 210 women were returned from private employment to the first class and 275 to the third class for various offences.[21] Those who went into the first class were immediately available for reassignment, which was of concern to the Factory Board of Management, suggesting that it believed some penalty ought to be attached regardless of whether women were guilty of offences. When penalties for masters were attached to the premature return of servants who had not been charged with offences, the number of 'offences' increased. The existence of female factories facilitated the working of the domestic labour system. They also helped assigned servants to use the system to their own advantage, to negotiate their transfer from difficult masters, and to exchange information which allowed them to develop strategies of survival.

Once formalised, assignment was regulated by law, and convict women could try to manipulate the system or use legal means to protect themselves. Regardless of the odds, convict servants did bring charges against their masters. Mary Anne Carberry's case suggests that sometimes this could be done out of naivety.[22] Carberry was a first offender, from Dublin, sentenced for arson ('house-burning')—the sort of convict woman historians have tended to treat sympathetically. She had only been in Van Diemen's Land for a month when in 1852 she alleged that her master had taken 'indecent liberties with her' one day when her mistress was in bed sick. She told her mistress what he had done and said that she would not stay in the house. A few days later she refused to do her work, and when the constable came for her she explained the reasons for her behaviour. Before the magistrate her master denied the charge, stating: 'I am the prisoner's master. I never took indecent liberties with her either by word or action.' And in reply to the prisoner: 'I did not put my hand in your bosom and blow the lights out.' She was not believed and was given six months in the Cascades Female Factory in Hobart with hard labour, alternate months to be spent in the separate cells, after which she was to be sent to the interior. Harsh penalties were designed to prevent convict servants bringing frivolous or dishonest charges against their masters, but must also have discouraged them from bringing legitimate complaints, especially without other witnesses to support their testimony.

While it was unusual to be able to substantiate a charge

against a master on the grounds of his sexual behaviour, it was not impossible, especially if the boundaries between private and public behaviour had been transgressed. Winifred Mackew may not have intended bringing her case to the attention of the Hobart authorities, but she was given very little alternative when during 1850 she was found by a constable in Shadwick's public house in New Town and accused of being absent without permission from her service for the whole night. Mackew defended herself by saying that she was not absent from her master but with him.[23] John Hughes, she said, often took her from his house to his mother's house to sleep. On this occasion they had gone drinking in the town, met up with some other people and gone on to the pub in New Town. There Hughes had left her in the company of his somewhat drunken friend Lawrence. The 17-year-old convict girl had not wished to go with Lawrence, but he had threatened her ('because I would not consent to remain with him all night'), and after he booked them both in as husband and wife and settled down to do some more drinking she had gone upstairs to the publican's bedroom and sought the protection of his wife. The publican would not or could not identify Hughes, but a cabman and another woman in the party identified both men, describing Lawrence as 'tipsy' but Hughes as 'perfectly sober'. This case is interesting not only because Mackew's master was acting as a pimp and offering her sexual services to another man, but because the public nature of the occasion allowed the young woman to seek protection and to provide witnesses to support her charges.

Finding protection was not easy, and hoping that the law would provide it either in a legal sense or in the person of the local constable could often result in disappointment. Constables (often ex-convicts themselves) sent to take convict women to and from places of assignment frequently assaulted or harassed them, getting them drunk, taking them to public houses or taking sexual liberties with them. Anne Reece, who was being transferred by steamer to Brickfields in Hobart in 1852, was detained by the captain in his cabin and sexually assaulted.[24] Mary Haigh, who had arrived in the colony in 1838, gave evidence at the 1841–43 Inquiry that when she was being taken from Richmond to Hobart the constable, encouraged by other women in the party, 'wanted me to have connection with him'.[25]

Haigh (at this time a married woman with a ticket of leave) said that there were many places in Van Diemen's Land to which servants should not be assigned, and where girls were 'allowed to be on the Town'. At the same inquiry Grace Heinbury told how she had left one situation 'on being insulted by the male servants'. At another she was asked by a lodger 'to prostitute myself to him', adding, 'he was a married man and his wife selected me herself from the Factory'.

The sexual vulnerability of female convict servants was increased by the unwillingness of colonial authorities to inquire closely into the character and habits of prospective masters, even though observers were aware that some masters (and mistresses) were not only uninterested in assuming a disciplinary role but were engaged in exploiting the women assigned to them. While surveillance and classification were key elements in the repertoire of convict management, they were seldom extended beyond the servant to the master. In the words of Hobart Police Magistrate John Price, the process of distinguishing between suitable and unsuitable places of service was 'too inquisitorial'.[26]

The refusal to permit a person to take assigned servants, or their removal from those who were not exercising sufficient discipline, was always fraught with difficulty. In 1834 Arthur instructed the Van Diemen's Land Assignment Board not to give reasons for not assigning convicts; to do so would be to place it 'in collision with every man in the colony who is not given servants'.[27] There is some evidence in the convict records of masters thought to be unsuitable who lost the right to have female servants assigned to them. When Mary Clifford (who had already been charged a number of times for drunkenness) was found out after hours in Hobart in 1832 she was 'returned to Government' and her master described as being 'considered to be unfit to have a female servant'. Mary Miller in 1830 'falsely accused' her master of 'assaulting her with lewd intention' and the complaint was dismissed. Curiously, however, the records noted that 'the woman's accusation appearing to be well founded, she is removed from her Master's service and placed in the Assignable Class'.[28]

Sometimes sexual exploitation and the absence of protection for convict women brought tragedy. Mary McLauchlan, the first woman executed in Hobart, who was hanged in 1830 for what was described in the records as 'the wilful murder of her male bastard child', had brought two charges against her master and mistress which were dismissed.[29] Married to a weaver in Scotland and the mother of two girls, she had often been heard to say (as the *Hobart Town Courier* reported) that she wished that her infant would not be born alive. The paper concluded, without speculating on its meaning, that the only motive for the crime was that of malice towards the father. Even so, it would be a mistake to conclude that because assigned servants were vulnerable (to the sexual advances of masters and of other servants) all such relationships were forced or that exploitation was always their most dominant feature. A decade after McLauchlan's execution, John Price stated his belief that the prevalence of abortion among convict women was caused not by their fear of punishment at the factory but by their wish not to be 'separated from the connexion formed'.[30] Mary McLauchlan, hanged before a large crowd in her white dress and black ribbon, may be the ultimate victim of laws which exacted harsh penalties but refused protection, but like the women who used abortion to stay with their lovers, she was not a passive victim.

Convict women with experience of the system were likely to use indirect methods to deal with what they called 'bad places' or with masters and mistresses they disliked and for whom they did not wish to work. A number of offences were used by convict women as a means of manipulating the assignment system. Offences such as insolence, refusal to work and short absences without permission carried light punishments and could be used effectively by women wishing to change places. Grace Heinbury found in her first place of service that she was to work with a shipmate she disliked, so she told her mistress that she 'could not do "housework"' and was returned to the factory.[31] The volume which lists charges brought in Hobart against convict women servants for the period 1850–54 records the words of one mistress complaining of a servant whose actions cut short the possibility of protracted negotiation: 'Prisoner yesterday told me that she had done enough work and she would not do any more—she said she was tired of the place and would not stop and she brought her clothes into the house and put them on the table.'[32]

At Cascades all the 'good places' in which women were allowed to do as they pleased were known, and ways to manipulate the system were taught—essential if women were to afford themselves some advantage and some protection. As Mary Haigh described it, 'The women with whom we trafficked told us all the "ways" of the Colony and how to manage if we got into bad places. Telling us that we must be insolent, disorderly or must run away.'[33]

Court records in Hobart for 1850–54 give some insights into the master–servant relationship. They are full of charges against the convict women: 'going into a brothel with a man'; 'not proceeding to be married'; 'having a man her fellow servant in bed'; being found in bed with another woman and two male ticket-holders in a common brothel; drinking instead of going to chapel; taking the master's child to a pub; giving a disease to a 14-year-old boy; dancing in the taproom; attempting suicide; being absent from her husband's house; not in the proper care of her husband. They also document the way some convict women responded to these charges (refusal to work; not cleaning but instead smoking a pipe) and some retorts: 'I'm as good as you'; 'I've worked for better mistresses'; 'the worse I'm punished the worse I'll be.'[34]

Narrative accounts which detail the way women experienced assignment are rare, but some remain in the convict records. Mary Haigh's description of her experiences as an

assigned convict servant is interesting less for the drama (for
her story is remarkably without incident) than for what it
reveals about her own responses.[35] Haigh arrived in Hobart on
the *Arab*. She waited for about a week at the Female Factory
and then was assigned as a nurserymaid to a 'Gentleman's
Family'.

> I had at this time plenty of clothes of my own. I
> remained in this service four or five months during which
> time I received neither wages or clothes with the excep-
> tion of one Gown which was taken away from me when
> I left this service. I never asked for my wages I had plenty
> to eat and drink being strictly kept to the House. I was
> returned to the service of the Crown as I refused to obey
> my Masters Mother in Law—no charge of misconduct was
> however preferred against me—At this house a freewoman
> was kept—She had a bed and bed stead mine was made
> on the floor. The free woman had sheets but I had none—
> The Servants dined together but at other times I was kept
> away from the free servant.

The 'Gentleman's Family' Haigh was first assigned to was a
disciplined household with gradations between family and servants, free and convict strictly maintained. Her next place was
very different.

> I then went to Brighton the mistress was a Prisoner hold-
> ing no indulgence the Master a Blacksmith. I had only to
> attend on a child. I might here do as I liked I was
> allowed to drink go to the Public House and might
> remain out all night if I pleased. I had no wages and only
> one pair of shoes from my mistress. If I applied for any-
> thing I was told that they were too poor to give it me
> telling me I might get it how I could provided I did not
> trouble them. I remained in this situation six months and
> was then sent to the Crime Class being charged with Inso-
> lence to my mistress with whom I had a quarrel—I was
> treated by her as her equal and could not respect her. I
> had a disturbance with my mistress in a Public House and
> the Landlady gave me into custody. My mistress tried to
> get me off but could not succeed—I was passed down to
> Hobart Town.

Haigh was next assigned to a person in the country (at the Clyde): 'This was a good place I was allowed clothes and was very comfortable. I was never "allowed out" but I was contented.' Later at Swanport she was also 'comfortable' and 'strictly kept', but eventually quarrelled with her mistress.

These experiences provide a catalogue of what was important to assigned women: food, clothing, shelter, wages, discipline, the relationships of the house. The significance of food to convicts generally is acknowledged. In New South Wales the resistance of male convicts to maize prevented it from becoming the staple in the convict diet in place of wheat, to the inconvenience of masters.[36] Space and living conditions within the house were also the subject of contention.

Clothing, however, had special importance. Clothes could be bartered and sold, and those women who brought clothing with them on the voyage, into the factories or into service had considerable advantages. Convict Sarah Bird, whose public house the Three Jolly Settlers was the first to be licensed in New South Wales, had brought goods with her and sold some of her clothes on arrival to provide capital for her business venture.[37] For female convicts clothing was currency. For women who had been subjected to the procedures of the penal institutions (its uniforms and short hair), dressing well was also a matter of self-respect and a way of reclaiming both individuality and femininity. Women who were able to afford clothes because of prostitution were envied, and it was their dress which was said to tempt younger women into the trade. One woman who was alleged to have earned money by prostituting herself on the *Duke of Cornwall* used it to buy clothes from an officer's wife at the New Town Farm Depot. Others on board the same ship accepted gentlemen's silk pocket handkerchiefs as payment for sexual favours. Grace Heinbury ran away from a position in Hobart where she wore all her clothes out and could afford no others: '[I] could not even obtain soap to wash myself with—No money was given me—my food was Potatoes and Herrings and cakes made with ration flour bought from prisoners in the Penitentiary.' Mary McLauchlan (who, as we have seen, was later executed for infanticide), when charged with misconduct had counterclaimed that she had 'not received the proper quantity of clothing'.[38]

Both female and male convicts were concerned with the way they dressed. Jane Elliott has suggested that very early in the history of Sydney, convicts 'began to assert themselves socially' by the money they spent on clothing.[39] Both men and women spent large amounts of their earnings on clothes, of good quality if they could afford it and in imitation of those of higher status. Dress obliterated the difference between the free and the convict. This and their habit of spending on other goods such as tea, sugar and tobacco mirrors the convict concern with the food and clothing they received while assigned as servants, and their tendency to place significance on the availability of these items when assessing a master.

Many of the 'offences' committed by convict women in the colonies which resulted in them being further punished were acts of disobedience committed while they were assigned servants, such as laziness, insolence, drunkenness or being absent without permission. One woman who gave a very detailed description of a dispute with her mistress which led to severe punishment was a convict woman called Jane Miller. She was a passholder, employed as a house servant and needle-woman at the Hobart house of Josiah Spode and his wife. Spode was a convict administrator and erstwhile member of the committee which inquired into female convict discipline.[40] She lived and worked in the house and waited on Mr and Mrs Spode, their family and their guests. She wrote to the authorities to put her own case:

> On the morning of the 3rd October I was very bad and said to the Laundress I am not able for my work this day. She was sorry for me and when she went to clean the parlour passage she went into the parlour and cleaned the grate for me. I then went into the rooms and finished them as best I could. I was then called upon to get breakfast ready for Mr Copeland and bring [it] upstairs. I was ordered to bring up hot water for Miss Scott. I told Mrs

Spode that I was very ill and unable for my work thin-
kin[g] she would allow the Laundress to assist me.
Without once *thinking* of leaving my place at that time.
Mrs Spode said it was false, that I only said so to get
away but she would send me to Mr Mason [the magis-
trate]. I came down stairs and went to my room. Miss
Spode came in after me and said '*Dear Me* I am very sorry
for you. You will be better [for] the dark cells and bread
and water. Out with you, you Convict wretch, you are
not fit to be in a room with me.' I said I will be glad to
get out for fear they would do to me as they had done to
the Cook. I went to go in to the kitchen but Miss Spode
said no, no—out of the house with you, you abominable
wretch. I took her advice as I thought it was the safest. I
asked Miss Spode for my book which she had the loan of.
She brought [the] book and threw it out to me and said
you need not be so careful for your books you will be
obliged to come back again. I said never if I should put
my head upon a block. Miss Spode went in and told her
mother what I had said. Mrs Spode came down stairs and
called me in and asked me what I meant. I said I was not
able for my work. Mrs Spode said she would do for me.
She said I will humble *your* pride. Mrs then asked me
what I had done with the purse and the 15 shillings that
was left in Miss Ellens desk last night. I then thought of
what I was told before I went to serve with them and my
heart sunk within me. I said O Mrs Spode take care what
you say for your conscience will not always sleep. She
told me to [give] her none of my cant. The constable
came up and I was given into charge.

Many convicts had been transported for less than stealing
fifteen shillings. When the constable arrived, Mrs Spode said
that she wished her servant to be searched. Because the
constable could not search her Mrs Spode offered to do it
herself and got Jane to remove her clothes, shoes and stockings.
Jane went on:

Mrs Spode ordered me to take down my hair which I
did. Mrs Spode then took up a knife and cut the trim-
ming of my cap … I was afraid of the knife and cried

murder. The door of the room opened from without and Mr Spode said my dear let Jane go.

Mrs Spode then accused Jane of wearing one of her daughter's petticoats, but Miss Spode said that it was Jane's. No money was found. Mrs Spode next accused her of being drunk. Jane was then borne off by the Constable, without all her clothes or her wages, which were due the next day. In the letter she defended herself against the charge of theft, saying that she was completely innocent and that everyone in the house had the same access to the desk as she, adding, 'I do not think a servant in the house would take a shil[l]ing belonging to them. They know too well who they have to deal with. Neither did I ever see as much ready money in the house of the cruel oppressors.'

By the time Jane Miller wrote this letter she had already been tried, convicted and sentenced to twelve months' imprisonment with hard labour in the Cascades House of Correction in Hobart. Miller was a 'passholder', and subject not to the assignment system but to the probation system which replaced it. No longer to be degraded 'Domestic Slaves', women like Miller were paid wages. She was not assigned to an ex-convict mistress or a single man but to a well-off and well-known family. The size and furnishings of the house and the presence of specialist servants (cook, laundress, housemaid) suggested urban gentility. In other respects, however, the situation seemed little changed. Her letter—owing something in style, perhaps, to her reading—was persuasive. Furthermore the authorities had received many complaints made by passholders 'of the ill treatment they state they have been subjected to in Mr Spode's service'. But to agree with Jane Miller was to undermine the authority of those who had convicted her, and the Comptroller-General was sensitive to 'the importance of not disturbing the verdict of magistrates who may be called upon to deal with Convicts'. She remained in the factory, where her behaviour was 'very good'.

The relationship of master (and mistress) and servant was

clearly a complex one, involving a variety of expectations—about payment and conditions, about personal space and intimacy, about sexual rights and the possibilities of long-term relationships, about social status and the entitlement to respect. Jane Miller was set upon by vindictive women. Mary Anne Carberry was outraged at her master's advances. Winifred Mackew tolerated her master's behaviour (it seems) until he offered her to another man. In exceptional cases the master seems to have become the dominated party, as in the case of Mary Ann Anderson, who disobeyed her master's orders, neglected her duty, was insolent to both master and mistress and 'threatened to knock her Master's brains out with a poker'. After a time in the factory she was returned to her master, 'who states that he wishes to have her'.[41]

Few women were able to pervert the assignment system as effectively as Ann Solomon, the wife of the famous fence, Isaac (Ikey) Solomon. He escaped to New York but she was sentenced in 1827 for receiving stolen goods, and transported to Hobart, bringing her four young children with her. Two elder sons went to Sydney 'as gentlemen to settle'. She was assigned first to a family, then to her husband after he joined her and on his arrest (and return to England for trial), assigned to her son. Assignment for Mrs Solomon did not mean that she became a domestic servant; instead it enabled her to reconstruct her household. Assigned to the family with whom her sons lodged, her 'mistress' did the work, as her record discloses: '1828 Assigned to Mr and Mrs Richard Newman where according to another servant, she was not required to work, Mrs Newman doing "all the Drudgery of the house".'[42]

Robert Hughes described the assignment system in Australia as 'by far the most successful form of penal rehabilitation that had ever been tried in English, American or European history'.[43] For all its faults and uneven results the 'assigned man' worked within a legal framework that protected his rights, he could be rewarded for his efforts, and he gained skills that were useful in the new environment. In contrast to the inhuman discipline of the penitentiary system, assignment was, according to Hughes, 'the early form of today's open prison'.

Is such an optimistic view of assignment also applicable to women?

Male convicts benefited from the value that was attached to their labour and the demand for the skills they brought to the penal settlements. In *Convict Workers: Interpreting Australia's Past*, the editors conclude that the convicts brought with them a cross-section of useful skills, that they were on the whole better educated than their working-class compatriots, and as healthy. Viewed in the context of emigration history, these coerced migrants had further distinct advantages when compared to the free immigrants: they were mainly clustered in the most productive age groups, were for the most part unencumbered by dependants, and most were men. Moreover, few returned. The age–sex structure of the convicts provided 'a unique workforce base on which to build economic growth'.[44]

These factors have different resonances for women than they have for men. The most productive age for workers is also the most fertile age for women, and the experiences of pregnancy and motherhood were of central importance in determining women's experience in the penal settlements and their contribution to the economy. Employing workers unencumbered by kin may have been a condition which had attractions for some employers of labour, though in some positions a husband-and-wife team had advantages. And notwithstanding the attempts of many male convicts to begin new families or reconstitute old ones, for some men freedom from family ties was advantageous. (The desertion of women and children and the evasion of family responsibilities is a not inconsiderable theme in Australian history.) But for many women, the absence of kin meant a lack of protection afforded by fathers and brothers, an absence of the support offered by female relatives and the assistance which came from wider kinship networks. It might also have meant severance from an economic unit as well as a social one. The presence of a child, on the other hand, often conflicted with the demands of potential employers (particularly those requiring live-in servants), who expected a woman to have no dependants. Assigned women who became pregnant were returned as 'useless': Ann Thomas, 20 January 1830, 'Being in a state of pregnancy she is useless in her service and is therefore returned to the House of Correction'; Ellen Fraser, 25 January 1830, 'Returned to the House of Correction, being unable to perform her duty in consequence of having a child which is not weanable, and refusing to tell the Principal Superintendent who is the father of the child'.[45]

Rather than providing labour that was valued or in short supply, women worked mainly in the two general areas mentioned in *Convict Workers* for which there was little demand: domestic work and unskilled urban work. New convict arrivals, assigned women, and increasingly young women born in the settlements and assisted immigrants competed in a narrow labour market frequently characterised by glut.

Assignment institutionalised domestic labour as the vocational destination of most women—like women's employment more generally, it was seen as an interlude before marriage and a preparation for it. It was prostitution rather than domestic employment that gave women the same capacity as men to trade their labour in the market, although the market they were operating in was clandestine and unregulated.

It is apparent that assignment was for male convicts a transition to a full wage-based economy in which they experienced some of the advantages of wage earners—including those benefits (particularly in the early period in New South Wales) which flowed to workers in an economy in which labour was in short supply. Male convict labour was measured and rewarded. Female convict labour was neither valued nor comparably rewarded, nor was it ever in such short supply that it commanded high wages. Paula Byrne, in her study of the legal records in New South Wales between 1810 and 1830, points out that while the colonial administration struggled with measuring and weighing male convict work and its payment, domestic labour was neither regulated nor quantified in the same way.[46] While convict men were able to deal in that part of their labour which was not owned by the state or their master (and continued to do so regardless of regulations), women were more constrained and their rights less clear.

Byrne concludes that because the work women did in the household could not be measured in the way men's work was, and was not limited by time or task, the female domestic servant was 'bodily owned'. She was 'owned by the employer and could not bargain over her labour'. Moreover, she argues, the policing of domestic service assumed this. In the case of female convict servants (if not of free women), while in the first decades of settlement they may have been given bodily to their masters, systematic assignment saw the state rather than the individual master assume greater control over convict women's bodies. It was the state, by attempting to curb female sexuality and exert moral and labour discipline, that became the 'master' of women's bodies. Assigned women, like convict men, worked within a legal framework, and while the master's authority extended into the intimate lives of his servants, this power was increasingly circumscribed by the law and contested in a multitude of ways by convict women themselves.

One illustration of this is provided by the case of female convicts assigned to their husbands. Because of their convict status, these women were able to seek greater protection from the authorities than free women. Although a husband could charge a convict wife with a range of misdemeanours and have her punished, she could also be removed from his care because of his mistreatment of her. And she could contrive to be removed from his charge and be given refuge in the factory. Although in these circumstances his powers over his wife might appear to be more extensive than those of a husband, in other ways his authority was more circumscribed. A convict wife could complain to the authorities about her husband's behaviour and raise matters that in other circumstances would have been seen as purely domestic.

The convict record of Margaret Burke is one instance of this and discloses the torrid nature of her domestic relationship with John Smith, a freeman she gained approval to marry in 1830.[47] Less than a year after their marriage he charged her with using abusive language to him, and for this she was admonished and discharged. In the same year Smith assaulted her, and although she was directed to go to the Female Factory the order was revoked because of her 'advanced state of pregnancy'. Just after Christmas four days later, because of his 'ill-usage' of her, she was removed from his charge. (Re-assigned to Smith in 1832 she was still his wife at the muster a year later.)

Sarah Roberts' series of relationships provides another example.[48] Roberts had been convicted for uttering forged notes in 1821 and though she was described in the records as being married to a horse-dealer named Robert Wintham and had been accompanied by her 2-year-old son to Van Diemen's Land, she married soon after her arrival. While the wife of George Crump she was found, in 1826, to be illegally at large and returned to the factory for assignment. By 1830, with her new husband dead, she was in possession of her ticket of leave and living with another man, Richard Brown. Accused of being 'disorderly in her conduct', she was ordered to 'part from Brown immediately', but a year later they were still together (and were described as having been 'cohabiting for a consid- erable time past') and she was deprived of her ticket of leave. An indication of the nature of her relationship with Brown is given in the records, which suggest that she had come before the authorities because of injuries she had received at Brown's hands. Her arm had been broken and she was 'otherwise ill from the ill treatment she had received' from him. Four months later she applied to marry a free man, John Weavis, and they were married a month later on 8 April 1832 at Green Ponds. The marriage was short-lived. By the end of June Mrs Weavis had refused to live any longer with her husband and was sent off to the Female Factory to be assigned. In 1835, after three other charges had been brought against her, she received her freedom from the Crown. In one sense Sarah Roberts as a convict was more confined than a free woman and more likely to be punished or incarcerated for minor acts of disobedience. On the other hand she seems to have sought, with some success, the intervention of the penal authorities to help her deal with domestic difficulties. She continued to live with Brown, though with the disapproval of the convict administrators, until his violence towards her led her to seek their help. When she tired of Weavis she had a refuge to return to—the Female Factory—and help in securing a position in service—through reassignment. The state, in the shape of the convict authorities, provided more assistance to her than they would for nearly a century and a half to many free women who were victims of domestic violence.

The history of female convict administration is punctuated by regular inquiries and investigations, but none was more extensive or more significant than the official inquiry Governor Franklin set up in 1841 into female convict discipline. The board established on 15 September included the Colonial Treasurer as chairman and both the Principal Superintendent of Convicts and the Hobart police magistrate, as well as the Lieutenant-Governor's private secretary. Signatories to the final report (which was never published and exists, with the evidence, in manuscript) included Dr Adam Turnbull, who had been secretary to Arthur, Josiah Spode, Principal Superintendent of Convicts, John Price, police magistrate, and F. H. Henslowe, then secretary to Franklin.[49]

The committee was as concerned to investigate assignment as it was to examine conditions within the female factories. Sensitive to the social expectation that women should meet higher standards than men, the committee's conclusions were very different from the earlier findings of the Molesworth Committee which had been so critical of assignment and women convicts in general (drawing extensively on the views of Franklin's earlier private secretary Alexander Maconochie, who was by then in charge of Norfolk Island). 'It is not fair', they concluded, to form an estimate of the general conduct of the convicts here by those at present in the factory and who are going backwards and forwards to it as there are many who are assigned on their arrival and who conduct themselves so well as never to come under the notice of the authorities except when applying for indulgences. I should think that one half of the women who arrive here may be included in the latter class.

Although there was much evidence in the body of the report that reflected poorly on assignment, the committee put forward the view that while nothing was more conducive to reform than marriage, assignment, which isolated women from one another but not from the 'respectable community', was the best method of dealing with convict women. Quoting Police Magistrate Price, they suggested that both marriage and assignment were desirable because they excited 'the better feelings' and 'called the affections into play'. Supporting this position was its highly critical evidence about the female factories in Hobart and Launceston.

The committee was aware that, politically, it was too late to win comprehensive support for assignment, and it tried to draw a distinction between assignment for men and for women, stating:

> the evidence now submitted to Your Excellency in favour of a *well* regulated female assignment is probably more con-clusive than any testimony ever offered in the British Dominions ... We are, however, quite aware that as assign-ment has been discontinued with respect to men it may be contended that impartial justice requires that it should be equally discontinued in the case of Women ... But if it be clear that the measure of discontinuing assignment could not be extended to the case of the Female Prisoners without manifest moral injury both to them and to the Public, we do not think that Your Excellency will be disposed to attach much weight to the argument to which we have alluded.

By the time the report was handed down Stanley had already made his decision to end assignment for women and to introduce probation. To the views of Molesworth and Maconochie was added the voice of Jane Franklin. Writing to Elizabeth Fry in 1841, she condemned the situation where assignment for men was abolished but the assignment of women continued: 'all the women who come out here are still sent into Assignment. And not a single voice ... has been raised in England to save them from this tyranny and this degradation.'[50]

Jane Franklin had formed an early view that the system of female transportation was both 'vicious' and 'faulty'. In her opinion the committee's report (which, as she wrote to her sister in September 1842, 'is said to be unfit for me to read') substantiated her criticisms of the female factories but proposed remedies that were in some repects 'absurd and weak and preposterous'.[51] Lady Franklin's opposition to assignment, which the committee strongly supported, was as implacable as the British Government's.

The new system was introduced for women from 1844. Under probation women who had spent some time in prison in Britain were to spend six to twelve months on arrival in a reformatory establishment before being given a probation pass and sent to a hiring depot for employment as a servant—if there was sufficient call for their labour. Passholders were paid wages but did not receive them until they had earned their tickets of leave. Institutional arrangements under the new system were designed to introduce a more complete reformatory regime, which is examined in the next chapter. But by 1850 the failure of the new system was apparent and critics urged the end of confinement on arrival and in its place the immediate hiring out of transported women. From 1850 'reformation' was undertaken in British prisons and women were sent into private domestic service as soon as they arrived in Van Diemen's Land. When, for instance, the *Aurora* arrived in 1851 with 232 female convicts, within three months 179 women had been hired, eighteen were confined under sentence or in the hospital and only thirty-five were at the New Town Farm still awaiting employment.[52]

It is unlikely that the fundamental experience of assignment was actually transformed by the new probation system. In many ways assignment simply continued in a modified form. Magistrates' reports and conduct registers reveal that women were punished in much the same way and for the same disciplinary offences as they had been earlier, and that they used the same strategies to manipulate the system. Among the cases referred to in this chapter many come from the probation period, suggesting that women's experience of service under that system was largely indistinguishable from their experience of assignment. Some modifications were significant. These related primarily to incentives, first wages and later a reward scheme which encouraged women to stay with one master by reducing their sentences. In introducing this scheme in 1850 (at a time when there was a shortage of domestic labour), Denison said that it would encourage 'settled habits'.[53]

In the early years female convicts had been abandoned by the state as long as there were individual men willing to take them. In contrast, systematic assignment (and the probation system in Van Diemen's Land) intruded into every aspect of women's lives. Moreover, patterns established under assignment left a mark on free labour practices. Immigrant women bound themselves for set periods of time as servants and, after they became subject to the strictures of the Masters and Servants Act, found that their lives were almost as circumscribed as those of convict women.[54] In the early 1850s free women charged with disciplinary offences under that legislation joined convict women committed for similar offences in the Cascades Female Factory.[55]

If we are to look for a parallel with later times it might be that the assignment of women convicts is best compared to the regime of state detention which was applied well into the twentieth century to young working-class and Aboriginal girls. These women, who were sometimes guilty of 'delinquent' acts but who were more likely to have been seen as in some form of moral danger (because of their family circumstances or racial background), were separated from their kin and associates, 'trained' in institutions and sent out to perform domestic work as servants or farm labourers. As state 'wards' they too were protected by a legal framework and learned domestic skills both in the institutions in which they were incarcerated and in the households to which they were assigned. They were often vulnerable to various forms of exploitation, including sexual exploitation and forced pregnancy, and to the grief that came from separation from their own families and, later, from their own children. For women, practices established in convict times persisted well into the modern period, leaving a deep imprint on the community.

It could be suggested, then, that while the state was building a free-market labour system for men for which assignment was a preparation, it was also building a welfare system for women and children (consisting of detention, training and indented domestic employment) of which convict assignment gave a foretaste and which persisted in its basic form as a part of the policy repertoire of state welfare agencies well into the third quarter of the twentieth century. The escape from this system was marriage rather than employment. Moreover marriage allowed the family, fractured by the intervention of the state as children were removed to institutions, to be reconstituted (which work seldom did). Women thus experienced the power of the state very intimately in their lives, and while family life provided the best opportunity for self-reliance or 'freedom', when family life broke down it was the state to which women tended to turn for help through either the law or the welfare system.

5

THE FEMALE FACTORIES:
THE FAILURE OF REFORM

The female factories were characterised by a tension between two opposing tendencies. They could not have existed in the form they did without the ideas of the prison reformers and their urge for discipline, order and the reformation of the individual. Yet in many ways these institutions recreated the chaotic conditions of the eighteenth century against which the reformers had reacted.

Those who were instrumental in the development of the colonial female factories increasingly saw classification according to behaviour, observation and the separation of individuals from friends and family and from each other as the key to reform. The apotheosis of that system was the model prison built at Port Arthur in 1848, which emulated in the beautiful rural setting of the Tasman Peninsula the carceral machine that was Pentonville. There the aim was the reformation of the individual through the application of the ideas of the reformers in their most refined form. The architecture of the model prison transformed observation into surveillance. Separation came to mean isolation, in individual cells and ultimately the dark cell. Hoods worn during exercise, partitioned boxes in the chapel and the command of silence were all designed to create anonymity and prevent prisoners from communicating with each other.[1]

The Pentonville model and the silent system itself were never fully embraced by those in control of female convict administration. And, in the institutions that housed them, the ultimate aim of the reformers—to expunge the culture of the prisoner—was seldom realised. Prisoners were not fully quarantined from members of their own class. Nor did the regime prevent the growth of a prisoners' subculture, in which the values that the prison system set out to subvert survived or were transmuted into new and strange forms. The female factories established in the colonies of New South Wales and Van Diemen's Land demonstrated these tensions between the old and the new. They were curious hybrids in which the ideas of the reformers competed for dominance with a vigorous culture which in some ways is more appropriate to the unreformed institutions of the eighteenth century. This is not to suggest that they did not change nor that ideas about the management of convict women remained static. During the period of transportation both the methods of handling women and the objectives of their custodians were altered in many, sometimes fundamental, ways. Yet this was not sufficient to transform fully the nature of the institutions or the experience of the women incarcerated in them.

This chapter looks at the intentions behind the establishing of the female factories and at the inevitable failure to achieve the high ideals of the reformers. Later chapters explore further dimensions of this failure by looking at the hidden life of the factories: the subcultures and relationships which provided an alternate structure to the official system described here.

While the aim of the proponents of transportation had been to find an alternative to incarceration, over the period that convicts were sent to the Australian colonies the management of criminals in Britain was transformed. Pain inflicted in public on the body came to be replaced by the hidden punishments of the prison. These trends were becoming evident in Britain in the last thirty years of the eighteenth century when the procession to Tyburn (but not public hangings) ceased and use of whipping declined.[2] In the early penal settlements the dominant forms of punishment were both physical and public. The first hangings were ceremonial, with the whole population mustered before the gallows, producing (as the Sydney press described one occasion in 1806) a 'spectacle' which was both 'awful and impressive'.[3] The display did not always stop with death, and bodies were sometimes hung on a gibbet.

From the beginning punishment was applied differently to male and female convicts. For women flogging was used much less, although Foveaux was said to have applied the lash with relish to women on Norfolk Island and Edward Lord to have punished a woman who insulted his wife in the same way. Ralph Clark recorded regular sentences of twenty-five to fifty lashes for women on Norfolk Island (in 1791) and watched them 'faint away' before the full sentence was applied. John Nichol reported the flogging of a woman on the *Lady Juliana* after confinement in a flour barrel with holes cut for head and arms ('a wooden jacket') failed to restrain her.[4] From 1817 women continued to be hanged but not whipped. The absence of secure places of confinement in the early period meant that punishments other than incarceration were used extensively. Fines were common, although for women in particular the only way of raising money may have been through prostitution. Rather than the lash, physical punishments included hard labour, the use of heavy iron (and sometimes spiked) collars and, less commonly, the stocks. Ann Ward, who arrived in Van Diemen's Land as a servant to Mr and Mrs Lang in 1813, was fined five shillings more than once for drunkenness and was forced to wear the iron collar twice for theft.[5] Jane Womack, on suspicion of stealing, was forced to sit in the stocks and to work for the government for three years (her husband received a hundred lashes and six months in the gaol gang).[6] Women's heads were shaved, which they hated, and clothes were inscribed, in a form of branding. A well-known case from the first years in New South Wales was that of a convict woman, 'her head having been previously deprived of its natural covering', paraded before the muster wearing a canvas frock with the initials RSG (Receiver of Stolen Goods) painted on it in large letters. This was a public punishment which began with a theatrical ceremony (there had been no trial) and continued through personal branding. The woman's male accomplice had earlier been similarly attired in a canvas frock with an R for rogue, but he had also been flogged.[7]

Three cases (two involving the whip) suggest that particularly harsh physical punishments were used for women who challenged male authority. In New South Wales Deborah Herbert was sentenced to twenty-five lashes in 1788 for bringing a false charge against her husband (she accused him of beating her).[8] In Hobart in 1806 Elizabeth Murphy (who had written a letter to Francis Dring 'containing the most infamous language and accusing him of a most heinous crime') was sentenced by the Lieutenant-Governor to be tied by her hands to a cart drawn by the gaol gang, stripped and given twenty-five lashes, after which she was to be sent to Risdon.[9] In 1818 Alice Robson (severely beaten while pregnant by her husband and asserting his brutal ill use of her), sought refuge from him in a relationship with the Principal Superintendent at George Town. The commandant at Port Dalrymple ordered this 'profligate adulteress', who was at the time nursing a 2-month-old child, to walk thirty-five miles with a 6¼-pound iron collar around her neck.[10] These punishments were visible, economical, and physically painful, but not reformatory, even in intention.

In New South Wales and Van Diemen's Land the transportation system could not continue to function effectively without places of confinement. Secondary punishment, efficient assignment and any pretence of providing protection for women depended on the provision of institutions to house them. The institutions that were built to accommodate convict women had to serve multiple purposes, and it was this that made it difficult for them to fulfil the expectations of the reformers. A major theme in the history of female convict institutionalisation consists, therefore, in the attempts to deal with this complexity either by separation within a single institution or by the creation of other, single-purpose establishments. The *idea* of the penitentiary (which itself changed over time) was important in these deliberations.

Female factories, as we have seen, acted as arrival depots and as places for women awaiting assignment or reassignment. Potential masters came to them to select servants. Prospective husbands sought wives there (the Parramatta factory was famous for this). They offered a refuge for convict women in times of illness and pregnancy, and asylum from intolerable situations outside. Formally known in Van Diemen's Land as 'houses of correction', they were also places of imprisonment, in which women served out sentences for colonial crimes or received additional punishment for acts of insolence and disobedience. Though called 'factories', and though a variety of work was performed within them, employment was the least significant of their functions.

The factories at Parramatta and at Cascades, in Hobart, were not the only female factories in the colonies (there were others at Newcastle and Port Macquarie in New South Wales, at Moreton Bay and at Launceston, George Town and Ross in Van Diemen's Land), but they were the biggest and attracted most public attention. In the first factory at Parramatta, work was of some initial importance. Women who were not wanted as servants or who were to be punished were sent there to weave a coarse woollen material which became known throughout the colony as 'Parramatta cloth' in the same way that cloth woven at the George Town factory later was known as 'George Town cloth'. Consisting only of the upper floor of the Parramatta Gaol, the factory was reported by Governor King as affording 'for the first time in this colony the most comfortable asylum' for convict women. Accommodating women within the gaol precinct was a practical, short-term solution, repeated later in other settlements, rather than an 'experiment', although King reports that the women on the transport of that name—Maria Lord's ship—were among the first to be housed there.[11] Except for several who had already been 'indented', these women were retained to manufacture woollen and linen cloth. The factory within the prison did not contain enough room to accommodate all the women who worked there. Those who could paid for lodgings in the town. Some found a male companion to provide a bed and a roof. Women were released in the mid-afternoon after they had finished their government work and allowed to make money for themselves. Some women earned money in the one part of the labour market where they had a competitive advantage—prostitution.

Revd Samuel Marsden supported the building of a 'public Place of Accommodation' to protect convict women and their virtue.[12] In Van Diemen's Land, Surveyor-General John Oxley put forward a similar proposal:

> It is well known that the greater part of the Women Con-
> victs have from their Youth been brought up in every
> scum of wickedness, destitute of Industry, unable from
> Ignorance to work, even if they possessed the inclination
> to render themselves useful. It will be evident that the
> Task of reclaiming and bringing into habits of Industry
> such Characters will not be an easy one, and that it will
> not be aided or assisted in the smallest degree by the
> endeavours and disposition of the Women themselves. To
> suffer such wretches to be let loose on society without
> any restraint would be a serious injury to the quiet and
> well disposed among them, and that [sic] any mode of
> employing them would be preferable to such an alterna-
> tive.[13]

He went on to suggest setting up what he called 'a Well regulated Factory', which he believed would be the only way to make the women useful rather than a burden on the public. It would not be necessary, he argued, for the factory to be 'converted into a *Nunnery*', for

> if the Women could be induced to Manufacture the
> Cloathing, that might be wanted for themselves and for

the Male Convicts employed by the Government, together
with some Canvas for the use of the Colonial Vessels, it
might be just as well not to be too strict in confining
them after their labour was performed, with the exception
of the very worst and most irreclaimable characters.

Oxley did not believe that such an enterprise would pay
for itself but he did think it would keep the women busy and
prevent them from 'doing Mischief', at the same time giving
them 'a chance of Individual amendment' so that they could
in the future find honest employment and not return to their
former ways of life. One significant characteristic of both the
early practice at Parramatta and Oxley's conception of a female
factory is the idea that most of the women who were to be
confined should be allowed out during the day once their tasks
were completed. In the old factory contact between inmates
and outsiders was extensive.[14] Nor was separation from the
community, except for the 'incorrigible', thought to be
essential. In that sense the treatment of female convicts was
less differentiated from that of male convicts than it was to
become later.

Macquarie was slow to provide adequate accommodation
at Parramatta and resisted Sorell's insistence that a factory was
necessary to house the increasing numbers of convict women
arriving in Van Diemen's Land.[15] Consequently some women
were sent to Sydney for secondary punishment, including in
1820 a woman who had stolen four rings from Mrs Lord (she
served out her sentence at Newcastle).[16] Eliza Bell, charged
with neglecting her duties as a nurse at the hospital, was
ordered to sleep there at night.[17] Eight female convicts were
sent to Macquarie Harbour when it was established in 1822,
but this was a short-lived experiment, and the women accused
of 'immorality' and preyed upon by the soldiers were sent back
to Hobart.[18] By 1825 there were about eighty women confined
in a makeshift factory in rooms adjoining the Hobart gaol.

While the female factories could provide an asylum for
women, the old Parramatta factory was a refuge for only a
few. In 1817 only sixty out of the 200 women employed at

Parramatta were able to be housed on the premises. In the following year when Macquarie ordered a new factory to be built, the building was planned as a penitentiary rather than as a refuge, although it continued to be both. In Britain prison reformer John Howard had envisaged the penitentiary as an institution in which an emphasis on cleanliness, order, discipline and the reformation of the individual would replace the filth and chaos of the old prisons. Solitary confinement at night, communal labour in the day and separation from the community were to be its cornerstones. Following the passing of legislation in 1770, a number of small institutions on the penitentiary model were built in Britain, the most influential of which was Gloucester. Some transported convicts had experience of penitentiaries in Britain and were familiar with the stricter rules, the dividing of prisoners into classes, and the use of isolation and silence as a punishment. Influential as Jeremy Bentham's Panopticon was on prison architecture, it was the Gloucester experiment that was of more significance to prison reform.[19] In New South Wales the term 'penitentiary' came often to refer not to the whole Parramatta institution but to its secondary punishment area.

When Elizabeth Fry wrote to the Under-Secretary of State for the Colonies in 1823 recommending the establishment of a female factory in Hobart Town, it was an establishment dedicated to the reform of the prisoner that she had in mind. Her letter outlined the essential requirements of the reformed system: a separate institution for women under the control and guidance of a 'respectable and judicious matron'; part of the building was to be set aside for schooling, with 'School Mistresses to be selected by the Matron from among the reformed Prisoners, provided they be sufficiently qualified for the office'.[20]

The emphasis on the reformation of the prisoner carried with it the seeds of the transformation of the prison system, not because it led to a process in which there was less recidivism and 'transformed' human beings were given the opportunity to join the respectable classes on their release, but because it changed the nature of the factories and shifted the emphasis within the institutions themselves from acts committed outside to the prisoner's behaviour while in detention. What is apparent from Fry's letter is the importance of watching and measuring the behaviour of the prisoners. On first arrival at the factory, she proposes in 1823, 'the deportment of every prisoner shall be scrutinized with exactness'. After that, those who 'merit a favourable report' will be 'selected' and sent into service with 'respectable inhabitants under such restraints and regulations as may be considered needful'. For the remainder instruction and employment are to be their lot until they 'evince sufficient amendment in habits and disposition to warrant the grant of similar indulgence'.

Elizabeth Fry's views on the management of female prisoners were published in 1825 in her book *Observations on the Siting, Superintendence and Government of Female Prisoners*, by which time she had developed a more sophisticated system of individual classification through numbered badges that would allow the continuous gradation of prisoners and the systematic application of punishments and rewards.[21] Under this system prisoners had no part in the running of the institution, which was to be in the hands of female officers reporting to a committee of female visitors. Fry's principles were influential, and although in practice their application fell far short of her grand design, the records reveal that for many women past life and past convictions ceased to be the determining factor once they entered the 'reformatory' world of the factory. How they reacted to their incarceration became more significant than the reason for their confinement. That itself represented one triumph for the reformers.

Once incarceration became common, the punishment of women usually took place within the factory. Other changes in the way women were punished over the period of transportation are less dramatic but nevertheless substantial. Fines and stocks were alternatives to incarceration and came to be used less as confinement was used more. An unwillingness to punish women by subjecting them to the same degree of physical pain as men led to the end of the lash and the iron collar, although the latter continued to be used for some time within the factories. Because the authorities believed that it was impossible to apply in the case of women 'those summary punishments which were found to repress so effectually violent or improper conduct' in male prisoners, the difficulty of finding punishments suitable for them continued. Detention, however, was never the only form of punishment to which convict women were subjected (regardless of Jane Franklin's opinion, expressed to Mrs Fry in 1841).[22] Within the factories a range of punishments based on periods of separate confinement, reduced diet and compulsory work (including hard labour), combined with forms of branding that distinguished different classes of prisoner, became key strategies within convict management.

Women convicts particularly resented having their heads shaved and their hair cut. In 1847 Alexander Harris observed of one woman he saw on the road that 'she was a rough brutal creature, but the cutting off of her hair', which she was about to experience on her return to the factory, 'she seemed to feel very acutely'.[23] Without differentiating between them, Joy Damousi has placed considerable emphasis on both head-shaving and hair-cutting as punishments for female convicts and sees both as a means of humiliating and intentionally 'defeminising' women. Advocates of this kind of punishment, which included Elizabeth Fry and James Mudie, she suggests shared the view that removal of their hair particularly distressed convict women and was effective because it humiliated them. 'Headshaving became a way in which women could be shamed, and women's feminine dignity could be undermined. Humiliation and disgrace was the aim of this punishment.'[24]

Head-shaving and hair-cutting present an interesting microcosm of the way attitudes to punishing convict women changed as policies came to reflect an increased concern with reformation and with constructing appropriately 'feminine' behaviour. While in Britain in prisons like Gloucester head-shaving was used both to cleanse and to punish, in the penal colonies it was at first dissociated from the 'hygienic ritual' of the penitentiary and was primarily punitive. But shaving convict women's heads as a punishment did not continue throughout the whole period of transportation. Most incidents come from the early period, as for instance in 1822 when Ann Hayes was punished for prostitution by twelve months' hard labour at Parramatta, where her head was to be shaved and she was to wear the 'caps of disgrace'.[25] In Van Diemen's Land head-shaving was rare by the 1830s. By 1832 when Janet Black was sentenced to six months in the crime class for insolence and disobedience to her master and had her head shaved for 'being a very bad girl', this was an unusual form of punishment.[26] Witnesses at the 1841–43 Inquiry mentioned that head-shaving had long been abandoned in Van Diemen's Land. Only Josiah Spode supported its reinstatement, though in 1841 Jane Franklin complained to Elizabeth Fry that convict women at Cascades were not even 'subjected to that most harmless yet most efficacious of female punishment, the being deprived of the ornament of her hair'.[27]

On the other hand hair-cutting had by that time become for certain groups of women so much a common part of factory routine at Cascades that it was unusual for it to be recorded as a specific punishment (as it was in 1830 when both Sophia Fitzpatrick and Sarah Wood were put in the cells at Cascades for a week on bread and water, had their hair cut off and were returned to service).[28] From the 1820s in both Parramatta and Hobart all women who were incarcerated for offences (not because they were awaiting assignment) had their hair cut. Women transgressing the internal rules of the factory could similarly be relegated to the crime class and have their hair cut. Close cropping of hair was clearly a punitive measure, a way of differentiating between the classes of prisoner and also a way of imposing discipline, hygiene and uniformity—all marks of the reformed institution. Fry advocated this measure in 1825 as a 'harmless punishment' and as a way of promoting 'the humiliation of the spirit' which led to reformation.[29] In 1826 when all crime-class women at Parramatta were compelled to have their hair cut short, inmates were also required to wash on entry. Darling introduced weekly bathing (replacing washing out of doors in a stone trough).[30] Both the hygienic and the punitive intention are apparent in Darling's policies. In Van Diemen's Land new regulations introduced into the female factories by Arthur in 1829 stressed cleanliness, quietness, regularity and submission. All women on entry were to be bathed, washed and dressed in the 'clothing of the Establishment', and women admitted for offences were to have their hair cut short. Further differentiation between the three classes was introduced at the same time.[31]

By the 1840s head-shaving and hair-cutting as an individual punishment had ceased altogether to have official sanction. In 1855 an inquiry was held by a visiting magistrate at the Cascades factory to report on the treatment of free women and convict inmates, 'particularly that regarding cutting their hair'.[32] It found that regulations required that all women under sentence, bond or free, with the exception of women committed under the Masters and Servants Act, should have their hair cut 'in such a manner as shall conduce to the health and preservation of cleanliness'. Their hair was to be 'kept regularly cut as when received', but never to be cut or shaved as a punishment. Asked if cutting their hair 'in any way disfigured' the women, both the matron and female receiving officer described how the women's hair was 'merely shortened behind their ears and behind their necks', emphasising that this did not happen 'in a manner to disfigure them'. Moreover, they said, because all women wore caps 'it cannot be perceived'. They were also asked if any woman's head had been shaved for punishment and assured the magistrate that there were no such cases. The magistrate, Edward Last, concluded that the rules and regulations were carried out with 'the greatest feeling and consideration, and nothing exacted but what is necessary for the cleanliness, good order and discipline' of the prisoners; 'none of the women are disfigured by the operation.'

The changing use of head-shaving and hair-cutting in the repertoire of convict administrators was part of a broader shift within institutions towards expert management, regulation, reformation, and the medicalisation of the individual. While the effect was still humiliation, the intention had shifted from an emphasis on separating out, stigmatising and punishing the individual towards an attempt to instil discipline and quell rebelliousness through regimentation and uniformity. Part of this process was a concern with the effect on women themselves and a wish to ensure that they did not become 'hardened' by punishment. Reformation for women was constructed around considerations of gender (which was why it was acknowledged to be more difficult for women to reform) and was expected to reawaken the feminine virtues, not to destroy them. By 1840 the thinking of Elizabeth Fry, whose approach to these matters had been so influential, had undergone a further change, as her response to Jane Franklin's letter referring to the utility of such punishment indicates:

> With respect to cutting off the hair we have not found its
> effect good in England, for whilst the poor prisoner
> should be humbled by her faults she should not always
> carry about in the view of others the crime she has com-
> mitted, it hardens and makes them worse than before.[33]

Fry's shift in language—the substitution of 'humbled' (in 1842) for 'humiliated' (in 1825)—is indicative of this change. Concern about the self-esteem of convict women is apparent from the committee's report in the 1841–43 Inquiry.[34] The opposition of convict administrator William Gunn to the proposal that all convict women be confined for two years on arrival arose from his view that they would be 'lowered in their own estimation' if so confined; his comments are alluded to more than once in the report. A wish to avoid policies that degraded women and inhibited their reformation and reintegration into society lay behind the Committee's belief that a 'more refined system of discipline than that required for male prisoners should be enforced in the case of females' and also behind their strong support for the continuation of assignment. The idea that practices that intentionally defeminised or humiliated women continued to be unselfconsciously endorsed throughout the period of transportation fails to take into account the seriousness of the debate about reformation. It also neglects the general shift in thinking (exemplified in the Molesworth Report) in which punishments that were immediate and physical were condemned as degrading and brutalising.[35]

A key principle in the reformers' lexicon was separation. One of Macquarie's intentions in establishing a new factory at Parramatta in 1821 was to separate inmates more effectively from the outside world and, within the establishment, into different categories along the lines recommended by the reformers: first two classes and then three classes of prisoner. As Annette Salt points out in her study of the Parramatta Female Factory, after Macquarie's changes women within the non-crime class could still earn money from working part-time and were allowed to retain some contact with friends and companions outside.[36] A more rigid classification system was introduced in the mid–1820s at Parramatta and a third class or 'crime class' was created to which women were consigned for secondary punishment if they committed a 'crime' outside the factory or if they transgressed the rules inside it. By the 1830s the Newcastle Female Factory was also divided into three classes.[37]

Demotion to the crime class was a significant element in the disciplinary mechanism of the establishment. Third-class women at Parramatta stood out because they were dressed differently from the rest, they received an inferior diet and their hair was closely cropped. At Cascades by the end of the 1820s women in the second class were distinguished by a large yellow C on a sleeve, while the same letter was more prominently displayed on the jackets, sleeves and shifts of the third-class women.[38] But the 1841–43 Inquiry found that there was no discernible difference in the discipline applied to first- and second-class prisoners, and that the 'only mark of distinction' between these and third-class women consisted in the latter being denied coffee made of roasted wheat. When

Charlotte Anley visited Parramatta in 1836 she noted a 'sub-division' of inmates but no effective separation of classes.[39] If, however, separation was often ineffectual and distinctions sometimes more apparent than real, the classification of women into classes was of consequence to the women themselves because it was usual only to assign women from the first class. Behaviour was the key to progression through the classes.

Although after its restructuring the Parramatta factory contained what was seen as a penitentiary, separation of individuals by solitary confinement continued to be restricted by the small number of cells available—still only eight after Darling's additions, two more than those originally built in Macquarie's time. By 1840 a new wing containing 72 cells had been built. Gipps thus brought to fruition Bourke's intention to extend the separate accommodation available to the third class, but he more than doubled the number of cells Bourke had planned. Gipps had conducted his own investigations into the reformed prison system in England before embarking for the colony, and after visiting the Millbank Penitentiary was convinced of the merits of silence and cellular separation. He also brought with him two administrators for the factory selected by Elizabeth Fry herself. In New South Wales, however, Gipps' cells were thought to have created an excessively harsh environment, and he was forced to moderate them to provide more light and ventilation.[40] Under both Bourke and Gipps the factory came to be seen primarily as a prison and one to which the strictest principles of reform should be applied. In Gipps' words: 'order, cleanliness, perfect obedience, and silence, may be said to prevail in the Establishment to a degree scarcely surpassed in any prison in England.'[41]

The development of the Female Factory at Parramatta charts the refinement of strategies for the reformation of the individual and the importance of separation, first in classes and then in single cells. Its history also suggests that although the factories continued to have a range of functions (including those relating to health, benevolence and employment, some of which came to be taken over by other specialised institutions for women), the ideas that transformed them derived from thinking about criminality and prison reform.

While the Parramatta factory was built specifically to accommodate convict women, at Cascades in Hobart the building used as the female factory had been a distillery. Before its completion late in 1828, women had been housed, as at Parramatta, within the old gaol precinct, with only a brick wall separating the prison from the factory. Classification and separation were impossible. The new factory's location, upstream on the Hobart Rivulet in the cleft of a shadowed valley, was ideal for its original purpose, but it was a damp and miserable site for a house of correction. In winter the building scarcely saw the sun. Even in its first year (by which time 200 women were housed there) the health problems caused by its situation were apparent. The solitary cells were described to the Lieutenant-Governor, George Arthur, by a visiting surgeon as 'extremely damp and unwholesome ... the beds being placed on the floors ... in the water which oozes beneath the walls of the building, so as to be frequently saturated with moisture'.[42] Arthur raised the beds but did not attend to the underlying problems.

Apart from staff quarters, nursery, hospital and kitchen, initially twelve cells were built. The factory was extended in the 1830s and again in the 1840s to allow the classification and separation of inmates to be carried out more effectively. In 1832 a hundred solitary cells were completed, and 112 cells were built in new two-storey blocks in the next decade. Solitary cells were a feature of the factory from the beginning, but their numbers meant that they were used for refractory prisoners as punishment rather than for general confinement.[43]

Health continued to be an issue at Cascades, especially the health of the children living there. Convict women who became pregnant while in service often returned to the factory to have their babies, and children stayed with their mothers before being transferred to orphan schools. Consequently children made up a large part of the population of the factories. In February 1845 at Parramatta, for instance, the number of women in the factory was 326 and children 118.[44] In 1829 the Hobart press attacked the convict administrators for the level of infant mortality at the Cascades factory, and new buildings were put up in response. Part of the problem was cleanliness. When Arthur inspected the factory in 1832 he found the children's bedding 'quite black with fleas'. Overcrowding was a major problem and the deaths continued. In 1834 a coroner's inquest into the death of an inmate was told of twenty adults and 42 babies living in two rooms at Cascades.[45] Ten children had died in the six weeks before the inquest. Overcrowding, unhealthy conditions and poor diet were the causes of the continuing deaths. In response to continued scandals the nursery was shifted out of the factory, first to Liverpool Street, then to Dynnyrne and then, after a further extension in 1850, back to Cascades. As late as 1855 there were claims that the high death rate among children at Cascades was the result of mismanagement and neglect.[46]

Work at both Cascades and Parramatta followed a similar pattern. At Parramatta all women were supposed to work, but sometimes third-class women had been sentenced to hard labour, such as breaking stones. Machines were set up in the factory for the spinning and weaving of flax and wool, but the capacity to employ women in this way varied, as did the contribution such employment made to the costs of the establishment. An early use of payments to staff based on the work of the inmates (a 'centage'), which contributed considerably to the salaries of officials, was stopped by Darling.[47] Apart from the production of cloth, quantities of clothing and other items for sale were also produced, such as straw hats and bonnets, window blinds and cushions. Washing for the soldiers and later for the colonists was done in the factory yard. Third-class women could not earn money from their labour, but women from other classes could. Often women were underemployed. Gipps, on arrival, regarded the women as mostly idle and introduced new work such as washing and needlework, some of the proceeds of which the women were allowed to keep. While at Moreton Bay, usual work was done (there was, for instance, a 'washing gang'), at Eagle Farm female convicts did field work, hoeing and picking cotton and husking and shelling corn.[48] At Cascades spinning, carding wool, picking hemp, ironing or washing all provided work, but seldom in sufficient quantities to keep everyone busy. Sewing, some of it fine work, could earn convict women money. It was not until the last decade of transportation that the need to provide employment as a systematic and routine part of factory life was seriously addressed. In 1851 a male visitor described the women's labours:

> One of the great yards of the factory was devoted to laundress work. Squads of women were up to their elbows in suds ...
>
> We had next a glimpse of a room full of sempstresses, most of them employed in fine work. It was not impossible, the matron admitted, that some of the elaborate shirt-fronts we should see at the Government house ball this evening had been worked in this, and washed and 'got up' in the last ward. A rougher fabric done by the less-skilled prisoners is a coarse kind of woollen tweed, only used for the material of prison-dresses.[49]

The gap between the ideals of the reformers and their realisation was attributable in part both to the inadequate resources for the upkeep and adaptation of buildings and to the deficiencies of administrators and staff. Unsuitable buildings housed women who were frequently ill or pregnant. Infant mortality was high. Suitable work to occupy the women's time was in short supply. Moreover, who could be entrusted with the task of reforming these women, if that was to be the serious intention of the colonial government? Authority over women in the convict system and more particularly in the factories was exercised by various guards and guardians (superintendents, matrons, turnkeys), not always outstanding for their skills or honesty. Among the managers of female convicts no one stands out as driven by either reformist zeal or vision.

Some of the most useful work the female factories created was not work for the inmates but the employment derived from the running of the institutions themselves. The factories employed numbers of convict women as well as other staff. The more care that was taken with the health, welfare and the supervision of the women, the greater the employment costs to government. If women were to remain healthy, midwives and nurses were necessary. If they were to acquire skills, a needlewoman and even a schoolteacher was needed. A store-keeper, a laundress, overseers, turnkeys, assistant matrons (often soldiers' wives), a clerk, a porteress, a gatekeeper, and convict monitresses were all employed at Parramatta. In the 1830s factory staff there included both a midwife and a schoolteacher. Overseers and turnkeys were often convicts, and ex-convicts frequently held other subordinate positions.

The complexity of administration and the difficulty with which appropriate staff could be employed was apparent early in the history of New South Wales. Francis Oakes, the first superintendent at Parramatta, left most of the supervision of the women to a convict overseer and managed to devote considerable attention to his other occupations, those of local constable and baker. In 1821 Governor Macquarie sought as superintendent of the new factory a 'Married Man of Good Moral Character', someone 'Sober' and 'Steady' who had a good knowledge of the weaving trade (in which the women were to be employed), a person who understood how to prepare wool and flax. He also wanted someone who could keep efficient accounts. In the end he made do with Oakes.[50]

The appointment of women to supervise the incarceration of other women was central to the thinking of Elizabeth Fry and her followers. The first matron at Parramatta was Elizabeth Fulloon, a widow, whose eldest son became for a short time the administrator. Such male-female combinations became common in institutions, although they were usually teams composed of husband and wife. Because the position of matron was a live-in one it was an ideal job for a woman with children to look after, or, as in the case of Mrs Fulloon, with children to support. John Fulloon had not been in his position long before he was accused of theft and 'immoral behaviour' with one of the women in the factory. Such scandals were frequent, but

Mrs Fulloon survived two official inquiries before she resigned. Her successor, Mrs Gordon, if not above reproach, worked hard and there were few serious complaints against her. The rest of her family, however, failed to meet acceptable standards of behaviour and Mrs Gordon lost her position.[51]

Governors in New South Wales and Van Diemen's Land continued the policy of appointing husband-and-wife teams to run the female factories. Esh and Sarah Lovell (strict Wesleyan Methodists) were appointed to run the new factory at Cascades. At Parramatta Sarah and George Bell were twice appointed there to the positions of matron and keeper. The Rogers became matron and storekeeper, followed by George and Lucy Smyth, whose subsequent dismissal arose out of complaints that a ball had been held at the factory involving drunken women. The last administrators were also a husband and wife. Unlike most of their predecessors they did not lose their jobs because of corruption, inefficiency or immorality. Their positions were abolished when the factory closed down in 1848. Even the two administrators chosen on the personal advice of Elizabeth Fry were dismissed.[52]

Right to the end of transportation, other factories were not free of problems with staff. Many of the people who took positions in them shared the lower-class background of the female inmates and some of their vices, particularly drinking. Misappropriation was common. At Cascades complaints and allegations were frequent, but few charges were proved and then largely for minor breaches of regulations, most of which related to gaining personal benefit from the work of needle-women—a common complaint in other factories. Sexual misbehaviour between officials and inmates was also reported (and was cause for dismissal), but rarely. In 1832 at Moreton Bay the assistant surgeon was dismissed for allowing the master of a visiting ship to associate and drink with women in the factory overnight.[53] Stories of sexual abuse by constables conveying women to the factories were accepted as fact by the authorities, but evidence of sexual abuse by staff within the factories themselves is very slight and one can assume (from the later experience of institutionalisation in Australia) that much more often than the documents reveal, male supervisors sexually exploited their charges. Perhaps the appointment of committed Christians (missionaries and Sunday school teachers) offered a better combination of strictness, sobriety and respectability. Wesleyan Methodists were particularly useful because they were respectable but not of such high social standing that they were above working in these positions. (All the staff appointed to Cascades during Arthur's time were Methodists.[54]) Sometimes jobs in institutions ran in families: both of the parents of Miss Elizabeth Snape (a Sunday school teacher recommended by both the bishop and the chaplain for employment at Parramatta in 1836) were turnkeys at the factory.[55]

The outstanding figure among convict managers was Francis Oakes' daughter, Mary Hutchinson, who was among those who could be said to have inherited her vocation. When Mrs Hutchinson became matron at Cascades in 1832, living among convicts was not a new experience for her. Her grandmother had been a convict and her mother, Rebecca Small, was said to have been the first female European child born in the colony of New South Wales. When she was eleven, her father became superintendent of the Female Factory at Parramatta, so that for most of her childhood female convicts were part of the background of her everyday life. Mary Oakes was not quite sixteen when she married the Revd John Hutchinson, a clergyman from Yorkshire nearly twenty years her senior, who, like her father in the 1790s, was about to set out to the Pacific Islands to convert the native inhabitants to Methodism. The South Seas adventure was a miserable experience, and Hutchinson developed a new plan to join the landed gentry in Van Diemen's Land, stocking his land with the sheep and cattle he had left in the care of a good friend, John Batman. Hutchinson sought a land grant from Lieutenant-Governor Arthur but was offered and accepted instead the position of superintendent of the Female House of Correction at Cascades. As matron Mary Hutchinson was given £50 a year and relieved of the drudgery of doing her own housework. With a combined salary of £200, free lodgings and fuel, their washing done and food cooked for themselves, their family and two servants, the Hutchinsons took up their new responsibilities. Mary Hutchinson was twenty-two. She was to be matron at Cascades for nearly twenty years, remaining until 1851 when the health of her husband forced him to resign. Until 1854 she was in charge of the Launceston House of Correction, by which time the transportation of convicts had ceased.

Although the local press on occasions demanded Mrs Hutchinson's dismissal, she was the great survivor among factory administrators. The strongest calls for her to be stood down related to the infant mortality rate at the factory and the emaciated condition of weaned babies. Mrs Hutchinson had twelve children herself, eight of them born while she was matron; six died in infancy. Colonel Mundy visited the factory in 1851 and described her as 'a dignified lady who looked quite capable of maintaining strict discipline whether in a public or in a merely domestic establishment'.[56]

Changes in thinking about the management of convict women are reflected to some extent in the patterns of employment of factory staff. While Mrs Hutchinson's tenure spanned the period of change, by the end of transportation appointments to manage institutions were increasingly made of people with experience in institutional management, such as Mrs Bowden and her staff (who had worked in British insane asylums). The appointment of medical practitioners as superintendents (for instance at Ross in 1848) reversed the process of appointing women—often with an evangelical or religious background—to manage institutions which had derived from the interventions of Elizabeth Fry.

In New South Wales the most serious attempt to impose an efficient reformatory regime within the female factories came with the arrival of Sir George Gipps. In Van Diemen's Land the story was somewhat different. The 1841–43 Inquiry revealed the chaotic and undisciplined conditions inside the factories. Moreover, the ending of transportation to New South Wales saw a vast increase in the numbers of women sent to

Van Diemen's Land and massive overcrowding in both the Cascades and Launceston factories. With more than 500 women in Cascades in 1842, a new establishment was created at Brickfields in New Town. By the beginning of the decade the management of female convicts in its entirety became the subject of debate and redefinition, as Franklin contemplated how to extend the probation system to women. Franklin's wife, Lady Jane, wrote to Mrs Fry in 1841 endorsing the probation system and the building of a penitentiary, and at the same time attacked assignment and the Cascades factory, which she said had 'no pretension to be a place of reformatory discipline'.[57]

The idea of a penitentiary continued to offer to those who opposed assignment and were critical of the female factories the possibility that incarceration might be transformed into a reformatory experience. Charlotte Anley had suggested in 1836 that a penitentiary might be established in New South Wales to take women on probation, allowing the factory to be reserved for punishment using the silent system.[58] The idea that the penitentiary should be built outside Hobart as a separate reformatory institution for newly arrived women also lay behind planning in Van Diemen's Land and was the core of the probation scheme proposed by Lord Stanley. There women were to be classified, separated and in John West's words 'trained for the duties of domestic life': 'The discipline intended rather to restore than to punish: those remitted in disgrace to the Government, were not to re-enter this place of reform.' By this means 'a more complete separation between those who may seem wholly irreclaimable and those of whom better hopes may be entertained' would be effected.[59] Graduates of the penitentiary would receive passes and later their tickets of leave. Freedom was dependent both on good conduct and the labour market—a capacity to find employment was as essential to this system as reformation. Secondary punishment would continue to take place in other institutions, such as the female factories.

Plans for the penitentiary were drawn up by Joshua Jebb, Surveyor-General of Prisons in Britain, and were based on

Parkhurst, built in 1843, which specialised in educating its inmates in both trade skills and religion. Costs were estimated at between £34 000 and £35 000. The penitentiary was never built, although a matron, Mrs Bowden, a medical officer (her husband, Dr Bowden) and some assistants arrived at the end of 1843. In Britain Philippa Bowden was familiar with the management of the insane and came with a formidable reputation. She had been matron at the Hanwell Asylum in Middlesex and six of her female assistants were from the same establishment, which was a large pauper asylum known for its commitment to moral rather than physically coercive treatment. But her activities were to be confined to the hulk the *Anson*, moored in the Derwent and sent out as a temporary depot for female convicts in 1844. Within a year the vessel held over 500 convict women, and over 3000 women spent some time there. From that time the older factories ceased to be the only major institutions housing convict women and shared that role with the hiring depots and the *Anson*. From 1844 to 1849 the *Anson*, with a staff of twenty, held similar numbers of women to the Cascades Female Factory.[60]

Changes to female convict administration under the probation system represented the most serious attempt at shifting the emphasis within the system to reformation of the individual Importance was attached not only to punishment ('secured by the due application of coercive labour and restrictive discipline') but also to reformation ('attained by means of religious and moral influences, and by the careful inculcation of industry and regularity'). New regulations promulgated in mid–1845 also paid considerably greater attention to the need for 'constant employment' of inmates in institutions, as well as to religious instruction and basic education (both neglected in the regime prior to the 1841–43 Inquiry).[61] The roles of both religious instructors and medical officers were extended and clearly articulated, with the latter obliged to visit the women in separate or solitary confinement daily and all other parts of the establishment twice a week. Religious instructors were to keep full and detailed records of their charges. Present in varying degrees in the new regime are each of what Michel Foucault has called 'the seven universal maxims of the good "penitential condition"': attention to reformation, classification, individual penalties, the centrality of work, education, the employment of staff with moral qualities and technical skills, and supervision following release.[62]

By 1847 it was becoming apparent that the new system was not working. The building of the proposed penitentiary at Oyster Cove had been suspended and though additional accommodation had been rented, it, like the *Anson*, was becoming overcrowded. The vessel was seen as being 'unfit' for its purpose, and the women confined in it were described as having 'deteriorated, both morally and physically'.[63] Suitable staff were difficult to find. Medical men were increasingly employed in female factories, but the salaries available for attendants and administrators reduced the appeal of such positions to trained people. When the superintendent at Ross in 1852 sought the dismissal of two of his staff because they were 'hopeless' and complained that the woman entrusted with teaching 'could not read writing at all' and so 'excited the contempt of the women', he was reflecting a general problem.[64] In the 1850s many of the difficulties that had been endemic in the early administration, including incompetence and dishonesty, continued.

Moreover, with the deepening depression there was little demand for labour. Male and female convicts languished in the hiring depots while ticket-of-leave holders, without work, trudged the country. Dr J. S. Hampton, the Comptroller-General of Convicts, regarded the *Anson* as marginally better than the other institutions but 'useless' for reformation and favoured its abandonment. He also expressed his belief that the system would be more effective if women could be hired out as soon as they arrived and encouraged to marry, thus reiterating the views of the 1841–43 committee.[65] More change was on the way. On the same page of the *Hobart Town Advertiser* (14 September 1847) that carried a discussion of Mrs Bowden's work on the *Anson* was a report of Sir George Grey's speech in the House of Commons debate over the Prison's Bill, in which he condemned the 'evils arising from the aggregation of masses of convicts' under probation and announced that in future the first period of punishment for criminals sentenced to transportation would be spent in British prisons (transformed by the separate system), after which they would become ticket holders and 'be placed in every respect in the same condition as the convicts now there, with this exception, that they would have gone through a reformatory instead of a demoralizing system of discipline'.

Spurred on by the spectre of the 'depraved' behaviour of incarcerated convict women, during the last ten years of transportation to Van Diemen's Land attempts were made to separate the newly arrived female convicts from old hands and to introduce stricter discipline. But just as Maconochie's penal experiment was tested and rejected on Norfolk Island, Mrs Bowden, who felt that her labour had met with little more than indifference at the highest level, returned to England when her husband died, without being able to implement her ambitious plans for reforming either female convict adminis-tration or the women themselves. She was convinced, John West concluded, that 'moral insanity is far more hopeless than the diseases of Hanwell'.[66]

The new system, while never fully implemented and fraught with difficulties, seems to have produced greater pas-sivity, if not reformation of character. Alexander Marjoribanks, describing women at Parramatta in 1847, commented on the silence and order that prevailed, with women prevented from speaking and kept busy sewing and washing.[67] West reported in 1852 that *Anson*'s matron and staff had found their convict charges generally 'submissive and docile', quite unlike many earlier descriptions of women in convict institutions:

> they were haunted with all kinds of terrors, and had less than the ordinary courage of women. Mere children in un-derstanding; some, such only in years; but their actual reformation, for the most part, only remained an object of

confident expectation, while their true tendencies were repressed.[68]

Submissiveness was also noted in 1851 at Cascades by Mundy, who commented on the 'dead silence' which was 'everywhere observed': 'women and children all silent! One would have thought them all deaf and dumb.' Mundy attributed it not solely to the 'avenues' of solitary cells which had been introduced in much greater numbers after the Inquiry but also to reduced diet and drugs, which had an enervating or sedative effect. According to Mundy the visiting surgeon prescribed half rations, solitude and 'gentle medical treatment (a grain or so of ipecacuanha, I suppose)': 'a prescription highly productive of nausea, occasions, it is said, a prodigiously soothing effect upon ladies with gross health and fiery temperaments.'[69]

It is apparent that the female factories, from their earliest days, embodied the flaws and difficulties that would later characterise and become chronic within the broader prison system. They were from the beginning inadequate as buildings, and they continued to be inadequately funded for achieving the purposes that were increasingly demanded them. The idea of reform pivoted on the concept of separation: separation between inmates, between the inside and the outside world, between the inmates and their custodians, between the incorrigible and the docile. Yet separation was expensive and seldom achieved. And without separation, 'sufficient amendment in habits and disposition' was impossible. The feeling persisted that far from reforming the unruly, the factories could also contaminate the weak, the young and the unformed. Factory life offered little chance of rehabilitation. Responsiveness to moral stricture, religious teaching and to discipline observed in some British institutions was remarked upon less often in the antipodes. If greater attention came to be paid to finding useful employment, there was little training in a useful apprenticeship. Any skills honed in the factory were for the most part in oversupply outside. Nor were those employed as the guardians and custodians of the convict women adequately prepared and educated for their tasks. Instead of enforcing discipline, their laxity often undermined it and continued to do so throughout the period of transportation. They were seldom models of probity or virtue.

With all these difficulties and inadequacies, by the time they relinquished their role as convict establishments the factories had nonetheless become more efficient institutions. The provision of solitary cells in greater numbers and greater attention to regulation and routine created the possibility of a more disciplined environment. Although concerns over health persisted, hygiene improved, to the extent that the cleanliness of Cascades (which had been bug-ridden and filthy when the Hutchinsons arrived) could be described in 1851 as 'almost dazzling', and its 'order and discipline appeared faultless'.[70]

If the implementation of the reform agenda failed, confidence in the reformed institution also faltered. Many inmates remained resistant to discipline and difficult to control, so that rioting, active sexual behaviour and a subversive subculture persisted within the factories, especially where the facilities for separation and confinement were inadequate (see Chapters 6 and 8). As some penal administrators showed themselves ready to embrace the ultimate discipline of the silent system (Pentonville opened in 1842 and the Port Arthur separate prison in 1848), Elizabeth Fry urged caution. 'There is', she wrote in 1842 in response to Jane Franklin's proposal of a penitentiary, 'so great a variety of opinion respecting the best mode of buildings and discipline' at present that she was fearful of plans to build a new prison. The Hobart factory, she believed, could be improved by adding to it 'something of a house of refuge' for those women hopeful of improvement.[71] Fry, who was increasingly critical of the inhumanity and excesses of the silent system, had said in 1835: 'In some respects, I think there is more cruelty in our Gaols than I have ever before seen.'[72]

Faith in the capacity of the reformed institution to transform the individual also weakened. Solitary confinement could pacify prisoners but not necessarily reform them. Reformation, in the minds of the prison reformers, was intensely personal.

At its heart was the salvation of the individual through self-reflection, repentance and the exercise of moral choice, encouraged by an environment of discipline and asçeticism. But the evidence of the penal settlements suggested that women could be 'reformed' more successfully outside institutions than within them, through their reintegration into society. Though they embraced the separate system as the best way of dealing with the 'incorrigible', the committee of the 1841–43 Inquiry was profoundly sceptical about the capacity of confinement to bring about a fundamental change in character and disposition:

> We could observe indeed that however conducive solitude may be to reflection and to the forming of resolutions of amendment religious principle itself does not often take deep hold of the mind except when it is worked into the affections through the trials the disappointments and the vexations the tear and the wear of everyday life ... Good resolutions ... will not alone carry her very far. Her continuance in a right course will depend more upon the position in which she may be placed and the nature of the associations that will surround her. The laws of simple suggestion which give to the separate system its power of expelling bad feelings by filling the mind with ideas of an opposite tendency render it equally certain, that there is no security that the latter will not also, upon a change of circumstances taking place, be expelled in their turn ... Habits, it might be observed change, not because they are either good or bad, but simply because chameleon-like, the mind is so constituted as to take on the hues of surrounding objects.[73]

Many convict women, the committee believed, arrived with the 'good resolutions' that the separate system was designed to produce, and to imprison them was unnecessary and degrading. Half the women, they argued, conducted themselves with propriety after arrival, a third never committed a single offence, and many married and became 'in every sense of the word, decent members of society—a result much more decisive than we ever remember to have seen attributed to the separate system'. In their emphasis on the importance of external factors rather than on willpower and moral choice as determinants of criminality, the committee's views cast into question some of the assumptions on which the idea of individual reformation rested and looked forward to ideas more common in later nineteenth-century thinking.

Having mounted what was in effect a strong rebuttal of the Molesworth Committee's views of convict women, their behaviour, the consequences for them of the assignment system and the efficacy of the reformed institution, the committee also argued against the view that assignment as a punishment was not 'sufficiently severe and deterring',

> when we reflect that its subject is in the case before us a female, that she has been separated from her friends and expatriated, that she is not allowed to select her own service, that she is amenable to summary jurisdiction, that she belongs to a degraded class and that she deeply feels her own degradation and longs to be emancipated.[74]

In the colonies, where marriage and family life might well be more conducive to reformation than institutional discipline and instruction (and assignment provided domestic labour), the penitentiary idea had a powerful and persistent competitor.

The fact that the factories did not achieve the particular and articulated goals of either the reformers or the colonial administration should not be seen to imply a more general failure. The female factories were always more complex institutions than their creators intended them to be. Their complexity derived from the number of functions they were compelled to perform and the paucity of other structures of support for women in the penal colonies. The activities of the factories in effect mapped the weaknesses of institutional structures in the wider society: the absence, for instance, of adequate institutional support for destitute women, for unsupported mothers, for lying in, for the sick; the paucity of benevolent assistance for the 'deserving' and particularly the 'undeserving' poor; the weakness of family networks, the absence of kin.

Edward Lord, by convict artist Thomas Griffiths Wainewright, 1846. (Allport Library and Museum of Fine Arts, State Library of Tasmania)

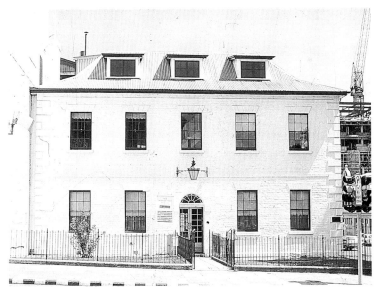

Ingle Hall, 89 Macquarie Street, Hobart, built c. 1814. Edward and Maria Lord lived in this house. (Australian Heritage Commission, photograph by Max Bourke)

Launceston Wednesday 15 18[--]

My Ever Dear Steaven

It is with great pleasure that I embrace this opertunity of addressing you hopeing it will find you well as it leaves me at present and I am most happy to inform you that I received your kind and welcome letter and likewise the things that you were so kind as to send and my Dear you must excuse me for not answering your letter before you did not tell me have you come to leave gibsons my dear yet I hope when I here again I shall get a good long letter and tell me all particulars and I hope it will not be long till I do I wish I could here every day from you till I come out I want to here that you have got a place for me for their is memorials gon to hobentown for migation of sentence for all that is senin 12 now

This page, opposite and over: Letter from convict woman, Maria Turner, written in the Female Factory, Launceston, 1841. (Archives Office of Tasmania)

I want you to come for me at 5 oclock in the morning the day I come out my dear you must get the person that you get to take me out to go to our every yard ofice in town and get me reserved for the 18th of January and then you come in on the 19th and get an order for to get me in the morning and bring up the order to the gate on the 19th and then you can get me in the mornin at 5 my dear I hope you will be able to get us a pig for cricmues and do not for get the tobaco and pipes and put a bottle of rum some may so as it cannot be seen I have a good miss and master they have fought many battels for me and kept me out of trouble my dear you had better direct the parcell to the factory and do not let the person that brings them to gate mention my name at all for I shall be sure to get them for you do not none he them and they will rat...

any thing to hvs when you
any thing my dear I want
shoes and dies and stays and if you
will send me the monney my
misis will by them for me
my dear my time seems longer
now then ever it did I wish
I could bring this myself
o dear I have so much to
tell you when I come out
god bles you I must conclude
with my kind love to you
yours sincerly and truly till
till death Ann Maria Turner

When love is planted their
It buds and blosoms like a rose
Their is no flower half so sweet
As absent lovers when they met

And we shall soon now I hope
my love
Maria

answer it as soon
as you can

Cascades Female Factory, Hobart, c. 1870. (Archives Office of Tasmania)

Cells at the Cascades Female Factory, Hobart. (Archives Office of Tasmania)

The *Rajah* quilt, 1841, made by convict women on their voyage to Australia. (National Gallery of Australia)

Detail of the *Rajah* quilt: dedication panel. (National Gallery of Australia)

Female Factory at Parramatta, watercolour by Augustus Earle 1826(?).
(National Library of Australia)

View of the Female Orphan School, Parramatta, by convict artist
Joseph Lycett, 1825. (National Library of Australia)

Catherine Bartley, tried in Roscommon in 1849 for stealing a cow. Her offences in Van Diemen's Land included insolence, 'being a Common Prostitute' and 'delivery of an Illegitimate Child'. (Archives Office of Tasmania)

Regardless of the often horrific conditions in the factories, for much of their histories they continued to be regarded as refuges as well as prisons, and women sought to return even to the crime class from what they considered less pleasant circumstances outside. Some women survived better in this environment than others and committed offences so that they could return. For many the factories provided companionship, a place in which they could mix with women of their own class, a place where they could be reunited with shipmates and exchange information which enabled them to survive more easily when they were released. The tension between their punitive function and their role as a refuge was evident from the beginning. The failure of administrators to suppress the prison subculture was for some inmates the factories' most attractive characteristic.

6

ROUGH CULTURE
AND REBELLION

─────────────────────

Central to the creation of the 'reformed' institution was the need to enforce a greater distance between the confined inmate and the community outside and to rid it of the internal subcultures which allowed the contamination of the novice. Attempts to achieve this within the female factories met with considerable resistance—resistance which was both individualistic and collective, and which posed a significant and continuing problem for penal administration.

Attempts to keep inmates in the female factories separated from the outside world were bound to fail because there was so much movement between the factory and places of assignment. But neither the physical confines of the factory nor the staff provided an impenetrable barrier. The capacity to maintain strong illicit links with the world outside the factory depended largely on one important element in the factory subculture— trafficking.

Letters and goods were regularly smuggled to and from friends outside, often through attendants. A few intercepted letters, almost illegible, survive in the convict records. They reveal the ways in which women, from behind the walls, tried to keep some control over their lives by continuing to orchestrate interactions central to their well-being. These are concerned primarily with their relationships with male companions and children, and with significant aspects of their lives as prisoners: applications for marriage, release and assignment, and the provision of food, clothing and 'trading goods'.

Some of these, like the letter written by Jane New just before her escape from the Parramatta Female Factory in 1829, represent quite desperate attempts to keep contact with male companions (a common-law husband or the father of a child). She wrote to her 'dear husband': 'I hear that you are in Parramatta; I hope and trust that you will get an order to come and see me, for I am almost out of my mind at not seeing you.'[1] A letter written in 1842 came from a young woman in the Cascades factory who had heard that the man to whom she was writing was living with another woman she referred to as 'Jiney Joncon', news which she described as making her 'very unhappy at present in my mind'.[2] Mary Jones wrote that she hoped he would not 'forsake the old one for the new one'; her time was to be up early in September when she would be coming out to her 'liberty', and she urged him to see the 'Clark', ending, 'If I ham guilty of aney fault it is loving the[e] to[o] well.'

Another woman, concerned that her male companion had not replied to her previous letter, wrote to tell him that he could get her out of the Hobart factory by making her his wife, advising him that in order to do so he would have to get a printed memorial from the office and bring it to Mr Hutchinson. She went on:

> Dear James i hope you will act as a man of Good principle and as a father to your unfortunate child by providing for your own. Remember it is in your power to make us a Comfortable home.

She said that while she was in good health the child was not because of 'this cold and miserable place'. She was concerned that at the end of twelve months she would have to send her 'unfortunate infant' to that other 'wretched' place (the Orphan School) unless James did something for them. She urged him not to forsake them now that she was in trouble and asked him to go to the Orphan School to see her other children and send her word of them. The trap in which she now found herself seems to have been precipitated by a minor incident (going out to 'see after' her clothes), although it was perhaps pregnancy that led to her apprehension and confinement. Dependent on the father of her youngest child not only to seek her release through marriage but to do so before the child was removed from her and placed in the Orphan School, she was also dependent on him for news of her other children.

Susannah Watson (the subject of Babette Smith's book *A Cargo of Women*) found herself in a similar predicament at Parramatta. The irony of the situation for many women lay in the fact that while incarceration had interrupted and perhaps endangered their most important personal relationship, it is likely that the relationship itself was the cause of their confinement: they had become pregnant while assigned, or had slipped out to meet a man without leave or had been found in compromising circumstances with a lover. Fear that return to the factory would destroy that relationship formed outside was said to be one of the reasons convict women resorted to abortion.

To deal with these situations women who were barely literate became learned in the rules of convict administration and provided expert advice to their friends about procedures and means of intervention. They also learned how to communicate with friends outside and how to bring goods into the factories, either for their own use or to trade. One letter from an inmate in Cascades refers to receiving the message 'that you sent to me by that young woman' and to seeing a mutual friend 'on the hill last Sunday week' (the factory yard could be observed from higher ground and people congregated there). Another letter written in 1841 and smuggled out by Maria Turner, an inmate of the Launceston Female Factory, to her boyfriend, suggests that regular communication was maintained between the two. While affectionate, the letter was also concerned to put in place a number of transactions, including her release. In addition Maria wanted money sent to her so that she could get her mistress to buy her 'shoes and dress and stays'. She said she had 'a good misis and master' who had 'fought many battles' for her and kept her out of trouble. She reminded Steven not to forget the 'tobaco and pipes and ... a bottle of rum', to be sent 'in some way so as it cannot be seen', and advised that when the 'parcell' was brought to the gate her name was not to be mentioned because she could not be certain who would be there at the time, reassuring him, 'I shall be sure to get them'. Maria's letter ended with the verse

> Where love is planted their it grows
> It buds and blossoms like a rose
> Their is no flower half so sweet
> As absent lovers when they meet

While these letters reveal the domestic and personal pre-occupations of women convicts (and thus conform to the traditional picture of feminine concerns) they also disclose another world. Smuggling, trafficking and trading in goods was a significant part of the complex social and economic life of the female factories. These arrangements required organisation, the compliance of staff and overseers, and sometimes the intimidation of other prisoners. Throughout the entire period of transportation officers were charged with trafficking offences (such as Mrs Cato at Cascades, who allowed letters to be smuggled inside parcels containing chickens for her dinner) or merely accused of them (as officers at Parramatta were accused of supplying luxuries to prisoners). The number of charges brought and proven against staff in relation to these offences seems, however, to have been insignificant compared with the prevalence of the activity.

The maintenance of the 'private world' of individual rela-tionships—which was usually one object of the letter writer—was supported by the survival of a rough prison subculture, tolerated but not acknowledged by the authorities. The robust subculture of the Cascades factory, in which trafficking played such an important part, is described in some detail in the testimony given by two women to the 1841–43 Inquiry—female convicts who during these investigations became informers and in turn were rewarded for giving evidence against their fellows. The narrative account of these 'jacketters', as they were called, is supported by the fragmentary evidence contained in the individual records of convict women and shows how trafficking was essential to the internal arrangements in the factory and to its power structure.

Mary Haigh had been sentenced to fourteen years for theft in 1835 and the records describe her as having been connected with 'a large gang of prostitutes and thieves'. She was sent to Van Diemen's Land on the *Arab*.[3] Selected to give evidence and promised 'certain indulgences in consideration of the most faithful and full disclosures', in April 1842 she was given a conditional pardon. She described how, on her arrival in the colony, she was sent with the other women to the factory to await assignment. In the week she remained there she was introduced to the commerce which underpinned the relationships within that establishment. Haigh described the way that a prisoner turnkey who 'attended' on them orchestrated the economic exchange, by allowing women from other yards to come in and barter goods for the clothes and other possessions brought in by the new arrivals. The women gave them tea, meat, sugar, tobacco ('eight pence per Fig was given for this latter article'). Haigh went on to describe her education at the hands of 'the women with whom we trafficked' and who, like the turnkey, had been in the factory long enough to understand the system. Later Haigh was returned to the factory for insolence and put into the crime class. She reported that on her arrival she had been searched by the matron, Mrs Hutchinson, ('but not strictly I could have passed in anything I liked') and as soon as she met up with two or three of her shipmates in the yard they asked her for money and tobacco.

> I had money and with it I purchased tea sugar meat
> and bread—The meat bread etc was brought by the Turn-
> key from the Cook House the tea she obtained from the

Messenger. Several of the women dealt with her ... Smoking is common in the Factory and I have known Rum introduced into the First Yard by the Servant in Mr Hutchinson's employ—She is 'allowed out' and obtained it at the Public House. She could pass into any part of the Building she liked ...

On a later occasion Haigh was sentenced to a month in the light cells, which had little effect on her capacity to trade:

I was almost as well off there as in the yards. I could obtain whatever I wanted through the Turnkey—Sometimes the Turnkey would let the Women under sentence out all day—Mr Hutchinson never visited us—Mr Cato would come once a fortnight or so. We could do much as we pleased as Mr Cato allowed us to get our clothes out of store and sell them—we could talk to one another and visit one another and could with the Turnkey's assistance see any woman in the building. I did not care for the Cells. The Factory is a great deal less severe than the English Gaols. The Turnkeys here have the keys they can take the other keys out of the Gatekeepers House and go out at the back of the wash-house getting thus anything they like even Rum Wine or Brandy— ... I have been in the dark Cells. That is a bad punishment but even there Tea Sugar etc can be obtained—it is the worst punishment except a long sentence in the light Cells which would be a punishment if the Women were kept strictly.

A second woman at the Inquiry was Grace Heinbury, who had arrived in Van Diemen's Land on the *Atwick* in 1838.[4] Heinbury had been a nurserymaid and needlewoman, sentenced for stealing, and like Haigh received a conditional pardon after giving evidence. Her experience was similar to that of Haigh. Soon after she arrived at the factory from the ship a woman came from the second yard 'through the Top of the Privy to traffick with the newly arrived Prisoners'. Heinbury said that she could purchase anything she wanted from the nurse at the factory but was not aware of how her contact obtained the goods. Some of the articles she suspected were stolen from other prisoners ('as is done in the other yards of the factory'):

'Those who have money can always get enough to eat whilst the others are Hungry.' On another occasion, sent back to the factory, she had no money and could get nothing for herself, but she saw 'plenty of fried meat and tea passed in by the Turnkey from the Cookhouse', which they pretended were their own rations. She could also smell spirits and believed that women with money could get them if they wished. Smoking, she said was common. While the turnkey, Mrs Livermore, kept the keys, two prisoner 'helpers' came around early each morning to empty the slops and at that time 'those Girls who have money are let out and can get what they like'. In Heinbury's words, 'Those who had money could here feast and do no work.'

Heinbury had also experienced factory life as a turnkey, and had traded on her own account:

> I was once in the dark Cells but I could get anything there that I required. I had money and my sentence was short, the punishment was nothing but it is severe when the sentence is long. I was once Turnkey over the Crime Class and used to sell and buy on my own account Tobacco, Tea, Sugar Meat etc. Two women after Muster were released, by me or by Mrs Hutchinson's Servants, from the Cells as I managed to abstract the keys I wanted and we were supplied from over the Wall with what we wanted—the Clerk at the factory was the person who supplied us. The overseer of the Building now going on there supplies the Women at present.

Occasional individual records of other women support these descriptions of factory life. In 1825, for instance, Johanna Leahy, who had been previously punished for abusing the Revd Bedford at the factory in Hobart, was placed in the cells on bread and water for three days for being found on the roof of the factory 'with intent to get something thrown over the wall'.[5] In 1820 Jane Lewis had her hair cut off after she was caught throwing a letter she had written over the wall of the old Hobart factory.[6] Ridding the female institutions of trafficking was as difficult as finding attendants above reproach. As late as 1852 E. S. Hall, attempting to dismiss incompetent officers at Ross, complained of 'things being admitted to the building'.[7] Even so, allegations of trafficking are not among the common charges laid against convict women, suggesting that women who used the established networks for moving contraband goods were unlikely to get caught. It is largely through inquiries into factory discipline or into the behaviour of attendants rather than from the individual records of convict women that a picture of these interactions emerges.

Trafficking undermined authority. Historians have tended to understate the subversive behaviour of female convicts, concentrating instead, as contemporaries did, on the multitude of individual acts of indiscipline, insolence and insubordination and the 'offensiveness' or 'unattractiveness' of the individual convict woman. Miriam Dixson encapsulates this second response when she says: 'Defined as outcast, the women became outcast, and their consequent ugliness put them further beyond the reach of kindness.'[8]

The image carried away by many observers of convict women was of the coarse and the unruly. Contemporary reports of the female factories are full of scandalised references to foul language, drinking, smuggling, violence between prisoners, dancing, singing 'obscene songs' and play-acting. In part this reaction derived from social distance, unaccustomed as many observers were to looking so closely at intimate and convivial aspects of working-class life. Moreover, the gulf between middle-class expectations and lower-class manners was greater than outward demonstrations of docility and obedience led reformers to believe. Convict inmates maintained their own distinct patterns of behaviour in prison, and it was the survival of this robust, 'rough culture' among women that so shocked upper-class observers.

While this bears witness to the fact that 'reform' was especially difficult for women because it was so closely concerned with manners and demeanour, to suggest that the 'offensiveness' of convict women's behaviour was merely unintended—a consequence of social difference—is to see only part of the picture.

From the time of the First Fleet many of those whose job it was to control female convicts were shaken by the impossibility of the task and by the women's aggressive sexuality, and their rough language and behaviour. Lieutenant Ralph Clark's panic as he struggled to maintain order on the *Friendship* in 1787 is evident; he was appalled by the sexual behaviour of his charges ('damned whores' and 'Bitches that they are') and by their language. Quoting one woman, who had accused the doctor on board of wanting 'to f–ck her' and who challenged the captain to 'come kiss her C–t', Clark wrote that 'in all the course of my days I never hard such exspertions from the Mouth of a human being'.[9] Words which may have been common among the lower class or among men were particularly disturbing from the mouth of a woman, but the offensiveness lay not only in the language but in the challenge to authority. Similarly, when Peter Murdock's wife was appalled at finding her assigned servant lying in bed with 'what she called a yard of clay in her mouth, and drinking a pot of porter, and blowing a cloud' (her own expression), it was the attitude of disrespect as much as the behaviour that was shocking.[10]

Convict women have for the most part been portrayed as disobedient rather than rebellious, and as motivated by individual concerns rather than those of the group. Moreover, while they 'scandalise', they seldom 'rebel', and their most extreme acts are seen as those that provoke disgust or shock in others. Female convicts are frequently, therefore, not only seen through the eye of the beholder but the observer's response is given more significance than their own actions. If, however, the focus is adjusted to look closely at the subculture and economy of the female factory, at the riots and acts of rebellion themselves, and at some of the ringleaders and their relationships, it is possible to develop a more complex picture of the actions of female convicts and of the convict system itself.

The continuum of refractory behaviour in the female factories stretched from minor lapses of discipline and less than punctilious behaviour to rebellion, riot and mutiny. In the former cases some women were clearly the victims of the unreasonable demands of those in authority over them. On the other hand, such behaviour could also signify resistance, and many women showed their unwillingness to conform to the demands of the system through a multiplicity of minor acts of insubordination and defiance. Just as assigned women did not always behave meekly in the face of injustice but spoke out like Jane Miller, or manipulated the system to their own advantage, in the factories individual rebelliousness was common, and on occasions large numbers of women combined together to confront the authorities.

Clearly many women were not passive victims of institutional authority and responded in a variety of ways to attempts to control and pacify them. Female convicts were more likely to be punished within the factories for riotous and disorderly conduct than for trafficking. Common charges included alleged acts of insolence, abuse and insubordination. Women were punished for breaking the rules of the institution, for using foul language and for refusing to work. Sometimes women damaged their cells or broke spinning wheels and utensils. In 1825 Mary Murphy broke out of the Female Factory in Hobart by making a hole in the wall.[11] Returned to the crime class, she beat up a fellow prisoner. Murphy had absconded alone twice before. Sometimes individualist acts of rebelliousness threatened the whole establishment as when, in 1832 at Cascades, Mary Garner set alight to the shingles by throwing a firestick into the second-class yard.[12]

Observers commented on the tensions between convict women. Arguments between women were endemic to institutional life, where women were crowded together in close confinement. Threats against fellow prisoners and staff and intimidation and violence between prisoners were not unusual and reflected the realities not only of life within the walls but of the hierarchy which existed among the inmates. What external matters influenced these relationships is impossible to determine, although testimony relating to the voyage of the *Duke of Cornwall* from Dublin in 1850 suggested that there was 'a very bad feeling' on board the ship between Catholics and Protestants.[13] Deciphering the nature of these relationships between prisoners is helped to some extent by the testimony of the 'jacketters', whose statements suggest a world in which the better behaved among the inmates could be preyed upon by the rest. In Mary Haigh's words before the 1841–43 Inquiry, other women swore and struck 'the well conducted' women if they attempted to remonstrate with them over their behaviour. Other evidence of group behaviour, however, suggests that this is a partial picture.

While historians writing about convict resistance have tended to see female convict rebelliousness as individualist rather than collective (in contrast to the protest of male convicts), manipulation of the system was almost universal, and it was from their companions that women learned how they could resist and work the rules to their own advantage. Collective knowledge, passed on in the factories, armed and prepared the individual. There is, as well, a collective dimension to many of even the most apparently individual acts. A violent incident in 1827 at Cascades involved Ann Wilson (or Bruin), who on being returned to the factory asked if her hair was to be cut off. When told by the superintendent, Mr Drabble, that it was, she screamed and swore, and seizing a pair of scissors proceeded to cut it off herself. Both Hughes and Damousi mention the incident (as an example of individual protest) but not its aftermath. Wilson, who was injuring herself by thrusting her fist through the glass windows of Mr Drabble's sitting room, was pacified with the help of some of the women; later other women tried to release her from her cell, either (in Drabble's words) 'to excite a fresh disturbance or enable her to effect her escape over the Wall'. On being sentenced to twelve months in the factory at George Town, Wilson replied, 'I thank you it is the very place I wish to go to.' This brought an additional sentence of four hours in the stocks, and her retort, 'That will not hurt me either. You shall not have my hair off for all that.' Then, sentenced to have her hair cut, she replied, 'That will not hurt me either. I don't care if it was cut off fifty times.' Wilson was punished on a number of later occasions for drunkenness and died while still in servitude in 1836. Just as her companions had helped her, one of her last offences (which brought another severe sentence) was giving tobacco to prisoners at Port Arthur.[14]

Convict women have been thought of as 'non-political', less likely than male convicts to be involved in large-scale acts of rebellion or challenges to authority and more likely to act from personal interest. The form of work women convicts undertook (domestic service) gave them less opportunity to meet together and act in unison or to make group demands. Yet women's experience of institutional life was more extensive than that of men, and while records of offences in the factories reflect for the most part individual responses to authority, the organised activities of groups of women presented a greater challenge to institutional authority than most individual acts of insubordination. While innumerable personal 'illegalities' structured institutional life and were essential to the smooth working of its system of personal rewards and punishments, group protest undermined the system and threatened its authority.

Trafficking, the major covert activity of women in the factories, was the work of groups of women rather than individuals. Organised trafficking required widespread complicity from staff and other inmates. Individuals acting alone tended to get caught, as the charge records show. Interference in these activities could lead to more violent group protests. The first riot at the new factory at Cascades was caused when women who had been calling out to soldiers on the hill had food that was thrown to them over the wall confiscated by an overseer. When he was hooted by the women (in his words '30 & 40 of the Women followed me clapping their hands and hooting me out of the yard'), the superintendent had to intervene, putting the ringleaders in cells, only to find the building set alight by the women in the crime class. Food continued to be thrown over the wall.[15]

Groups of women, too, were punished for putting in place a variety of arrangements which were intended to subvert institutional procedures, including 'mutinous conduct', which usually involved refusal to work. In 1823 at Cascades a number of women were charged with wetting the wool they were spinning so as to increase its weight and reduce their working hours.[16] At Parramatta in 1833 women rioted over having their hair cut. Revd Marsden, who was determined that their hair should be cropped, reported that it took all day to restore order and finish the task. Two years earlier they had cropped the hair of the matron, Mrs Gordon, when they seized her during an attempted escape. In 1836 the women rioted when Mrs Gordon was replaced, disqualified for her position as matron not by her own misconduct but by that of her family. In the debacle that led to complaints being brought against both Mrs Gordon's husband and her daughters, convict women denounced the Gordons' detractors, turning on the midwife, Mrs Neale, who described their behaviour later to the Factory Committee headed by Samuel Marsden: 'Maria [Gordon] then crying with passion, turned towards the women, and said, how can you bear to see me used so. The women shouted at me one and all, some said you old thief, and some you old whore.' Mrs Neale was a free emigrant whose efficient work had so met with Marsden's approval that he sought an increase in her salary. The Gordons, on the other hand, seem to have been closer (in morality and manners) to the women in their charge.[17]

Though the press may on occasions have treated riots involving convict women with some amusement, the authorities did not. They responded by taking steps to ensure that the women were not provoked, as a letter from the Chief Superintendent of Convicts in Van Diemen's Land in 1832 suggests. Spode advised Arthur not to allow 'refuse potatoes', which were too poor to be served to the navy, to be given to female convicts at the factory, commenting that it would be 'impolitic in the present agitated state of the Females in that Establish[men]t to do anything needlessly to cause any excitement of their passions'.[18] Just as male convicts had resisted the imposition of the maize diet, convict women exerted some influence over what they were fed. In 1848, soon after the first female convicts moved into the new Female Factory at Ross, a riot occurred during the visit of the visiting magistrate, Robert Pringle Stuart, which led to alterations being made to the buildings, including the erection of 9-foot fences to separate the women. A constable conveying a prisoner across the yard to the solitary cells was attacked first by the woman in his charge and then by most of the women in the crime and nursery classes. Order was regained only with difficulty and after batons had been drawn. The superintendent and staff at the factory argued against the ringleaders being tried for rioting on the grounds that it would lead to further 'exasperation' among the inmates and it would be impossible to control them.[19]

The most significant evidence of the role played by organised groups of women convicts within the factories comes from examining some of the riots in which large numbers of women were involved. In 1841 a riot occurred among female convicts in the Female House of Correction at Launceston which was of such ferocity that it was only brought under control after an assault on the crime-class ward by fifty men hastily enlisted from the male prisoners' barracks. The men, who had been sworn in as special constables, were armed with crowbars and sledgehammers, and with the assistance of some regular constables forced their way into the ward in which the women had barricaded themselves. The 'most refractory and violent of the female prisoners' were captured and put in cells in the Male House of Correction and the gaol. The internal report of the riot stated that the 'utmost resistance was offered' by the women and 'every description of Missile that could be procured was brought into operation by the females'. The male prisoners who helped to re-establish law and order were commended for their 'extreme forbearance and proper Conduct'.[20]

The riot had been provoked by the treatment of one woman, Catherine Owens, who had been confined in the solitary cells. Complaining that she was unwell, she convinced the sub-matron to visit her and as she went in, a group of women from the crime class seized the sub-matron and burst in and rescued Owens. The riot was striking for the solidarity maintained between the convict women, the numbers involved and the boldness of its execution.

After the women rescued Owens, they took her to the mess room, and in the words of the official report they then 'bid defiance to the authorities in the factory. One and all stating they would not allow her to serve the remainder of her sentence in the Cells'. When the superintendent, Robert Pearson, demanded to see the ringleaders all 85 women in the crime-class resisted. They barricaded themselves in the ward and fought off the police constables sent in to seize them using bricks prized from the floor and walls, knives and forks and quart bottles, and the legs and spindles from the spinning wheels to defend themselves. Nor did their resolve weaken as the day went on. The disturbance had begun in the morning. By evening the women, deprived of food and water, demanded that the superintendent give them rations and promise that Owens not be returned to punishment. They also demanded that the ringleaders not be tried. Unwilling to agree to their conditions, Pearson withdrew. At daybreak the prisoners became 'very outrageous' again, breaking furniture and windows, and trying to burn down the building. The intervention of the male prisoners brought an end to the women's rebellion but not to their defiance. When the ringleaders were brought to trial in Hobart and sentenced to hard labour at the Cascades factory, they once more 'exhibited the most outrageous Conduct abusing and threatening the Magistrates to their face'.

Of the known riots, one of the best recorded occurred at Parramatta in 1827 when the third-class women, whose food rations had been reduced, broke out of the factory. About forty 'took to the bush' and another hundred charged into Parramatta itself, grabbed as much food as they could and only returned when confronted by the soldiers of the 57th Regiment.[21] The *Sydney Gazette* described their recapture:

> Constables were seen running in all directions. A Captain, a Lieutenant, two serjeants, and about forty rank and file, were in immediate requisition by the Magistrates, and were seen flying in all directions with fixed bayonets, for the double purpose of securing the fugitives, and staying the mutiny; and so violent were the Amazonian banditti, that nothing less was expected but that the soldiers would be obliged to commence firing on them. After a little time, however, numbers of those who had broke loose were secured and conducted back to the old quarters under a military escort, shouting as they went along, and carrying with them their aprons loaded with bread and meat … On their arrival at the Factory, Major Lockyer, the Superintendent of Police, at Parramatta, directed the ringleaders to be selected and confined to the cells, but so determined were the rioters, that, though opposed by a military force, they succeeded in rescuing their companions, declaring, that if one suffered all should suffer.

As well known as the Parramatta riot is the mass display of disobedience by convict women during Divine Service in Hobart in 1833. The service, led by the Revd Bedford, had been attended that day by the Governor's wife, Lady Jane Franklin. Three hundred women present pulled up their clothing and smacked their bare bottoms (underclothing was not part of the ration at the factory)—an act not merely 'indecent' but synonymous with contempt in many cultures, whether performed by a man or a woman.[22]

The same mass, organised action was evident in riot at the Cascades Female Factory described by District Constable Brice to the committee of the 1841–43 Inquiry. Brice, who tried to calm the women, was completely unnerved by what he described as 'a regular confederacy amongst them'. He recounted how all the women acted in concert, pronouncing themselves to be, as they had done in the 1827 breakout at

Parramatta, 'all together'. In his evidence Brice described how he had gone with Mr Hutchinson and the chief constable into the crime-class yard where he found that

> the women upstairs kept up a tremendous clatter with their tongues but did not hurrah after we went into the yard. They refused however to listen to the Superintendent when he endeavoured to speak to them but continued in a riotous and disorderly state.—Mr Hutchinson desired them in my presence to give up the Women who were dancing in the ring and first causing the disturbance and the only answer Mr Hutchinson received was we are all alike, we are all alike, and this preceded from a great number who had clamber'd up to the Window.—I heard however two different voices call out silence. There was no attempt by any woman to give up the name of the rioters nor did any Woman from the Windows declare herself not to belong to the riotous party.—The Constables by this time had come into the yard and the Chief Constable—Mr Hutchinson and myself and another constable or two went upstairs leaving the remaining body of Constables in the yard—When we got up in the room I found the whole of the Women excepting two or three had seated themselves in a round ring on the floor and they were all very quiet.—Mr Hutchinson demanded the women be given up as before and after some delay I saw two Women talking together who appeared deliberating in my opinion to give themselves up. I spoke to them and told them to go out, they said there are two of them and they said there are plenty more in the room—The moment I entered the room I was convinced by the way in which the women were sitting that there was a regular confederacy amongst them. The ring consisted of three or four deep and I was quite surprised to find that such a body of Women could have placed themselves in such a regular manner in so short a time …

The solidarity demonstrated in this incident is striking, yet it is a characteristic of each of the four incidents described above. Both the church service demonstration and the riot at Cascades which Constable Brice described involved large groups of women executing what was in effect a planned manoeuvre in unison. The superintendent of Cascades, Revd Hutchinson, was surprised by the capacity of the women to organise themselves so quickly in a mass formation. Brice's use of the word 'confederacy' suggests, too, that their behaviour had political resonances for him, recalling other unified bodies (guilds, unions, a 'brotherhood' of conspirators) and their challenges to social order.

There is also an element of theatricality in the women's actions which recalls the prevalence in eighteenth-century British prisons of play-acting and the mock trial. As Michael Ignatieff suggests, these 'burlesques of official ritual', which represented an institutional version of the charivari, 'attested to the vigour of a competing and countervailing system of order' within the older prison system.[23] Reform did not wipe out these activities. At Brixton in the middle of the nineteenth century women prisoners danced and whistled and made up songs about all the officers.[24] In the colonial female factories play-acting, dances and songs mocking the authorities persisted well into the nineteenth century and were a feature of the internal institutional subculture. Grace Heinbury described how, at Cascades, after she had finished her day's work, she and the other women would sing songs, run about and 'do anything to pass the time'. 'Some of the women', she said, 'would act Plays, dress themselves up'.[25]

The authority of the convict system was challenged by the mere survival within the factories of this resilient culture. It is apparent that for all the prison-like constraints of the penal system, it was the capacity of convict women to recreate a semblance of their everyday lives within the institutional environment that made life on the ships and in the female factories bearable. In Mary Haigh's words:

> In the ships we were under but little restraint. We had
> but one Matron she had the charge of the Hospital and
> the whole of the Prisoners. We were locked down in
> the Prison every night, but we could talk to the men

constantly. The Middle Hatchway of the vessel could be lifted up and the Women would thus gain access to the Sailors. Rum was passed into the Prison through the Bars—thieving was common amongst the Women at night. Singing, dancing and telling the Histories of their past lives beguiled the time away—noone was present to check us, in fact after being 'locked down' we did just as we pleased.

In his evidence to the 1841–43 Inquiry, Hutchinson described how, on the evening before the riot, while investigating a noise at the factory, he looked through a window and found five female prisoners who were dancing. They were, he said:

> perfectly naked, and making obscene attitudes towards each other, they were also singing and shouting and making use of most disgusting language ... The disgusting attitudes towards each other were in imitation of men and women together.
>
> What the women now say about their washing themselves is quite untrue, they had no right to have the tubs in the rooms and when I went in there were none there ... The language they used and the attitudes they made use of corresponded in obscenity so that no mistake could be made by me as to the nature of both.

One of the women alleged that the behaviour had begun as a 'mere joke'. If the women's behaviour was 'a dirty beastly action', neither was the behaviour of the superintendent (who, in his own account, had observed his naked charges through a window, before he spoke or made himself known) particularly decorous. Joy Damousi has commented of this episode that it was 'obviously sexual play'.[26] But it is not clear that the women were engaged in sexual rather than satirical activity; certainly the combination of parody and bodily display, in which the women mocked conventional sexual behaviour, was profoundly shocking to the watcher on the other side of the windowpane.

This 'theatre', in which the order of the world was reversed, was common. Observers and inmates at the Launceston factory confirmed that singing, telling stories and dancing took up much of the women's time, while in Hobart John Price talked about how the women spent time 'composing songs ridiculing the authorities'. Price (on whom Marcus Clarke based the character of Maurice Frere and who was to become commandant of Norfolk Island) was an expert on flash language and convict culture and better placed than most to understand these songs. In the case of female convicts, there is no remaining evidence that allows us to become intimates of that culture, to hear the songs and the voices. Some remnants of flash speech remain in the records, but the authorities for the most part are likely to have shared Watkin Tench's view that the continuance of 'this infatuating cant' led to depravity and that its abolition 'would open the path to reformation'. Still used in everyday life, this 'unnatural jargon' was abolished in the official records, which use a sanitised language almost bereft of idiom.[27]

While among male prisoners mock trials inverted the dominant power relationships, and on Norfolk Island language itself was inverted so that 'good' meant 'bad', among convict women parodies of sexual behaviour inverted and mocked accepted domestic relationships. The Cascades disturbance had begun with dancing in a ring and ended with a deep circular formation of women. The silent circle in reformist discourse carried multiple allusions (to domesticity, to the circle of personal reformation and to the circle of surveillance, in which women performed domestic tasks under the gaze of the authorities), but it became, in the hands of large groups of mutinous women, a powerful mechanism of intimidation. The watched became the watchers. This was a subversive culture rather than an accommodating one. Through these acts women claimed space for themselves and reconstructed the values of those who sought to reform them.

Joy Damousi, in writing of order and disorder on board the convict ships, has argued that women's protests were different from those of male convicts.[28] She locates their rebelliousness primarily in boisterous and recalcitrant behaviour, playing down group actions such as the forming of mutinous committees as more conventional (that is, less specifically female forms of protest). While rough and aggressively sexual behaviour in women clearly threatened male authority, it would be wrong to ignore the more organised and collective challenges women made, especially when those actions demonstrate not an imitation of male behaviour but an adaptation of it. Damousi pays a little more attention to collective resistance in her book (although she still regards 'unified action' as less relevant to convict women) but emphasises how it was perceived—by the press either as a 'frolic' or eroticised—rather than what it meant. In seeing all transgressive behaviour as resistance, and resistance largely as an expression of 'pleasure and desire', Damousi does not attach any specific significance to collective resistance. The factories, however, are 'societies', not just a transitory clustering of individuals motivated by their own interests. Collective acts, like the riots just described, enable us to decipher the subculture and underpinning relationships within that world and the serious threat they posed.

Intrinsic to the reformatory ideal was the idea that individuals should progress through the cycle of reform by contemplation of their faults and by exercising greater personal self-control and discipline (a process best achieved through isolation from other influences). The number and type of individual transgressions were indicators both of failure and of progress. Collective rebelliousness and the maintenance of a subversive subculture, on the other hand, threatened not so much the institution itself (for the women, in the end, could always be controlled by the use of force) but its fundamental purpose. And it was that which most disturbed the authorities and led them to take steps to control such behaviour by the use of separation and isolation, by accommodating some of the women's demands and, ultimately, by their rejection of institutional confinement as the best means of reformation.

Who were the pivotal figures in this subversive culture? What sort of women led the riots and organised the economy of the factories? They were certainly not meek victims who took their punishments passively. Nor were they easily reformed by discipline and industry, as Mrs Fry hoped. The authorities might deny that any group called the 'Flash Mob' really existed at the Cascades factory, but Mary Haigh's description of these women gives some idea of what the 'ringleaders' in the crime class were like. She reported that

> in the Factory are found several Women known by the name of the 'Flash Mob' who have always money and wear worked caps silk Handkerchiefs earrings and other rings. They are the greatest blackguards in the building, the other women are afraid of them. They lead away the young girls by ill advice ...[29]

Of these women, two can be clearly identified. Catherine Owens, the central figure in the Launceston riot, had been transported for fourteen years for receiving stolen silver spoons.[30] A housemaid from Liverpool, she was said to have been 'on the town' in Lancaster before her conviction, and a member of a gang of burglars. She had other convictions, including the theft of her father's property. In Van Diemen's Land she was violent (to her fellow prisoners as well as to others). She was charged with more than fifty offences between 1829 and 1846, and her existing sentence was extended three times. A drinker, she was punished on a number of occasions for acts committed while drunk, including breaking the windows of the colonial hospital while drinking with whalers. Some of those punishments were quite brutal. On one occasion she was sentenced to three days in the iron collar and to repeated spells of solitary confinement.

Owen's friend Ellen Scott, who probably organised her daring escape, had a very different background. She was a 'lifer' from Limerick in Ireland.[31] She had only one conviction, for vagrancy, before she was transported for the theft of a watch chain. She was 18-years-old, small in build, and single. Her record in the colony was more impressive: refusal to work, refusal to proceed to service, absconding, dancing in a public house, out after hours—all evidence of a rebellious rather than a criminal disposition. Her first severe punishment was seven days in the cells on bread and water for the most 'serious' crime of 'Being out of bed at an unreasonable hour'. Because she neglected a child left in her care she was sent to the factory in Hobart for six months and there forced to wear the hated collar. In 1833, after the church service at the factory when the Governor's wife was insulted by the mass display of bared bottoms, Ellen Scott was one of the women put in the solitary cells for 'indecent behaviour'. During the seventeen years it took before she got her pardon she spent time in the factories in Hobart, Launceston and George Town and in gaol in Hobart and Longford. When the authorities were searching to find some place with separate cells to confine Scott and her associates after the Launceston riot, they declined to return her to Hobart because she had been sent to Launceston after an attempt on the life of the matron at Cascades, and it was thought to be 'perfectly dangerous for Mrs Hutchinson to have her returned'.

Ellen Scott and Catherine Owens had very different backgrounds before they were transported. From their criminal records one could be described as merely an unfortunate young woman, poor and without the means to support herself. The other fits the description of the 'professional criminal'. Their lives as transported convicts resulted in both becoming 'incorrigibles', although that word understates the role they played within the convict system. They were among the most difficult women the authorities had to deal with in Van Diemen's Land and in response were subjected to brutalising physical punishments. By the time of the Inquiry they were the ringleaders of the crime-class women. If there really was a 'Flash Mob' they were among its leaders. The fact that their relationship was also a sexual one and the significance of lesbian relationships to the politics and economy of the factories will be explored in the next chapter.

7

SEXUALITY

Overwhelmed by their concern with the issue of prostitution, few historians have shown a serious interest in the sexuality of convict women. Even Robert Hughes, who discloses so graphically the rampant male sexuality of the 'fatal shore', is less concerned with women as actors than as respondents.[1] Female sexuality has for the most part been seen to exist only in reaction to male desire. In the sexual history of the Australian colonies the priapic male dominates both the contemporary and the historical debate. The concept of active male sexuality provides the explanation for the penal society's harsh responses to homosexuality, sodomy and bestiality as well as its tolerance of prostitution and its encouragement of marriage.

While the behaviour of men has been seen in sexual terms as 'natural', the behaviour of women has more often been seen in cultural terms, as deviant or immoral. Consequently, in relation to prostitution, the male client resumed his everyday persona after a sexual encounter; his female partner, however, 'became a prostitute', and was henceforth branded as such.[2] In viewing relationships in this way Australian historians were taking on the perspective and double standard of the time which allowed singularly less sexual freedom to women than to men. Victims of myth rather than analysts of discourse, they assumed the ambivalent attitude to women and to female sexuality evident among contemporary male observers. Men were seen as sexual beings, whether they were from the upper or lower classes. The active sexual behaviour of women, on the other hand, was either ignored or treated with suspicion and disapproval.

Feminist historians have not dispelled the image of female asexuality. One unintended consequence of feminist writing has been to portray men as sexual and women as primarily economic creatures, the latter led toward prudent marriages, cohabitation and prostitution more by the need for freedom, security, protection, even survival, than by desire or attraction. Yet true though this picture might be in its analysis of the motivation of many convict women, it also serves to suppress another dimension of female convict experience. Among all the conflicting emotions felt by Lieutenant Ralph Clark about the convict women in his charge, his fear of their aggressive sexuality is dominant. Threatened by their anarchic demands (and mindful of his wife's complaisant virtue), Clark restored order and authority at least to his personal world. He took a convict mistress, made her pregnant and deserted her. If his failure to record the liaison in his diary might be seen as hypocrisy, the act itself can be seen in less compromising terms. Female sexuality was restored to its rightful place—confined as a response to a single male's demands.[3]

Ralph Clark the hypocrite is less interesting (and more conventionally 'Victorian') than Ralph Clark the late eighteenth-century man fearful of 'the damned whores'. Historians concerned with changing customs and practices in modern Britain have observed a major shift in middle-class thinking over the period from the mid-eighteenth to the mid-nineteenth century, at the heart of which is a changed concept of femininity. Davidoff and Hall put it succinctly when they refer to the triumph of the Victorian belief in female purity over the eighteenth-century preoccupation with rampant and voracious female sexuality. Just as interesting is their choice of an occasion in which the two views come into dramatic conflict: the trial in 1820 of Queen Caroline, in which she (incongruously) came to represent the virtues of middle-class domestic life and morality and her husband the upper-class vices and debauchery of the Regency—particularly the open enjoyment of and indulgence in sexual pleasure.[4]

Central to the management of convict women from the beginning of transportation was the issue of their active sexuality. This chapter looks at the changing context of ideas and behaviour in which this took place and examines more closely the later period in which aspects of female sexual behaviour threw up new complexities for convict administrators.

Historians writing about the convict period in Australia have not vigorously pursued the idea that the colonies were founded at a time in which concepts of female sexuality and morality— femininity itself—were being reformulated and contested. The views that later became equated with Victorianism were not, at the beginning of the period, dominant. Australia was not born Victorian, but nor did it wait until the Victorian period for the virtues of sexual restraint to become influential. Many looking back at the morality of the early settlements from the vantage point of 1820 were as uncomfortable with the appetites of early governors and officers as the supporters of Queen Caroline were with those of the Regency debauchee.

In Britain the period of roughly sixty years in which female convicts were sent to Australia was a time of considerable change in both sexual practice and morality. It was a time during which the expanding middle class created patterns of domesticity which increasingly excluded less respectable forms of behaviour and in which attempts were made to draw both the upper and the lower classes into that sphere of gentility. Changes in the behaviour of the working class suggest an increase in moral respectability beginning as early as the 1790s. Michael Mason argues that 'anti-sensualism' became a key element not only in conservative religious thinking but also in progressive social thought, and it is to this that he attributes its temporary cultural ascendancy.[5]

Three areas of change in Britain are of particular relevance to the history of convict women in Australia: the sexual behaviour and attitudes of the lower classes from which the convict population was drawn; the embracing by the middle classes of 'respectability' and their estimation, in the light of these new standards, of lower-class behaviour; and changing concepts of sexuality and in particular female sexuality.

Historians looking at the lower classes in Britain in this period have concluded that there was an important shift in sexual morality and behaviour, although the timing and explanation of these changes is the subject of debate. Lawrence Stone suggested that an increase in premarital chastity in the seventeenth century was followed by greater prenuptial intercourse in the eighteenth century (most of which led to marriage, although an increasing number failed to marry after pregnancy), concluding that there had been a breakdown of community controls on premarital sex. The number of prostitutes was fed, according to Stone, 'not only by poverty, but by the growing culture of promiscuity in the large submerged class of the very poor'.[6] At the very end of the eighteenth century and early in the nineteenth century, however, Stone discerns what he calls 'a new wave of sexual prudery', beginning with the lower middle classes and spreading downwards to the respectable poor, with only the lowest social groups remaining unaffected by this change. The reasons for this are complex, for while Stone suggests that there is evidence that a small group of the poorest stratum of society were 'bastardy-prone' over generations and that many women from this group found themselves on the streets, he also argues that an increase in the propertyless poor at the end of the eighteenth century led to a rise in the group for whom virginity had no economic value. Moreover, men were increasingly removed from the constraints traditionally exercised by family and community, and women from the protections these afforded.

More recently Michael Mason has argued that, as suggested

by the observations of Francis Place, moral respectability among the lower classes was on the increase well before the Victorian period.[7] With the proviso that diverse and divergent moral cultures existed within the working class, Mason locates this change in the first two decades of the nineteenth century. In reference to the later period, Françoise Barret-Ducrocq's study of the archives of the London Foundling Hospital (covering three decades from 1850) discloses a range of sexual behaviours but no sign of the chaotic licentiousness contemporaries attributed to the poor. Instead she discerns a common set of moral rules relating to sexual behaviour, distinctly different from those of the middle classes, in which sexual relationships outside marriage were an acceptable and common preliminary to marriage and women in such relationships were not ostracised from family or community. On the other hand the understanding that women who became pregnant would not be deserted was, she argues, increasingly undermined as men evaded the consequences of this arrangement. Women were the victims of 'a new balance of forces' which left them particularly vulnerable and 'barely able to reconcile the defence of their material interests with the unpredictable demands of sexual desire'.[8]

The extent to which respectability was embraced rather than imposed, reshaped rather than absorbed by sections of the lower classes is difficult to establish either in Britain or Australia. While distinct lower-class codes of morality are evident, some groups appear to have been more susceptible than others to middle-class values. And as behaviour in the middle classes became more refined, the differences between middle-class behaviour and that of the working class, particularly the rough working class, became more distinct. Respectability is defined by differentiation, and the respectable classes required the 'other' behaviour of a 'rough' labouring class and a 'debauched' upper class from which to differentiate themselves. Regardless of any change in their customs and attitudes, the alleged 'sexual depravity' of the lower classes continued to be the subject of graphic exposure in Britain throughout the century. The morality of codes exclusive to the lower classes were for the most part invisible except to the most perceptive middle-class eye (such as Mayhew in the *Morning Chronicle* articles), and moral 'self-improvement' (as suggested by Francis Place) tended either to attract little attention or was attributed to missionary work and middle-class persuasion.[9]

Convicts were drawn from a disparate social group within which we would expect wide variations in cultural practices and moral patterns distinct from those prevailing within the middle class. But the early environment of the penal settlements accentuated rather than reduced the conditions which made women vulnerable and sexual restraint unlikely. Men both from the upper and the lower classes were less constrained by community pressure and family obligations, while women were commonly deprived of moral and physical protection. Virginity held little economic value—in fact loss of it and even pregnancy out of wedlock could bring rewards while women and children were supported and pregnancy was accommodated by the state. Whatever moral codes prevailed among the transported convicts, they came under considerable pressure in the penal colonies.

From the time of Macquarie tangible rewards were offered to those who showed their capacity and willingness to embrace forms of sexual behaviour acceptable to the administration. An official emphasis on respectability drew added impetus from the wish to differentiate the free from the convict, the reformed from the incorrigible. Michael Sturma argues that after transportation ceased the convict code was largely displaced by 'a code of middle class propriety' which regulated the boundaries of 'socially acceptable behaviour'.[10] For convict women middle-class respectability meant not only a condemnation of sexual activity outside marriage but a set of new behaviours which conformed to middle-class ideas of appropriate feminine behaviour.

Evolving views of femininity and female sexuality were central to defining the boundaries of respectability. New standards of feminine behaviour were expected of convict women in the factories and while assigned, and they were discouraged from various forms of public and sexual behaviour when free. By stigmatising the 'convict whore', other women could come to be regarded as respectable. The new emphasis on restraint was particularly espoused by groups involved in missionary work in the colonies and was influential among prison reformers, with officials at female factories often drawn from these groups. As institutions became more efficiently controlled, the role of chaplain and of religious instruction became central to routine. The reformist zeal of the convict system, once focused, was applied with particular vigour to women, and with particular intent to their sexual behaviour. It was here that the most substantial change took place in the management of convict women and where new middle-class expectations about the moral behaviour of women rubbed up against the disparate and different behaviours of the lower classes.

The emphasis on respectability made greater demands on women than on men. Women were called upon to take on broad responsibilities of moral leadership. Higher standards of public behaviour, cleanliness, modesty, polite speech and sobriety were expected of them.[11] In all these areas there was a stark contrast between what was expected of middle-class women and common patterns of behaviour in the lower classes. Moreover, while middle-class women were increasingly confined to a private world, lower-class women freely inhabited public space. They mingled in the streets and carried on their domestic life in open view; they moved in search of work, changed lodgings, formed relationships, discussed sexual matters, were sexually active.

In relation to sexual behaviour, contemporary images (internalised by many historians) of the middle-class woman as asexual, allied to the stereotype of the 'abandoned' convict woman, imply a class difference not only in sexual behaviour but in sexual appetite—with the effect of making the sexual behaviour of convict women appear more anomalous than it in fact is, so that female sexual desire itself appears to be 'deviant'. Regardless of the actual experience of middle-class women, the ascendancy of the view that all women should embrace the ideals of sexual restraint and feminine purity, combined with assumptions about the rampant sexuality of the lower classes, created the new terrain on which official convict policy in Australia was reconstructed.

The management of female sexual behaviour became central to convict administration as systematic assignment replaced the laxity of the early period and institutions were established to accommodate more women. Underpinning these practices was a belief, endorsed by both the secular reformer and the evangelical moralist, in the efficacy of sexual restraint and the appropriateness of confining female sexual activity to marriage. Segregation of the 'immoral' from society and regulation of relations between the sexes were the strategies used to control the sexual behaviour of convict women. Any active expression of sexuality outside marriage was defined as deviant.

In the context of assignment the apprehension and punishment of convict women for sexual transgressions was common, but the enforcement of strict moral standards was difficult, dependent as it was on their acceptance by master and mistress. Surveillance was incomplete, and often the system broke down because values were not shared. Within female factories greater surveillance of women's behaviour was possible, and incarceration became an increasingly important tool in managing transgressive behaviour. Officials, including the chaplain, played a key role in defining what was 'normal' or feminine; rewards and punishments were meted out accordingly. At the same time it became apparent that segregation from men did not curtail female sexual activity. Sex between convict women in the factories became as difficult a problem for the authorities as male homosexual relationships, although it was less publicly acknowledged and more difficult to accommodate within the prevailing set of assumptions about feminine and female sexual behaviour.

The way in which early colonial history has been both obsessively concerned with sexual behaviour and neglectful of the sexuality of women is exemplified in the way it records convict homosexuality. The discussion of homosexuality among convicts has almost entirely been about male behaviour, regardless of one paragraph by Robert Hughes and his comment that Cascades 'swarmed with lesbians'.[12] Yet evidence suggests that the sexual relationships formed between women confined in convict institutions were as much a concern to the convict administration as male homosexuality. Moreover sexual relationships between convict women were an important aspect of the way in which the culture and politics of the female institutions were constituted, and in that way raised additional and complex issues for convict administration, particularly in the last decade of transportation.

A detailed analysis of sexual relations between women convicts in his care is provided in the correspondence of the superintendent of the Ross Female Depot, Dr W. J. Irvine. In 1850 when Irvine wrote to the visiting magistrate, Robert Pringle Stuart (at his request) giving details of the 'unnatural practices' he considered to be 'occasionally' carried on in the Ross factory and elsewhere, he offered both a description of one aspect of the subculture which developed in the female factories and a clinical analysis of certain forms of female sexual behaviour which he said had, to a degree, a physiological basis.[13]

Irvine spoke of some female convicts who he believed 'even when not debarred from access to those of another sex' had 'an earnest desire to procure an artificial substitute' for the 'natural' relations between male and female. He divided the women in this group into two classes. The first group, he suggested, could not be distinguished from other women except in so far as they often had 'an apparently much stronger feeling for the woman acting the male's part, than for a veritable male himself'. The second class he called the 'pseudo-male' or 'man-woman' who he believed had distinctive external physical characteristics. Convict women who had a masculine appearance, hoarse voices and the 'development of a pair of imperfect moustaches' he placed in this latter category, although he could not say with any certainty whether any women without these characteristics could be so categorised.

He also pointed out that he believed some of these women possessed a 'preternatural development' of the clitoris which enabled them to assume at least partially the function of the male in sexual relations. 'And', he continued, 'in other cases I have learned that artificial substances, mechanically secured to the person form the substitute for the male organ'.

Irvine was clearly intrigued by the attraction these 'pseudo-males' held for other women, commenting that the 'most passionate appeals are frequently made' by women when they suspect the 'pseudo-males' of infidelity or fickleness:

> Indeed an amount of jealousy seems to be aroused as great as possibly could be, if an actual 'male' was in question, promises, threats, are alike lavished on the objects of their loves, and they are habitually in the practice of making numerous presents to their '*lovers*', so that an individual who acts the infamous part of the pseudo-male, is most comfortably provided for by the presents bestowed, with every procurable luxury

It was, Irvine suggested, the youngest and most innocent of the female convicts who were chosen by these women.

> These young girls are in the habit of decorating themselves, cleaning themselves scrupulously, & making themselves as attractive as they can, before resorting to the 'man-woman', if I may so style her, on whom they have bestowed their affections; I believe, a large proportion of the quarrels which too frequently occur amongst women (with such ill regulated tempers, as the women in the factory) are occasioned by, or take their rise from disagreements concerning the choice of a pseudo-male, or jealous feelings consequent on, some of these disgraceful transactions.

Irvine's information was based not only on his own observation of behaviour but on what he described as 'repeated and careful inquiries of many women whom I considered likely at once to know something of this matter'—women he considered to be reliable in that they were unlikely to conceal or misrepresent anything they had seen or heard. Letters had also been intercepted which demonstrated 'the warmth and impetuosity of the feelings excited in women towards each other, when allied in such unholy bonds'.

Irvine had written to the authorities in Hobart at the end of 1848 about the misconduct of three prisoners who had been caught leaving the beds 'of those to whom they acted in the capacity of men', and had raised the idea that they were able to 'fill the vile part above described' either because of some physical abnormality or by artificial means. This made the Comptroller-General of Convicts, Dr J. S. Hampton, write in the margin that all three should undergo a medical examination on arrival at Cascades. The results are not known.[14]

In the literature of criminology Irvine was not alone in ascribing special physical characteristics to the female criminal. Theorists of criminal behaviour, such as Lombroso and Havelock Ellis, put forward ideas of this kind in the late nineteenth century. But as Foucault and others have pointed out, the scrutiny and surveillance of the new institutions of punishment allowed the clinical observation of the inmate and the construction of a new criminology. Medical officers employed in colonial penal institutions were well placed to make such clinical observations. In place of Mayhew's picaresque 'biology' of the criminal world (with its 'species' and 'sub-species') a new scientific analysis of 'the criminal' and his physical characteristics began to emerge, with doctors playing a major part by mid-century in formulating these new 'scientific' discourses.[15] Irvine was doubly advantaged as an observer of female convict relationships. He was medically trained and, as was common in penal establishments, his wife was the matron and intimately involved in the everyday lives of the female convicts.

Dr William John Irvine arrived at the beginning of 1840 on the *Canton*, which carried male convicts to Hobart.[16] He was surgeon-superintendent (his only journey in that capacity) and his wife accompanied him. Later that year he established a private practice in the Cameron Buildings in Launceston. This seems to have been short-lived, because in July 1841 Dr Irvine was appointed again to a medical position within the convict service, this time as assistant surgeon at Jerusalem on a salary of £136 17s 6d per annum. A second attempt at a private venture in mid–1843 lasted nearly two and a half years. Irvine's advertisement for his new 'chemist and druggist' business in Liverpool Street, Hobart, gives some information about his experience and professional background. Promising that he would attend to the preparation of prescriptions himself, give medical advice at his own house and also perform the operations of a dentist (for which he had 'many years' experience'), Irvine described himself as a member of the Royal College of Surgeons of Edinburgh, Doctor of Medicine of that university and late president of that city's Royal Medical Society. The 1840s economy was not conducive to new enterprises. Nor were the colonies short of medical practitioners, many of whom, like Irvine, came out on convict ships as surgeon-superintendents, a position which after 1820 carried considerable responsibility for disciplinary as well as health matters. By late 1845 Irvine's 'very eligible little RETAIL BUSINESS' was up for sale ('in consequence of the state of [the proprietor's] health and other circumstances'), and in 1846 Irvine was back in the employ of the Medical Department as assistant surgeon on the Tasman Peninsula at the Coal Mines. When Irvine was appointed to Ross as superintendent and medical officer in February 1846 on a salary of £170, his wife (described as 'well educated, energetic') was also appointed matron. In 1850 questions were raised about Irvine's behaviour, in particular his alleged drinking and misappropriation of the medicine and alcohol kept for patient use. It was found that he did not possess 'the requisite degree of firmness and decision of character to enable him to control such an establishment', and he was removed to the position of medical officer on the *Lady Franklin*, which plied the route to Norfolk Island.

What is striking about Irvine's observations is his linking of physical characteristics not only with criminal but also with sexual behaviour. Moreover, he adds to his analysis a 'sociology' of homosexual relationships, locating his clinical observations in the social context of the prison milieu. He believed that a large proportion of the juvenile convicts were, through their association with these 'pseudo-males', 'irretrievably ruined' morally and 'frequently much injured in health, physically'. Physical damage as well as moral harm resulted from these liaisons, and women who were 'prone to these habits' or who indulged in masturbation were diagnosed by Irvine as likely to suffer from palpitation and functional diseases of the heart. This condition could not be treated successfully as long as the 'exciting cause' persisted.

Irvine's observations about female sexual behaviour are exceptional. Documentation of the sexual relationships between women in the female factories occurs most frequently not as a result of studied clinical observation but in the context of other investigations, often concerning allegations of assault. At Ross, for example, in the year following Irvine's letter, a prisoner was charged with assaulting a fellow convict in the water closets while the other women were picking wool. A witness saw one of the women with her hand up the other's clothing 'having connection with her'. She testified that the woman, who was crying, later became ill and accused the other woman of 'destroying' her. When questioned by the authorities, the 'victim', who had only been at Ross for a month, gave a different account in which she claimed not to have given way to the other's advances. She alleged that the other woman had pursued her, speaking 'smutty words' to her, asking her to 'let her do something to me, [saying] that she would show me the way'. While the accused woman had followed her and tried to put her hand under her clothes, she said she had not let her:

> I walked away because I knew she was after me, because she used to follow me and ask me to set down with her, and walk with her, I would not because I heard she had the name of being bad behaved and spoken—I used to shun her. I did not let her destroy me.[17]

The protagonist on this occasion was said to have six or seven other girls who liked her, and when the other woman claimed that she rebuffed her advances with the comment 'I would not have that sin upon me', she replied 'it was no sin'. Both women were married after their release.[18]

In 1843 Ann Fisher described another incident (this time at Cascades) when she gave evidence against two prisoners charged with gross disorderly conduct.[19] Fisher shared a hammock with one of the women, Jane Owen, and during the night the second woman, Eliza Taylor, got into bed with them. She asked Owen 'in language which no one could misunderstand to be indecent with her'. Owen replied that she would not because she was 'unwell'; 'Taylor then said will you when you are well she said yes.' The following night the two women (according to Fisher) washed themselves in a bucket of water and put on clean linen. Owen asked Taylor if she was coming over 'to give her a yarn'. Taylor later joined them and, after talking with Owen for more than two hours in what Fisher said was 'a very indecent way', asked her

> to give her that she asked for the night before Owen replied she would get out of bed and go home with her if she liked Taylor said no that was not what she meant. Taylor then called her a b—dy little wretch and said she could pull her out of bed and pull her to pieces for getting her in such a way as that for nothing at all. Owen said to Taylor that she never had been nailed and never would be, and Owen said to Taylor that it would make no difference to her as she had done it to her before. The expression they mean by nailing is indecently using their hands with each others persons. Taylor and Owen did behave on that night in the way I have above described Owen made use of her hands on the person of Taylor indecently. They behaved in this indecent manner for four or five minutes when I got out of bed and called Taylor a nasty beast. I then went to Sarah Berbeck's bed with whom Eliza Taylor slept and got into bed with Berbeck and remained with her about a quarter of an hour when Taylor came back to her own bed and I went to mine. I asked Taylor how she could let Stump meaning Owen have anything to do with her, she begged me not to say anything to anyone about it. When I returned to my own bed I called Owen a nasty beast for what she had been

doing, she told me she did not mind me talking to her about it but if any of her own sort spoke to her about it she would wallow in her own blood for it.

Charges were dismissed when witnesses called were unable or unwilling to support Fisher's testimony; but the description of the kind of physical relationship which took place between the women is given in some detail and is unusual because vestiges of convict language remain in the written record—perhaps because there was no legal terminology, such as 'Criminal Conversation', to substitute for her words.

Not all 'indecent assaults' were sexual in their intent. Grace Heinbury in her evidence to the 1841–43 Inquiry described how money was 'generally' taken into the Cascades factory in 'the Privates of the Women'. When two prisoners were charged with gross misconduct for 'committing an indecent assault upon the person' of Mary Newell in 1843, Newell made it quite clear that the motive of the assault was to search for contraband. She had been woken in her hammock by someone covering her face and head with a rug. She was then held down while another woman searched her to see, she thought, if she had hidden inside her body either money or tobacco. The search was so violent that she fainted. Later that night she

> got up and went to the night tub but found that I could not make water and on feeling with my hand I found that something was protruding out of my privates nearly the length of my finger ... I did not know what it was but I have since been informed by the nurse that my Womb was down ... I told what had happened to one of the Women who was a country woman of mine and she told me as I had a long sentence to do if I said anything about it the Women would lead me a sad life.

Newell was warned by her bedfellow (the women shared hammocks) that if she suspected her she'd 'stick' her through the heart with her scissors. Because a 'great many of the Women in the Ward' were on the side of her assailants, she had declined to make any accusation until the turnkey informed the superintendent. Newell's injury was similar to that suffered by the woman in the Ross assault. It is probable that incidents such as this came to the attention of the authorities when an injury resulted which could not be concealed.

Irvine's picture of the sexual relationships between women and the social hierarchy within the factory at Ross is supported by testimony from convict women themselves at other institutions. Grace Heinbury described a similar situation at Cascades earlier in which some of the women who were 'very bad' 'led away' young girls. They in turn, from her account, would commit offences when outside the factory so that they could return to their lovers inside. 'Unnatural intercourse with each other is common', she said, 'but those who practise it are despised by the rest of the Women'.

Whether or not the so-called Flash Mob who Mary Haigh said were 'the greatest blackguards' at Cascades, and who 'led away the young girls by ill-advice' were also involved in lesbian activities, they fit Irvine's description of the women at the apex of the factory hierarchy: their rings, money, silk handkerchiefs and worked caps are appropriate symbols of their position. Moreover, their possessions may well have come not only from their own trading but from 'tribute'. Irvine described one woman at Ross as being the 'purse keeper of her successive admirers'. This woman, whom he described as a 'large size masculine looking woman', was, according to one of the other prisoners, in the habit of never going out to service when she was in Hobart. She was, he said,

> in the habit of inveigling the very young and inexperienced and of seducing them and it appears the scenes that take place from the depraved habits of such creatures as this woman are to the last degree disgusting and offensive to the better disposed, both breaking their rest by their nocturnal orgies, and offending their sense of common decency by their licentious and unnatural practices.[20]

The descriptions of behaviour at Ross and Cascades are supplemented by evidence given to the Inquiry in 1841 about similar behaviour within the Launceston factory. The lives of two of the women at Launceston who were said to be involved in a sexual relationship have been outlined earlier: Ellen Scott and Catherine Owens were well known to the authorities and leading figures in the Launceston factory riot.

The superintendent at Launceston, Robert Pearson, alleged that the behaviour of the women in his care was generally 'depraved' and that sexual relationships between them were common. Girls and women, virtuous and modest as they may have been on entering the factory, must 'inevitably' under the 'present system ... become corrupted', he suggested.

Pearson's comments were supported by two inmates who gave evidence at the same time. Of some convict women it was said that they would not remain outside the factory 'while others remain in'. Mary Kirk alleged that 'unnatural conduct' was frequent and had increased considerably in the time she had been there, stating that the 'well-disposed' women were unable to avoid being corrupted as none could avoid associating with the others: 'The flash characters compel the others to follow their example.' A second inmate supported Kirk's belief that there were 'many' women in the factory who would not stay outside while the women 'with whom they carry on unnatural connexion are in the building'. Among the six couples she went on to name in this context were Catherine Owens and Ellen Scott.

These women are quite jealous of each other. The other women are afraid to interfere although they dislike such practices, they are never carried on openly but at night, they are never associated with by the other women. They generally sit together on one side of the yard ... The well disposed women would prefer they separated into parties of twelve but the others would not if any attempt were made to separate the women whose names I have mentioned and others of similar habits a riot would be got up immediately, I heard Ellen Scott say so last night if Catherine Owens were sent to Hobarton ... The women will not go out of the yards when wanted except taken by force. Some of them are quite desperate and would not hesitate to take a knife to any one.

Another inmate at Launceston said she could pick out eight women who she was certain were 'in the habit of indulging in improper practices'. This behaviour was generally talked about and was, she thought, more widespread, with perhaps about thirty women involved. Others were, however, 'afraid to complain, as their lives would be in danger. I have known women severely beaten for talking'. She also pointed out that practices of this kind had been common in Hobart when she was there four years previously.

There is an irony underlying much of the behaviour of these women that may not have escaped the notice of the authorities. The relationships between women both inverted and mimicked those more conventional relationships which existed outside the factory walls: the authority of the 'male' partner, who did not 'work' but held the purse, and the intense loyalty which marked these relationships. Virtues such as cleanliness, which the penal establishment hoped convict women would acquire as part of their reformation, were, in this context, avidly embraced, as the women scrupulously washed and put on clean linen for their female lovers. Michael Ignatieff has written of the 'new hygienic rituals', such as body examinations and bathing, which were introduced into institutions as health measures and which became a means of stripping individuals of their personal identity.[21] Concern with cleanliness became another reason for subjecting women's bodies to the demanding gaze of the authorities. But when women danced around the tubs naked or washed and dressed in clean clothes before sexual encounters, they were creating other, more subversive, rituals as well as reclaiming their identities in ways which challenged accepted notions of the female body and being female.

Most of the references to these women claim that the sexual activities of the 'bad behaved and spoken' offended their fellow prisoners and that they dominated others through intimidation and thuggery. Revd Hutchinson reported that women had come to him and begged to be put in the cells to escape the 'cursing, swearing and obscenity' of the wards. Informers were careful to state how disgusted they were by the sexual behaviour they described, and Irvine went so far as to suggest that these women were also notorious among men 'of their own rank', and that, when outside the factory, they were 'despised and detested and almost hooted at'. Yet the 1841–43 Inquiry provided substantial evidence that homosexual relationships in the female convict establishments were common and engaged in openly, even to the extent that two women were said to have been 'detected' during divine service in the chapel 'in the very act of exciting each other's passions'. Commentators also asserted that those engaged in these lesbian practices were powerful figures within the institutions and that young women would 'inevitably' be corrupted by them. Irvine, moreover, attributed the frequent quarrels among women at Ross to the jealousies and rivalries arising from these relationships. Governor Eardley-Wilmot confided to Colonial Secretary Stanley in 1843 that the women were 'generally of the most violent passions and abandoned characters' and did not disguise their behaviour. The women in the factories, he said, 'have their Fancy-women, or lovers, to whom they are attached with quite as much ardour as they would be to the other sex, and practice onanism to the greatest extent'.[22]

I have described earlier the subculture of the factories in which a thriving internal economy based on trafficking both undermined the authority of the prison system (by weakening the process of punishment and cementing relationships between staff and prisoners) and entrenched the authority of subgroups among the female convicts. Convict women whiled away the time exchanging information about masters and mistresses (and how to pilfer their possessions), and places to go to avoid apprehension. According to one observer, those who 'represented their conduct as having been the most daring, nay it may be stated the most corrupt' were 'held in the highest estimation amongst their fellow prisoners'. The 'ringleaders' or 'flash characters' could command considerable authority and even loyalty among large numbers of the women, and were on occasions the instigators of mass displays of disobedience and rioting. To add a further, significant dimension to this subculture, relationships between a number of these women and between them and their followers often appear to have been sexual, with younger female convicts being drawn into this network and supporting it. Far from succumbing to the 'vegetative misery' and 'stagnant leisure' of the factories (as Robert Hughes suggested),[23] or becoming (in comparison with male prisoners) unresisting victims of the system, concerned only with their individual welfare, these women reshaped the environment of the factories to their own ends. Officials were not unaware of these links between rebellion and sexual 'depravity' and juxtaposed in their reports descriptions of both. Pearson, describing how he had to 'carry pistols' if he wanted to take women out of the wards at Launceston, went on to say:

> I have had my shirt torn from my back. In almost every case, I am obliged to use force to take a woman out, as they will seldom come out when called, but will call the others to their assistance. Their conduct generally is most depraved and disgusting, and their language most obscene, unnatural intercourse between them is carried on to a great extent.

If in many ways these colonial institutions recreated the chaotic conditions of the eighteenth-century prison, they also became laboratories in which some of the new ideas of the prison reformers and their urge for discipline, order and the reformation of the individual were pursued. While the rough subculture survived, it did so in a changed environment. Surveillance and the documentation of the history of the individual took new prominence in the years of transportation. Although continual visual observation of individuals was seldom possible, the documentation of individual histories by centralised record-keeping was thorough and was increasingly supplemented by other reports, including the reports of medical practitioners who came to play a much greater role in the institutions.

The large number of medical practitioners in New South Wales was remarked upon in the 1833 Select Committee on the Medical Practices Bill, and Jan Kociumbas has drawn attention to the impact of their intervention in (and the consequent medicalisation of) various areas of public policy.[24] Their increasing role in convict administration, first on the transports and later in the penal institutions, is striking. Dr Hampton had been a shipboard surgeon with a medical diploma from Edinburgh, and had been surgeon-superintendent on several convict transports before taking up his position in Van Diemen's Land. Dr Turnbull, chairman of the 1841–43 Inquiry, was another graduate in medicine from Edinburgh. At Ross, Irvine's assistant superintendent, Mr Imrie, was also a medical practitioner, and his successor Dr Edward Swarbreck Hall, who had similarly tried unsuccessfully to establish a private practice before entering the government service, went on to become a significant figure in the history of public health in the colony. Ross's last superintendent, Dr Everett, was medically trained and had worked at both Port Arthur and Norfolk Island. Their experience contrasts to that of the Hutchinsons, who like Mrs Fry's protégés had an evangelical background, and the numbers of untrained women and men like Robert Pearson at Launceston, who had been a gatekeeper at the prison barracks before becoming superintendent. The new emphasis on the medical expert also involved a diminution of the power of the matron and a shift from female to male authority within institutions holding women.[25]

Medically trained observers such as Irvine subjected the body to new scrutiny, developing in the process theories of female sexual behaviour. These observations, while fragmentary, foreshadow the much later and well-known work of writers such as Lombroso and the English writer strongly influenced by him, Havelock Ellis, who believed that outward physical appearance provided indicators of criminality and that, in women, body hair, a man-like appearance and deviant sexual behaviour were all associated with a 'criminal type'.[26] Irvine's observations also predate the work of Lombroso's British precursors, such as James Bruce Thompson, who in the 1860s and 70s postulated that criminals had distinctive physical characteristics, commenting on the women that 'all have a sinister and repulsive expression' and that female criminals in particular are 'ugly and have a luxuriant head of hair'.[27] Like Irvine, Thompson was a member of the Royal College of Surgeons in Edinburgh and a prison surgeon.

Irvine's views of female sexual behaviour were not the casual opinions of an official shocked by a particular incident but an analysis compiled over time through observation and inquiry. It is improbable that Irvine would not have been aware of the revelations about sexual behaviour made in the earlier inquiry. The Ross factory gave him the opportunity for further exploration.

The control of female sexuality clearly required more than the segregation of female convicts from men, but specialised and expensive accommodation which separated crime-class women from each other continued to be in short supply. Though established late, Ross allowed for the separation of classes but insufficient separation of individuals. Few colonial penal institutions were able to emulate the Pentonville experiment (even if Port Arthur did so in part and with singular speed and enthusiasm). The female factory in which innovative penal design was used was Parramatta, where Gipps (confronting the end of assignment in New South Wales) introduced not only cells based on the separate system but a structure, later used in Australian prisons, that allowed ease of surveillance.[28] In Van Diemen's Land the octagonal plan of the Launceston House of Correction gave it a superficial resemblance to the architecture of the new penitentiaries. When the factory was built in 1834 specifically to hold convict women and to replace the dilapidated factory at George Town, the press, while applauding the arrangements which allowed the separation of classes ('so that, even in the chapel, though all will be under the immediate observation of the minister officiating, the women of the different wards will not have an opportunity of seeing each other'), was critical of the inadequate number of cells. There was, in addition, no central point from which prisoners could be watched, and the twelve cells were placed within the yards in which prisoners congregated.[29] The riots which took place at the factory were assisted rather than inhibited by the physical arrangements of the institution. The substantial addition of cells at Cascades in the 1840s after the Inquiry allowed much greater isolation of individuals, which Mundy observed in 1850. But temporary and less than suitable arrangements continued throughout the probation period and well after the time that the authorities became aware of homosexuality as an issue.

If the architecture of the Ross establishment was not innovative, Irvine brought to it a new sensibility. There are other intimations, too, that the treatment of convict women in this period was being influenced by increasing medicalisation and new ideas about institutional care, in the process of which women's minds and bodies came to be subject to increased scrutiny. Mrs Bowden's work at Hanwell—which, with nearly 1000 inmates, was one of the largest of the British pauper asylums—had influenced the development of 'moral therapy' which (in contrast to physical coercion) increasingly became the approved way of managing mental illness. Under the influence of Benthamite and evangelical reformers (and parallel to their influence in the penal arena), whips, chains and the older mechanical paraphernalia of restraint came to be regarded as cruel and dehumanising; order, discipline and encouragement to conform to socially acceptable behaviour became dominant. At Hanwell pioneering work was being done in the 1830s and 1840s relating to moral therapy. In the 1830s the system of classification used there (which was based on phrenological principles) and its 'humane and enlightened management' impressed Harriet Martineau and others who visited the institution. While phrenology itself became less influential, the idea that mental disease had organic and physical causes continued to grow, eventually undermining the authority of 'moral treatment'. It is likely that (as implied by John West) Mrs Bowden applied to her convict charges not only ideas about moral therapy but a knowledge of what had become known since the 1830s as 'moral insanity'—weakness of the will (lack of self-control) rather than of the intellect.[30]

How did men in authority within the convict system reconcile these pictures of active female sexuality with the images they had of women? Within medical discourse, if not more broadly, the complex nature of female sexuality was debated. Where, for instance was the physical site of female pleasure—was it the womb and ovaries? What was the role of the clitoris? Was conception, as popularly believed, dependent on female orgasm? Did sexual abstention bring risks to women's health or was female sexuality only fully aroused by intercourse, so that its absence had no deleterious physical effects? Mason suggests that on balance (and in contrast to the views of social theorists) Victorian medical opinion tilted towards the view that for men and 'even more for women', physical disorders arose if sexual appetites were thwarted.[31] These ideas sit uncomfortably with the views of those who advocated a more sexually restrained society where female purity was the ideal and female sexual activity should be pursued only within marriage.

Irvine's analysis of the sexual behaviour of female convicts, while novel in the links it made between secondary sexual characteristics and criminal behaviour, posed fewer challenges to current social thought than more progressive medical opinion. His picture of aggressive sexual behaviour (where even the more 'feminine' and 'innocent' of the partners were unusually passionate), although conflicting with widely held views about female sexuality and sexual arousal, reinforced the popular idea that sexual excess was a characteristic of the lower classes, while at the same time suggesting a more subtle 'pathology' of female convict behaviour. Irvine thought that both masturbation and the sexual arousal of young women by the 'pseudo-male' led to overexcitement and were injurious to physical health. Female sexual activity, in his analysis, was made problematic in clinical ways (in the figures of the 'pseudo-male', the masturbating female, the sexually excited young woman). Control of such behaviour therefore had medical as well as moral justification. Without diagnosing insanity, Irvine's analysis in effect constructs his convict charges as mad women (remembering that at this time, as Elaine Showalter points out, women were confined in Britain in institutions for the insane for rebellious and overtly sexual behaviour and in the next decade clitoridectomies were performed to cure these forms of female lunacy).[32]

Irvine was not alone in shifting the boundaries between insanity and criminality. Writing in Britain in 1862, Francis Robinson noted that while male prisoners were influenced to some degree by reason, female criminals seemed 'to act more like mad women'.[33] (Even the restraints used for convicts by the end of transportation—silent confinement, reduced diet, drugs and strait waistcoats—resembled the methods used to control the insane.) But by attributing the most extreme 'unnatural' and 'licentious' sexual behaviour mainly to women with distinct and masculine physical characteristics, Irvine confined the relevance of his central observations to a small deviant group and provided, at least in embryonic form, an acceptable explanation for female sexual deviance and criminality. In sexual terms the 'incorrigible' female convict could be distinguished not only by her behaviour but by distinct (and masculine) physical characteristics. Other women remained potentially receptive to the 'feminising' processes of reform; outside the institutional environment it could be expected that their sexual behaviour would be moderated and more appropriately redirected—confined, through marriage, as a response to a single male's demands.

What constituted the female in the view of the nineteenth-century penal authorities was for the most part a set of behaviours, usually defined in class terms. When women deviated from these forms they were thought to be behaving inappropriately. Irvine diagnosed inappropriate behaviour and in its most extreme form branded it as masculine (rather than unfeminine) and found physical manifestations which accompanied if not caused this behaviour. This coincided with a tendency in institutions after the middle of the nineteenth century to see organic and physical causes for conditions such as criminality and insanity—a movement which had implications for 'moral therapy' and other treatments which took the mind as its subject rather than the body, and for criminal reform. If such behaviour had physical origins, what could reformation of the individual character do to change moral behaviour?

While it is unlikely that convict administrators were unduly distracted by the implications of Irvine's hypothesis, ideas about the pathology of the criminal encouraged an environment of scepticism in which the reformatory capacity of institutions was increasingly questioned. As Martin Wiener suggests, if will had 'a diminished role in causing crime', it was also likely to have 'an equally reduced role in curing it'.[34] Ongoing questions about the nature of 'moral insanity', the physical causes of female deviance and the relationship between female sexual desire and criminality became of increasing interest to the guardians of institutions which confined women and young girls.

The active sexuality of convict women was from the beginning regarded as problematic by convict administrators, but public discussion concentrated on its heterosexual manifestations. The issue of male homosexual behaviour, on the other hand, was more openly discussed and was a recognised factor in official thinking about convict policy. By the 1840s the issue of lesbianism in the institutions confining women had become a serious (if not public) concern. Gladstone's recall of Eardley-Wilmot was in part caused by his failure to deal adequately with the lesbian issue.[35] In the report on homosexual behaviour commissioned by his successor, La Trobe, lesbian behaviour was commented on: for instance, Cascades was said to be free of lesbian behaviour but the Brickfields Hiring Depot in Hobart was not.[36] By this stage observers were sophisticated enough not to require the information of 'jacketters' but noted instead familiar symptoms which suggested 'the extraordinary and unnatural link existing between individual women': 'One absconds the other follows immediately; one receives punishment for misconduct the other commits some offence with the hope of rejoining her companion.' Even at the Orphan School, 'unwearied vigilance' was not enough to prevent incidents arising (it was thought) from the acquaintance with this behaviour, which 'all of the lower classes in the Colony, young and old, possess'. Irvine's reports from Ross confirmed that the earlier patterns of behaviour observed at Cascades and Launceston persisted.

Homosexual behaviour between women within the convict institutions was not merely a moral issue but posed a multi-dimensional threat. It underpinned the subversive subculture that continued until the end of transportation to challenge the authority of the convict administration and the concepts of 'femininity' the administration tried to instil. It also reinforced the view that integration into the community rather than incarceration was the best way to manage convict women.

8

PROSTITUTION

Considerable attention has been paid to women as prostitutes in the Australian colonies. At its most simple the argument is that in the penal settlements (and later on, the rural frontier), there was a considerable imbalance in the sex ratio. Marriage was restrained by demography, inclination and the law. Many convict women had been 'on the town' before arrival. In the colonies they resumed their trade and were joined by other 'incorrigibles' from the convict system.

The discussion of prostitution in early Australian society is more often a discussion of deviant behaviour than of sexuality. To some historians prostitution is largely a question of morality. Manning Clark, for instance, in his discussion of prostitution among convict women, refers to them as both unfortunate and dissolute, those 'on whom the hand of the potter blundered'. Others, more interested in numbers, simply assume that women designated as prostitutes who were shipped to Australia (about one in five of those were so described in the records) were in some way 'worse' than other women. Portia Robinson offers a refinement of the moralist's perspective by suggesting that these women, perhaps victims in their own society, were nothing more than 'incorrigibles' in the new land, failing as they did either to appreciate or to seize the opportunities held out to them.[1]

The ease with which historians have categorised women as 'whores' on the one hand and 'family women' on the other belies the reality not only of early colonial experience but of present-day Australian society as well. Caught in the trap of looking at women in the early colonial period through the eyes of those of their male contemporaries who left their imprint most forcefully in the written records, Australian historians for a long time looked neither beyond the stereotype nor at the condition which led women into prostitution. Some early feminist history in the 1970s reinforced rather than challenged that approach, and while others struggled to explain rather than to condemn that behaviour, a new wave of feminist history from the 1980s began to reclaim convict women for the family rather than explore the complexity of their behaviour.

The debate about whether convict women were in general prostitutes was one joined rather than initiated by historians writing specifically about women. The view of the convict settlement as a vast brothel was suggested in early commentaries and was a powerful weapon in the armoury of those wishing to end transportation. The report of the Molesworth Committee embedded in historical discourse the image of female convicts as 'with scarcely an exception, drunken and abandoned prostitutes', 'public prostitutes', and 'the common property of the convict servants'. Prostitutes, moreover, were equated with immoral and abandoned women. In historical writing this image persisted longer than that of convict men as members of the criminal class. For women there was no strong countervailing idea of the 'village Hampdens'—economic victims, 'torn from their native heath by harsh landed-class legislation'—to challenge if not dispel the dominant picture. In the early 1960s detailed research showed that the generalisations about female convicts were ill founded. H. S. Payne's analysis of a sample of convict women arriving in Van Diemen's Land between 1843 and 1853 proposed that only 24 per cent were prostitutes. Lloyd Robson, also using a statistical approach, concluded that the vast majority of women transported to

Australia, though of 'generally bad character', were not prostitutes: the proportions of women who had been prostitutes when sentenced varied with location, with 13 per cent in one sample and one-third in Lancashire.[2]

The approach is, of course, problematic, as later research on prostitution and its documentation through criminal records makes clear. In addition, because women were not transported for 'being prostitutes' or for being 'on the town' but for other illegal acts, the records may or may not disclose past activities. The annotation 'on the Town' in a convict record is not robust enough as an indicator to enable statistical conclusions to be reached with any certainty.

This weakness of the statistical approach is even more evident in examinations of the behaviour of convict women after transportation. Robson calculated that as many as one in eight women transported to Van Diemen's Land were convicted for acts of 'misconduct' relating to sexual behaviour. These women, he suggested, were also convicted of more offences than other convict women—an average of sixteen charges compared with five. While many of Robson's sample of convict women 'continued to lead immoral lives', Payne calculated that only 3 per cent of female convicts were charged after arrival with offences relating to prostitution, and that some at least of the women who had previously worked as prostitutes 'settled well' in the colony. Undoubtedly Payne's conclusion is right, though whether the colonial records inflate the amount of prostitution by confusing it with cohabitation and with other forms of behaviour thought to be immoral, or whether the records underestimate prostitution because it was so prevalent and condoned, is impossible to establish.

This chapter explores some of the stories of women who were described in their convict records as having been 'on the town' and others who, in the penal settlement, became involved (or were alleged to have become involved) in prostitution.

A number of women who were transported to Van Diemen's Land on the *Sovereign* fall into the first category. This vessel carrying 81 convict women arrived in Hobart Town in November 1827. All the women who embarked from London four months earlier survived the voyage; 32 of them (nearly 40 per cent) were recorded as having been prostitutes.[3]

Catherine Bannister was one of these women. She was described as a prostitute who had been 'twenty months on the Town'. Aged twenty when she was sentenced, she had stolen a brooch and for that received life. Single and literate, she came from Basingstoke in Hampshire where she had worked as a needlewoman, a dressmaker and a kitchenmaid. On the ship she was found guilty of so many acts of disobedience 'in defiance of the repeated warnings of the surgeon-superintendent', that on arrival she was sentenced to fourteen days in the cells on bread and water, her hair was cut off and she was dispatched to the Female Factory at George Town, in the north of the island, and kept there on hard labour for twelve months. This was the most severe sentence meted out to women who had been troublesome on the journey out, and the surgeon-superintendent said of her:

> Has been at all times turbulent, unruly and disorderly. Is in the constant practice of using the most blasphemous language, and on several occasions has attempted to conceal herself when out of the prison in order to have intercourse with the seamen. No mode of treatment, neither harsh nor kind, has had any effect in improving her.

In May of the next year Bannister, still in the factory, was confined to her cell for creating a disturbance and fighting. To this point she conforms to the image of the 'incorrigible' convict woman and would undoubtedly have been so described. In June 1829 she married James Jackson in Hobart Town. After that time her convictions were minor: she was disorderly; she was out after hours in a public house; she was illegally at large. Bannister received her ticket of leave in 1836 and her conditional pardon at the beginning of 1840, when she was described as 'Well married and recommended by many respectable inhabitants of Hobart Town'.

Margaret Jones had also been sentenced to life for theft, this time for stealing a watch. This was not her first conviction and she had been imprisoned for picking pockets on another occasion. Aged seventeen, a housemaid from Islington in London, she had been on the town eighteen months. In the colony no year passed between 1828 and 1843 without between one and six charges being laid against her. Usually she was absent without leave, sometimes insubordinate or drunk and disorderly. In 1830 she was sent back to the Female Factory to be reassigned 'up the Country' because it was discovered that she had formed 'a certain connection' with her master's son. In 1831 she left her master's premises 'for the purpose of prostitution'. In 1842 she applied to marry but was refused and her record marked 'Not at present. The woman must give additional proof of amendment.' Less than a year later a second application to marry another man was successful and when in December 1845 she applied for a conditional pardon it was recommended, Jones 'having been a long time in the Colony and her conduct having been very praiseworthy during the four years she has held a Ticket of Leave'.

These women were prostitutes in Britain and difficult prisoners in the colonies. After they gained their tickets of leave they did not merely evade the gaze of the authorities. By the 1840s concern with respectability and reformation had assumed considerable importance, and both Bannister and Jones were observed, judged and designated in official documents as reformed women. Moreover, in reaching this conclusion, the views of others were taken into account.

How many other women from the *Sovereign*, described as having been prostitutes, married and in the eyes of the authorities became 'respectable'?

Few had such unblemished records as Elizabeth Taylor, who did not commit a single offence after arrival and who was described as being married and 'a deserving character'. Taylor was a prostitute from London, with a prior conviction before she was sentenced to life for stealing a watch. Though not as perfect as Taylor's, Mary Ann Sullivan's record reported that she had never been charged with 'an offence of importance' and that 'by her police character and the certificates in her favour [she] appeared to have reformed'. Sullivan was a prostitute who had robbed one of her clients of a ring and an umbrella. She married in 1832.

Elizabeth Jordan, described in the records as a prostitute from Norwich, was like Jones sentenced to life for stealing a watch. She married in 1830 and only reappeared in the records to receive her conditional and then, in 1841, her free pardon. At that time she was described as 'well and respectably married and being well conducted'. Margaret Lowry, from Carlisle, a 'notorious pickpocket and common prostitute' transported for highway robbery, was punished in the colony on a number of occasions for absenting herself, for drunkenness and on two occasions for having a man in her bedroom. She married a free man in 1840 and was pardoned, as she had 'appeared by her conduct to have determined on reformation—her Mistress spoke highly in her favour'.

Described as a 'very bad character' and a 'Common prostitute', Elizabeth Vick had a list of misdemeanours in the colony, including being found in a 'known house of ill-fame', but by 1832 she had in part reclaimed her reputation and, for being absent, received only a reprimand 'In consequence of her good character'. In May 1835 she died in New Norfolk. Jane Morgan had, like Vick, been tried in Gloucester and had once been in custody with her. She too was described as a common prostitute and a 'most abandoned character'. From Trowbridge in Wiltshire, she had been a broadcloth weaver. Three minor charges against her in Hobart Town deprived her of permission to marry a free man in 1829, but she was allowed to marry a convict three years later. Sarah McGill was similarly described in her gaol report as a 'notorious pickpocket and common prostitute'. She had been in custody four times before. Unlike many of the other women who had been on the town (in her case, for three years) she was married and her husband was in the Royal Artillery. For some ten years she had worked as a farm servant and could milk, make butter and cheese, wash and iron. She married in 1831 and in 1837 received her conditional pardon with the commendation 'Two trifling offences only recorded, married and favourably reported'. When Elizabeth Clarke, from Exeter in Devon, received her conditional pardon in 1841 the Revd Bedford and 'another Gentleman' 'testified to her steady habits'. In England she had been on the town for three years. Sentenced for theft, she was charged with only minor misdemeanours and married in 1831.

The language of these reports suggests that the reformed woman was someone whose conduct in the colony (whatever her past record) came to be viewed favourably by the authorities and other respectable people. A number of these women had committed offences in the colony, but this alone seems not to have been enough to deny someone the status of a 'reformed' woman. Phoebe Clowes' record suggests, however, that some offences were less easily forgiven. With one exception Clowes committed not even a minor offence in Van Diemen's Land. Aged twenty when she was convicted, and from Birmingham, she had been a cotton-weaver. Like many other women who had been on the town, she had taken a man to her lodgings and robbed him. Her only 'crime' in the colony was to become pregnant, for which she was returned to the Female Factory. Six years later, in 1835, with no other charges against her, she married. A lifer, her conditional pardon was not approved until 1851.

While many of the women mentioned above offended after their convictions, and their behaviour in Van Diemen's Land ranged from the virtuous to the refractory (enough at the time to designate them 'incorrigible'), they appear to have achieved, at least in the eyes of the penal authorities, a degree of respectability as wives. Others, while not singled out for commendation in the public record, disappeared from it after they married.

Little is known about many of the women. Two nursery-maids, Maria Rivers, sentenced at seventeen, and Sarah Robinson aged twenty, had been prostitutes in London. Both married convicts within a year or two of their arrival. Rivers was still with her husband six years later. Robinson committed no crime or misdemeanour in the colony. Ann Smith, who had been on the town nine months and who attracted the attention of both the captain and the surgeon on the *Sovereign* as one of the best behaved women aboard, was less impeccably behaved in the colony but was neither reprimanded nor admonished after she married in 1832.

Hannah Ryles, a potter and housemaid from Stoke-on-Trent in Staffordshire, had been sentenced to death for the theft of wearing apparel. She had been on the town. Though she was only seventeen, there were three other charges against her and she was said to be connected with a gang of thieves in the Potteries. She could both read and write. Ryles had what was described as an 'exceedingly bad character' when she arrived on the *Sovereign*, and she 'maintained her title to it'. She was one of the group of women tried and sentenced on arrival for repeated acts of disobedience on board ship, although her sentence was not the most severe of those meted out. Nor was her punishment: she received fourteen days' confinement on bread and water and three months in the crime class. In Van Diemen's Land she was charged five times: for absconding, disobedience, insolence, and neglect of duty, including riotous and disorderly conduct in the Female Factory when she also obstructed the constables in the execution of their duty. None of these occurred after her marriage to a convict from the *Arab* in 1832.

Sarah Hay, from Durham, was a widow and a common prostitute. She described herself as being able to cook, wash and 'iron very well'. She was said to be 'Used to her needle'. Before her marriage in 1830 there were only a few charges against her for absenting herself. With similar skills, Charlotte Dwyer from Dublin, aged 30, was said to have been on the town for two years. Like Hay, there were a few charges against her for drunkenness and insolence, but none after her marriage in 1832. She died in 1834. Sarah Gates, a washerwoman from London, had been a prostitute for nine years. Four charges for drunkenness, insolence and disobedience occurred before her marriage in 1830, after which she disappeared from the records.

On the journey out Mary Wilkes had set 'all rules and regulations at defiance' and encouraged others to 'follow her example', so that on arrival she was sentenced to fourteen days in a cell on bread and water and three months in the crime class at the Hobart Female Factory. A housemaid and hawker aged twenty-two, she was sentenced to life at the Warwick Assizes for highway robbery. She was single and had been on the town. For seven years after her arrival she was punished for a series of offences mostly relating to drunkenness and absconding from service, although in 1831 she assaulted her master. During 1829 she absconded. Disguised in men's clothes and accompanied by a runaway male convict, she remained at large in the bush for five months. At the 1835 muster she appears as the wife of J. Laurance and thereafter only appears in the records to receive her ticket of leave and conditional pardon (1840).

Few of the women from the *Sovereign* were as rebellious and independent in their behaviour as Mary Wilkes. Yet without other information it is possible to describe her as one of the women who 'settled well', although she was not singled out for a special commendation by the penal establishment. It is apparent from the records that many women who had been prostitutes in Britain became 'settled' married women in the penal settlement, although this description covers a range of behaviour. Some, like Sarah Robinson and Elizabeth Taylor, had completely unblemished records in the colony, though that was unusual. Others were insolent and refractory while under assignment, but after they married no further charges were brought against them. Some were applauded for their good behaviour when it became time to give them a ticket of leave or a pardon.

Not all the women who had been prostitutes in Britain achieved this degree of respectability or disappeared from the public record after marrying in the colonies. Jane Toms, who had worked as a prostitute in London, had a number of charges for drunkenness and for disorderly and 'indecent' behaviour after arriving in Van Diemen's Land. She was returned to the factory after she had been found in the men's bedroom at her place of assignment and again when she was discovered to have been 'sleeping part of many nights with three men in Robinson's barn'. In 1832 her new master refused to take her because of her disreputable appearance. Freed in 1834, she was committed for trial two years later for theft.

Mary Lamb was a widow from York who had been a prostitute and the keeper of a disorderly house in her native town. York was a garrison town and known for the widespread existence of prostitution. Charged more than once with being drunk and disorderly in the colony, and with violently assaulting her mistress, there is no record of her marrying. She was freed in 1841 at the age of 43. There is no record of Elizabeth Draymin marrying before she received her freedom. A dressmaker from Cork, she had been a prostitute before she was convicted in London. Her behaviour seems not to have improved by 1832 when she was returned to the House of Correction on a number of complaints including 'general bad conduct'. Sarah Davidson, a widow aged 33 from Carlisle, was described as having been on the town for four years: 'A notorious pickpocket and a common prostitute.' Well behaved on the voyage out, she married in 1831, but there were various charges after this, including keeping a disorderly and infamous house and being in 'a beastly state of intoxication'. After she was freed in 1841 she was convicted again for receiving stolen goods and imprisoned for two years in Hobart Gaol.

Louisa Cutler had a variety of occupations including three years on the town. She had been transported for picking pockets. Her drunkenness and absences led, in 1831, to her banishment to the interior; she was not to be assigned within fifty miles of Hobart. The next year, for 'Gross neglect of duty, getting beastly drunk and using disgusting, obscene and filthy discourse', she was sentenced to solitary confinement on bread and water for fourteen days, seven days in the iron collar and six months in the crime class at the factory. Later that year her master said that she had been drunk four out of the five days she had been with him and she was sent back again to the factory, where she died in 1834. She was 28.

Elizabeth Castle was a nurserymaid and a prostitute from St Luke's in London. Her most severe punishment in the colony was for having let a male convict into her bedroom, for which she received twelve months in the crime class; other charges related to drunkenness and disobedience. In 1833 she was sentenced for 'general intoxication' and the next year for having been found in a disorderly house. There are no details of marriage and in 1834 she received her free pardon. Harriet Smith was married with one child. She had been a prostitute in London. Her only charges were for intoxication. From these cases it would be hard not to conclude that for many convict women, regardless of their previous records, drunkenness, not sexual behaviour, was the cause of their later problems with authority.

Of the women transported on the *Sovereign*, 47 were reported in their convict records as having married, which meant for the most part that they married while they were still prisoners of the Crown. Twenty-three women did not marry during this time and another eleven applied to marry, sometimes more than once, but were refused. Permission to marry was refused not only because of doubt about a woman's marital status but because it was thought that she had not behaved well enough to warrant it—marriage could be seen as a reward for reformation, not a means to it. Women who had been prostitutes appear to have been no more likely than other women to be refused on these grounds.

Mary Wright was aged only twenty and could not write, but she had other skills: she was a 'plain cook' who could wash, iron, milk and make butter. She was married with one child; her husband had been transported to Sydney separately for the same crime of receiving stolen property, for which she had received fourteen years. This was her only conviction, but she described herself as having been on the town before she was married. Her misdemeanours in the colony were minor, but when she applied to marry the authorities sought a report from a clergyman about her marital status. A year later she applied again to marry the same man and did so in the rural parish of Jericho, where her countrywoman's skills were no doubt valued. Mary Wright had come from a small town near the city of York, where she was convicted. Most women working as prostitutes in York were, like Wright, immigrants to the town and largely drawn to it from surrounding towns and villages; most also came, as she did, from the poor working class, and had worked or were seeking work in domestic service or the needlework trades. These occupations supplied most of the limited work available for women in York, and were notorious for poor wages and as a source of supply for prostitution.[4]

Mary Sawyer had stolen a watch from a man in her lodgings—presumably a client as she had been two years on the town. A servant of all work, she was 29 when sentenced. She continued to get into trouble for minor misdemeanours. She was insolent, she absconded; once she was accused, though not convicted, of theft and once of 'being tipsy'. None of the charges was serious, but when she applied to marry a free man in 1831 she was refused permission until she had been 'twelve months in service free from offence'. In the muster of 1833 she was back in the House of Correction.

The application of this rule about marriage appears to have been somewhat arbitrary. Like Sawyer, Sarah Simmons, from Colchester, had been on the town for two years and had robbed a person in her lodgings. She too was a servant of all work, though she also said that she could plait straw. Simmons had not been 'very orderly' in prison but had behaved well on the voyage out. Her colonial record was much worse than Sawyer's. Not only did she abscond and remain absent until she was apprehended, but on one occasion she struck one of the witnesses giving evidence against her and used 'gross and violent expressions' in front of the convicting magistrate (for which she was given an extra twelve months in the factory). A second similar sentence in the crime class arose from her refusal to work and from 'outrageous insolence and filthy and beastly conduct'. She was charged with harbouring a prisoner 'at unseasonable hours' and in the same year returned to the government as a person unfit to be employed in a public house. Not long after this, however, she was allowed to marry a convict who had arrived on the *Medway*. This did not bring an end to the charges against her and she was subsequently charged with drunkenness on more than one occasion, and once with forcibly breaking out of the police lock-up.

Maria Pearman had been on the town for six years before being transported for theft from a person. A nurserymaid from Norwich, she was sentenced in London. She married after she had been in the colony for only a short time but reappeared in the charge books for a few minor acts of disobedience. Rebecca Peavoitt also married soon after arriving in Hobart Town, first to John Robinson and four years later to a free man, Francis Williams. Like a number of other women who had been on the town, she had moved from her native town in the country (Somerton in Somerset), where she had been a dairywoman (who could milk, make cheese and butter) to the larger urban centre of Bristol where she was charged with enticing a man to her lodgings and robbing him of his watch. She was described as a 'notorious bad character'. After her first marriage in the colony she was charged with keeping a disorderly house.

Eliza Smith was a 21-year-old staymaker from Hampshire. She was literate and had been three years on the town before her conviction for the theft of a watch from a man at her lodgings. She was one of the group of women who were sentenced on arrival for their conduct on board ship on the way out. In Smith's case 'repeated acts of disobedience of orders' and 'violent and disorderly conduct' led to her being confined for fourteen days in a cell on bread and water; her hair was cut off and she was sentenced to twelve months' hard labour in the factory at George Town. She had attacked the first mate of the *Sovereign* and tried to strangle him, and at the factory in Hobart she created a disturbance and threatened the superintendent. In 1832 she received another six months' sentence for 'drunkenness, obscene language, indecent exposure of her person and turbulent and disorderly conduct'. Smith's aggressive behaviour was not softened by punishment. She remained insubordinate to the authorities, she formed 'bad connexions' in the town and she ill-treated a fellow servant. She married a transported man in 1839.

Whether or not a woman was a 'common prostitute' in Britain was a poor indicator of whether or not she would marry or become 'respectable' (at least in the eyes of the penal establishment) in the colony. On the *Sovereign* a better indicator of marriage was age, with three-quarters of the youngest group of women (under twenty) marrying and only one-quarter of the oldest group (forty and over). (These two groups were the same size.)

None of the women referred to as having previously been on the town were by occupation 'prostitutes'. Most gave as their trades occupations that were common to convict women generally. They were general servants (frequently), housemaids (frequently), and occasionally dressmakers, needlewomen and dairywomen. A number of women described themselves as having skills rather than a trade; that is, they could wash, cook, iron and 'get up linen'. Approximately half of the women who so described themselves had worked as prostitutes. Of the women on the *Sovereign* with more specialised skills, some—for example an upholsterer, a dressmaker and schoolmistress, a pastry-cook and a button-maker—had not been on the town. But others had, and these included a potter, a cotton-weaver, a broadcloth-weaver and a staymaker. More striking was the fact that all the women who gave 'nurserymaid' as their sole occupation were also described as having been on the town. Servants who nursed young children were becoming more numerous in Britain in the nineteenth century, making up, after the general servant, a large category of domestic workers.[5] Themes familiar to readers of nineteenth-century fiction might lie behind such statistics: a young woman with few skills tending children in a family in which the wife was taken up by child-bearing; this combined with a demanding master, the loss of both character and job, leading to life on the streets. For these young women the colony offered another chance. Most married quickly and whatever their fate, ceased to be of interest to the penal authorities. Whether or not they worked again as prostitutes or made happy or miserable marriages is for the most part unrecorded.

It would be foolish to try to ascertain in any statistical way whether women who had been prostitutes in Britain resumed that occupation in the colonies or whether other women who are not recorded as having worked as prostitutes before their convictions took up that work after their arrival. The criminal records of convict women routinely comment on their status in this regard. But while crimes of public disorder came under increasing notice, the colonial authorities were not particularly active in policing prostitution among the non-convict population, and it is not until later in the century when the Contagious Diseases Acts were passed that a serious effort was made to register and confine women working in brothels or on the streets.[6] Moreover, as studies of prostitution have revealed, women (particularly before health legislation began to stigmatise them as prostitutes) tended to move in and out of prostitution, few working for five years or more. Whether or not they came before the law could depend on many factors: their relationship with the authorities and the police, whether they worked on the streets or in brothels, and the social status and contacts of their clients. Criminal records disclose more about how prostitution is policed and managed by the law than about which women have worked as prostitutes or about prostitutes' lives. If women did work as prostitutes in the Australian colonies, it is likely that they did so not because they were 'incorrigible' but for the same reasons that British women did—because of poverty and lack of other work which would enable them to support themselves or their children.

Information about individuals working as prostitutes in early colonial society tends, therefore, to be sparse, and it is rare to find enough information to put together even a meagre biography. In the case of Jane Torr, whose story is outlined below, a few unhappy events left sufficient mark on the public record to make that possible. Torr is not recorded as having worked as a prostitute before her transportation to Van Diemen's Land.[7]

In January 1840 when the barque *Prince Regent* left Van Diemen's Land for London, on board, sailing alone, was a female passenger returning to the country she had left just over a decade before. A recent, tragic experience had undoubtedly influenced her decision to leave. For nearly eighteen months before the incident, Jane Torr had been living in Launceston in a relationship with a man called Thomas Johnson. In May 1839 she had left her small daughter Margaret in their house while she went shopping for potatoes. On her way back she met Johnson running up the street with Margaret in his arms. The little girl's muslin frock and petticoats had caught alight and she had been severely burnt. Johnson was carrying her to the hospital. He and her mother were with her there when she died later that night. Jane 'was weeping and appeared very much distressed'.

Margaret Torr was just under five years of age when she died, and while Johnson was not her real father, they were a close and affectionate family. A visitor, Sarah Williams, told the inquest into the child's death that she had often seen the three together and that both Torr and Johnson seemed 'exceedingly fond' of the child. Just after the accident she had met Johnson coming out of his stable in tears and he had said to her, 'Oh! Sarah, my Child is burnt to Death, I have taken her to the hospital.' Johnson told the inquest that Jane was very fond of Margaret and added that she 'always called me Daddy'. To the missionaries armed with their own technical vocabulary of moralisation, Jane Torr would have been a 'fallen woman', whose absence of shame at her lack of chastity was barely comprehensible. Yet to other eyes she appears to be remarkable only in that she had, under difficult circumstances, established a loving family—albeit not one that was strong enough to survive the tragic loss of her daughter.

Jane Torr's early history in Van Diemen's Land had held little promise that she would 'settle well'. Sentenced to transportation for theft in Exeter in Devon, where she was born, she had three previous convictions of a minor kind, including one, as she said, for 'leaving my place'. She had worked as a dressmaker and a milliner and then as a child's maid. Her employment background makes her one of Deborah Oxley's 'skilled workers' whose talents were squandered in the colonial environment. In actuality she was, in both Britain and the new settlement, a member of a precarious female workforce, whose tenuous hold on the labour market sometimes forced its members into prostitution, sometimes into vagrancy.

In Van Diemen's Land the charges against Jane Torr were largely concerned with absences and other disciplinary matters, but in 1831 she was involved in a prostitution scandal which also enmeshed two well-connected young men in the colony. One was the surveyor Thomas Scott, who had come to Van Diemen's Land in 1820 at the age of twenty and who had by 1831 already mapped large tracts of the island. When he left the colony seven years later he was a married man and a substantial landowner, and included among his possessions the pastoral property Mount Morriston. The second man was the assistant surgeon at the Colonial Hospital in Launceston, Dr James Spence.

Early one morning in March 1831, Jane Torr was apprehended by Constable Benjamin Rogers near the hospital. She was dishevelled, without her bonnet, and her gown was 'loose behind as if just put on'. It emerged in the subsequent inquiry that she had been at Dr Spence's house where she said she had, for the sum of £1 in silver, 'slept all night' with the surveyor, Mr Scott. She also told the constable at the watch-house and his wife that she used to go there to 'sleep with' Dr Spence. Since her arrival in Van Diemen's Land Torr had been the assigned servant of Ronald Gunn, at that time assistant superintendent of convicts at Launceston. Gunn was later to become secretary to the Lieutenant-Governor Sir John Franklin, a member of Parliament and a noted botanist. Gunn had arrived in the colony only in the previous year, as Torr had, and like her he was young—in his early twenties—at the time of the 1831 Inquiry. Far from being surprised by her behaviour, he was aware that she had gone to Spence's house, for she had told Mrs Gunn that she used to get out of the window at night after the family had gone to bed. Gunn said that he had 'always concluded' that she went to Spence's house, and added: 'My further reasons for supposing that she went to some respectable individual was, that she had always a great deal of money, and was continually getting new clothes.'

Jane Torr, for whom a stolen gown had meant transportation for seven years, earned money and spent it on clothes. Making clothes and hats had been her trade. She dressed her little girl nicely too, in the muslin frock and petticoats which caught alight and led to her death. While it is inconceivable that Torr, who had been convicted twice for vagrancy before she was transported, could have earned enough money to spend on good clothes except through prostitution, it is likely that without Dr Spence prostitution would have been for her a much less lucrative occupation.

Evidence at the Inquiry made it clear that Spence tolerated part of the Launceston Hospital being used as a brothel, covering up for the overseer, John Ayton, who resigned rather than face charges. Ayton was alleged to have allowed 'strangers to visit Female wards' and to have had and to have permitted others to have 'illicit intercourse with female patients'. Torr was an assigned servant and convict patient at the hospital on the night she was apprehended, and should have been confined within the hospital gates. Because those who let her out were anxious not to become the scapegoats for Spence and Ayton, their testimony to the Inquiry gave a detailed picture of the way the hospital premises were used as a 'bawdy-house'.

Ayton habitually slept in the women's ward and frequently sent in spirits, drank and played cards with the women there. He allowed 'strangers' to go into the ward. On the evidence of Francis Shaw, the hospital messenger, Ayton had on one occasion brought 'four or five China men' into the ward: 'one went in at a time into the women's ward, they stopped about ten minutes each.' Ayton had brought them into the hospital and saw them off afterwards at the gate. Shaw's evidence was corroborated by a patient, Mr Hamilton Wallace, who was confined to the hospital recovering from wounds he had received fighting with the Aborigines. Wallace described the hospital as 'more like a Bawdy-house than anything else', with frequent drinking sessions in the wards and men seen walking with women in the hospital yard.

Ayton himself had been attacked within the hospital building by the jealous lover of a convict nurse who was living with her child at the hospital. John Laverty was a freed convict who had been a cotton-weaver in Manchester before he was sentenced to seven years' transportation for stealing money. Laverty gave evidence at the Inquiry that he intended to marry Mary Sample and had become suspicious about her drinking at the hospital and about certain 'irregularities' he had noticed between her and Ayton. He decided to keep watch on her through the hospital window. Late one evening he saw Ayton 'whispering to her' at her bedside where she was with her child. She had got up and put on a petticoat and gone with Ayton to his bed. When the light was put out Laverty ('my passion was inflamed') broke off a paling from the fence, burst open the door and struck them both. Dr Spence convinced Laverty not to pursue the incident further.

Convict women who were inmates in the hospital were allowed out to drink, walk the streets and meet men. Jane Torr was admitted to the hospital for 'fits', though Ronald Gunn had never known her to be ill previously, and had been allowed (or encouraged) to behave in this way. She had been apprehended on an earlier occasion late at night on the green adjoining Government House—the Inquiry asked no further questions about this incident. On the evening of her last visit to Dr Spence's house she had first gone to the barracks to visit a sergeant in the 57th Regiment.

Spence did more than close his eyes to Ayton's behaviour. He intervened to enable it to go on unhindered by the complaints of people like Laverty. Furthermore he seems to have not only contrived to have Jane Torr admitted to the hospital and to have slept with her himself but to have allowed her to prostitute herself to other men and to have arranged for her to meet 'respectable individuals' like Mr Scott at his own house for the purposes of prostitution. Perhaps it was through Spence that Jane Torr was introduced to prostitution. Or perhaps he did her the favour of enabling her to meet a more affluent clientele. There is nothing on Jane Torr's previous record to suggest that she had been on the town before she was transported.

It is apparent from the behaviour and the responses of all the men involved in the Launceston Hospital scandal that prostitution was both expected and condoned. Because each of the men involved was in a position of authority over the women, it is likely that coercion was also involved. Torr's master, Ronald Gunn, though intrigued by her earning power, made no pretence of being particularly perturbed by her behaviour, as might have been expected from someone in his position of authority in the penal settlement. The main problem for all involved was being found out in circumstances that made an official investigation inevitable. Spence was suspended from his position and demoted as a result of the Inquiry, which found that 'his misconduct has consisted in taking out of the Hospital under his charge Female Convicts for the purpose of prostitution'. Ayton evaded facing charges by his resignation. Jane Torr was sentenced to six months in the Hobart Female Factory for repeatedly absenting herself from her master. A short time later she was given a similar sentence in the George Town Female Factory for refusing to proceed to her master's service. From that time until the inquest into her daughter's death she disappeared from the official records.

What of the other woman named in the Inquiry, Mary Sample? Sample had been transported for picking pockets, and once in servitude soon fell foul of the criminal system. Her first gaol report spoke of her 'violent disposition', and her record in the colony contained a range of charges which seem to confirm that opinion. On one occasion she was punished for ill-treating the children left in her care, and on another occasion, while imprisoned, she was punished for 'breaking down her cell' and smashing the spinning wheels. The disciplinary offences for which she was convicted included absences, insolence and drunkenness. Her head was shaved for her first offence—disobedience and insolence—and she was sentenced to this humiliating and hated punishment again a little later, along with fourteen days in the solitary cells. Sample may well have been one of those convict women whose rough manners and rebelliousness offended middle-class observers. Though she 'settled', in the sense that she married John Laverty early in 1831, whether she could be said to have 'settled well' is open to dispute. Two months after their marriage she was sent to the George Town Female Factory for drunkenness, and within a year her husband had been bound over twice for assaulting her. In 1836 she was sentenced to hard labour as a 'reputed prostitute'. Yet amid this common saga of brutal and brutalising behaviour, a few sentences in the public record hint at another dimension to Mary Sample's story. After he saw his intended wife go to Ayton's bed, John Laverty went to the Revd Browne, who was to marry them, and told him that he was not going ahead with the wedding, for he would not marry her 'after having connection with others'. But he returned soon afterwards and, according to Browne, 'told me that he would marry her and that he hoped she would make a different woman, and that she would break her heart if he did not marry her, as it was not her fault'.[8]

Both Miriam Dixson in *The Real Matilda* and Lloyd Robson have described female convicts as outcasts, looked down on even by men of their own class.[9] In Robson's words, they were 'not the sort of women to attract men into marriage'. While everything in her record might suggest that Mary Sample was one of those women, nothing that had happened to her made her 'unmarriageable' in the eyes of John Laverty. Nor do the marriage habits of convicts suggest that convict women were seen generally as unlikely partners or that women who had worked as prostitutes were spurned by prospective male partners. The matter-of-fact description by John Nicol, who as steward on the *Lady Juliana* lived with and fell in love with convict woman Sarah Whitlam, indicates a less moralistic view of prostitution than is usual among middle-class observers: 'There were not a great many very bad characters. The greater portion were for petty crimes, and a great proportion for only being disorderly, that is, street-walkers, the colony at the time being in great want of women.'[10] There are innumerable stories of women convicts whose histories are as complex as that of Mary Sample and Jane Torr. The latter took money for sex and was, by that definition, a 'professional whore'. Yet, but for her daughter's death, she too might have 'settled well'.

Writing of the period 1810–30 in New South Wales, Paula Byrne suggests that the courts were 'automatically suspicious of women's use of their bodies' and that in the case of adult women their bodies 'were assumed to be immoral and were to be proved innocent'.[11] It is apparent from looking at prostitution and its policing and at charges of rape and assault that women who worked as prostitutes were deprived of many of the protections the law afforded against assault and abuse, and that all women whose virtue might be suspected were vulnerable in this way. Class and criminality are relevant here. Women convicts were doubly suspect. Their criminality had deprived them of their 'character' and made them open to the charge of being whores, and their class background made it less likely that they would conform to the increasingly dominant expectation among the middle class that women should be virtuous before marriage and monogamous after. As well, assumptions about the sexuality of middle-class women ensured that suspicion of women's bodies was focused primarily on those of the lower classes.

This did not mean that convict women had no protection against male violence. Even from the earliest days in the settlement in New South Wales, as Marion Aveling has said, 'a kind of order was maintained'.[12] When the convict women disembarked at Sydney Cove, Phillip threatened that men would be fired on who tried to get into the women's tents (in Lieutenant Clark's phrase 'the whore camp'). Two men were caught doing so two days later; one, a sailor, was drummed out of the camp to the tune of the 'Rogue's March', while the other, a marine, received 200 lashes for assaulting a woman with whom he had 'connection' on board ship and who had refused to go with him 'into the woods'. These punishments should be seen as reflecting the importance attached to breaches of naval discipline rather than to protecting women from violence. Later in the year when a convict was charged with attempted rape and the charge proven, the case was heard before the magistrate's court, not the criminal court, and the sentence waived.[13]

Severe punishments were meted out to those guilty of a range of sexual offences in the penal colonies. In Van Diemen's Land carnal knowledge continued to be treated as a capital offence long after it had ceased to be so treated in Britain, and the use of the death penalty for both sodomy and bestiality was seen as essential in a place where an undersupply of women might encourage varieties of 'unnatural vice'. In contrast, as if to give tacit recognition to the view that women were sexual commodities, leniency was shown to men who raped women of 'doubtful' character. A case which exemplifies this was that of Mary Ann Stock, a 'nurse-girl' sentenced in York in 1848 to ten years' servitude for stealing three pieces of ribbon. Transported to Van Diemen's Land, by 1860, her marriage to a ticket-of-leave man over, she was living with James Brock in a hut in the district of Hamilton when she was savagely raped by an ex-convict William Fisher, known as 'Bill the fencer'. She was so badly injured she could hardly speak, and the Hobart *Mercury* reported that the assault had occurred in 'circumstances of unusual atrocity'. Although the case was proved and Fisher sentenced to hang, petitions that alleged that Mrs Brock's character was 'far from good' convinced the authorities that she was 'nothing else than a common prosti-tute'. Fisher was freed and Mary Ann Brock was sentenced to two years' hard labour at Cascades for perjury. She said of her situation that she 'had no one to speak up for her': it was 'a made up case amongst the men'.[14]

If the innocence of adult women was subject to constant scrutiny, at what age did the innocence of female children cease to be assumed? An early recorded rape case in New South Wales in September 1789 involved a young girl of eight. The accused was a private in the marines, Henry Wright, who was duly convicted and sentenced to death, later commuted to a life sentence on Norfolk Island. There, two years later, he attempted to 'deflour' a girl of ten, and (as recorded by Ralph Clark) was made to 'run the gauntlet throu all the men and women'. While strict penalties were seen as essential to deter 'unnatural acts', Collins reduced the sentence for Wright's earlier offence because 'the chastity of the female part of the settlement had never been so rigid, as to drive men to so desperate an act', and it was his belief that no other man was likely to attempt it.[15]

In 1796 Andrew Hamilton Hume, who had come to the colony as a superintendent of convicts, was charged with raping an 11-year-old girl employed as his servant. The child had come to New South Wales with her convict mother. She gave evidence that Hume had 'placed her on a chair, pulled her Petticoats up, unbuttoned his Breeches and put his Nastiness between her legs, he put her in Pain, she did not cry out, being her Master she was afraid he would beat her'. Hume in defence said he had suspected the child of having relations with another man and had told her mother, who would do nothing about it. A woman convict told the court that the girl had come to her house at Parramatta and she had seen her 'go under a rug' with a soldier, who, when he emerged, buttoned his trousers and said 'the girl was fit for a small Man but not for a large one'. Dr Balmain gave evidence that there was the suggestion of a venereal complaint and of attempted inter-course, but the girl was still intact. While Hume was acquitted, the evidence suggests that the convict woman and perhaps the child's mother had been involved in prostituting the little girl; this is likely to have influenced the judgment.[16]

Some attention seems to have been paid to child prostitution in the early period when it related to the conduct of convict women. For instance, Hannah Selsby was convicted in 1821 and transported to Van Diemen's Land. Three of her daughters accompanied her and she was joined there by her husband. In 1827 she was sentenced to fourteen days on bread and water and three periods in the stocks for 'conniving at the prostitution of her two daughters', who were both, at the time, under sixteen years of age, and 'encouraging them in their immoral practices'.[17] The introduction of their daughters to prostitution by parents who had been involved in the trade themselves was a pattern observed among a minority of prostitutes in Britain and is likely to have happened in the colonies.[18] Comments by the headmaster of the Queen's Orphan School in Hobart about some of his charges lend support to this. Revd Ewing was appalled that one of the young girls had often talked about wanting to be a prostitute. Her mother worked as a prostitute and he believed the girl had also been impressed by 'having seen girls who she knew to be on the town well dressed'. He reported that her mother had been heard to say that she would wait until the whalers came to town and then 'she would take her daughter out'. 'The day after she took her out she was seen in the street with three whalers.' He believed that convict parents paid less attention to their male children, who were in his care because they were thought to be 'useless'.[19]

In the early days of settlement there seem to have been some steps taken to protect children from sexual assault but less with child prostitution, although it was his concern that orphan girls were turning to prostitution that led King to establish the first orphan school in Sydney. Just as prostitution was seen as inevitable and was not thought of as a 'social problem' (requiring rescue societies, refuges and magdalen homes) until the middle of the century, scant public attention was paid to the prostitution of children. Ewing's observations were made in the 1840s, by which time concern with respectability and the moral welfare of children had assumed greater importance, and hard times and unemployment in the colony had driven many into poverty.

Have historians paid too much attention to prostitution in the history of early Australia?

In relation to the origins debate, just as male convicts have ceased to be seen as the detritus of British slums—members of the 'criminal classes' whose 'aversion to labour had driven them to crime' (Manning Clark, echoing Mayhew)—and come to be viewed as representative members of the labouring classes, female convicts have ceased to be viewed primarily as prostitutes (their 'criminal' counterparts). In relation to their colonial experience, while Robson spoke for the majority of historians of his time in endorsing the continuing 'immorality' of convict women, more recently historians have tended increasingly to follow Payne's emphasis on the reclamation of convict women by means of the family. Portia Robinson sums up this trend when she argues that convict women as a whole were given an undeserved reputation by a small group whose 'criminality was strongly linked with immoral behaviour—prostitution, brawling and fighting'.[20] While in earlier interpretations convict women *en masse* were seen as deviant, now only the 'incorrigibles' among them are so characterised. The prostitute no longer represents all convict women but is recast as a marginal figure.

Something is lost in seeing convict women merely as representative members of the labouring classes if that serves to overemphasise their skills and underplay the nature of the economic arena in which those skills were employed. Most female convicts may have been first offenders guilty of petty criminal acts, not habitual criminals, but they were also members of the most economically vulnerable sections of the labouring class, women whose family circumstances and skills (whatever they appeared to be on paper) were not sufficient to provide more than a precarious existence. Ironically it is Mayhew, whose views of prostitution in *London Labour and the London Poor* did much to create the stereotypes accepted by Australian historians, who best describes how in Britain the insufficiency of income and the casualisation of the labour force reduced both men and women (with skills) not only to a state of penury but to an improvidence bred of poverty. And it is Mayhew who, in looking at slop-workers and needlewomen, describes how perhaps half the women in that trade without parents or husbands to support them 'resorted to the streets to eke out a living', how others lived with men to gain lodgings, 'resorted to private or public prostitution', or had been 'drove to prostitution … through the bad prices'.[21]

In some ways the historians' rescue of the female convict from the 'undeserved reputation' of being a prostitute mirrors the removal from the male convict of the stigma of being seen as a member of the criminal class. In the case of women convicts, however, the rescue was twofold. Apart from the conclusions arising from statistical work that sought to show that prostitutes were a minority of female convicts and continued to be so, historians such as Michael Sturma argued that the term prostitute was used so loosely in the nineteenth century that many women who were not (in his words) 'professional whores' were so called in the contemporary record. Practices such as cohabitation, concubinage and 'unchaste' behaviour that were common among the working class in both Britain and Australia were not differentiated by middle-class observers from prostitution itself. Sturma thus distinguished the 'professional prostitute' from the rest of the convict and working-class population in a more precise way than either contemporary observers or those historians who have looked at early colonial society through their eyes.[22]

Sturma's work established, from another perspective, that there were fewer prostitutes among the female convicts than had hitherto been thought, and re-established the prostitute as a marginal figure: contemporary observers had been mistaken about the numbers of whores, and those who followed them, like feminist historian Anne Summers, reproduced their mistake. Two different concepts of deviance, one middle-class and one working-class, are juxtaposed, the inference being that while a wider range of sexual behaviour was acceptable to the working class, prostitution was deviant behaviour in both contexts.

In making the convict prostitute a marginal figure who can be named and counted, historians have moved from overemphasising prostitution in convict society to neglecting its significance. Convict women were not just called whores by mistake, any more than women are now. I have used the phrase 'purposeful ambiguity' to describe the way the terminology of prostitution was used in the nineteenth century by men about women and by the middle class about working-class women.[23] Convict women, like other women, were frequently called prostitutes or whores when they transgressed the norms of behaviour of the observer. This transgression might take the form of sexual behaviour or it might involve social and cultural practices alien or disturbing to the observer: swearing, drinking, being 'rowdy' or 'lewd' in public. Describing some women as prostitutes or whores was intended to differentiate them from other women. The intention was, however, not directed at the 'branded' women alone but was a means by which all women could be disciplined and coerced into conformity.

Contemporaries could be precise or loose in their use of this terminology. Maria Lord was called a whore at first because she lived with a man and bore children out of wedlock, and later because she was alleged to have had an adulterous relationship, not because she was thought to have worked as a prostitute. The Launceston servant who was described as living 'in a state of Prostitution' was so described because she was living with a sergeant of the Buffs. Lieutenant Clark's whores were marked out for their licentious and aggressively sexual behaviour, not because they asked to be paid for their favours. The missionaries from the Hobart City Mission whose self-appointed task in the 1850s was to convince couples living in long-term 'unlawful concubinage' to either marry or part were shocked at the 'slight regard' which was paid to either the sanctity of marriage or the absence of chastity, and concluded that 'hence prostitution is carried on to a reckless extent'.[24]

On the other hand, precise distinctions could be made when the occasion warranted it, as in the case of an inquiry into the behaviour of the master and surgeon of the *Vestal*, an emigrant ship which brought a number of pauper women from a Bristol workhouse to Hobart. The captain was described by the police magistrate as having cohabited with a woman who had previously been 'on the town', while other women were described as being of 'very easy virtue before they embarked', 'if not actually common prostitutes'.[25] The descriptions of the women preserve as much as possible of the reputations of the men, just as the description of Maria Lord as a 'convict whore' was intended as much as a slander on her husband as a description of her moral state.

It is difficult to argue that convict women had an 'undeserved reputation' as if, when all the 'facts' are known, we would find them to be morally better than we thought. If we mean that many of the women called prostitutes were not receiving money for sex, that was undoubtedly true, but we would lose significant insights into colonial society if that became the sole focus of our attention. Reputation—its giving and its taking away—is part of a complex cultural interchange (between men and women and between people of different classes). When women lost their reputation or became branded as 'whores' they suffered other consequences. They were likely to lose some of the protection the law afforded against assault and violence. If still under sentence, they were likely to be incarcerated or suffer further punishment. If destitute they were less likely to receive assistance from charitable agencies who discriminated between the 'deserving' and the 'undeserving'. If designated as a 'common prostitute' their public behaviour came under surveillance, and public behaviour which was legal for others could lead to their apprehension. Their children were more likely to be taken from them as being 'in moral danger'.

Undoubtedly, prostitution *as work* flourished in the penal settlements. As Peter Murdock stated to the Molesworth Committee, it was 'quite evident that there was a great demand for prostitution'. Moreover, while the report chose to condemn female convicts *en masse* as 'public women', the evidence given to the Moleworth Committee suggested that colonial circumstances could turn women 'without natural protectors' to prostitution (circumstances which included the fact that even free women could be incarcerated—and lose their respectability—for minor misdemeanors as servants).[26] Condemned by moralists, prostitution was accepted as inevitable by the authorities, preferred to other more deviant behaviour and managed in various ways (as it continued to be), to the disadvantage of women but so that its practice did not upset social sensitivities. Targets of disapproval shifted over time and came to include activities once condoned by a lax assignment system and various forms of public behaviour (that made women particularly prone to charges of 'disorderly behaviour' and vagrancy). For women faced with limited employment opportunities, prostitution was both an important source of earnings and an indicator of their economic vulnerability. And while historians might turn from prostitution with relief, having decided that the term was 'misused' by contemporaries and applicable only to a small minority of women, the suspicion of women's sexual behaviour and the branding of women as whores had consequences for all women but particularly for those with convict or lower-class origins.

Shifting the gaze from prostitution serves to make less visible the insights it gives into the experience of convict and lower-class women in colonial society. What we see when we look at prostitution are the layers of female vulnerability—as well as aspects of their resilience.

9

FREEDOM

Threaded through much of the discussion about the fate of convict women in the penal settlements is the idea that transported men and women were better off in the colonies than they would have been had they remained at home. This has been used by historians to support the benign interpretation of nineteenth-century Australian society and the position of women within it. There is no better expression of the view that the colonies were bountiful places of opportunity than the letters written to family at home by convicts themselves. Many suggest that ex-convict men and women believed they had gained considerable benefits from transportation. The idea that they had been given a second chance is prominent in these letters, as it continues to be in recent histories.

Of the letters written by convicts to relatives at home, most that remain were written by men. They give a glimpse of everyday life among the social group in the colonies into which convict women married, and a sense of their changing fortunes and expectations. The absences as well as the words are telling.

Sometimes these letters are well written, such as one sent by Richard Taylor to his father in Burnley, Lancashire in 1843, which began: 'I take this favourable opportunity of writing these few lines to you, Hoping to find you all in good Health as I am at present ...'[1] Taylor had arrived on the last convict ship to dock in Sydney, the *Eden,* in 1840 and had been put to work as cook at the Colonial Hospital. He described Sydney as a handsome town with 'shops large and splendid'. He wrote in 1841 that a short time earlier tradesmen had been earning ten shillings a day, and though the large numbers of free emigrants had lowered wages they were still 'far higher than at home'. Taylor used the services of more than one accomplished scribe in this and other letters, commenting not only on the economy but the politics of the settlement. 'Next year', he wrote home in 1841, 'the Colony will have a House of Assembly of its own and then it will be impossible to keep Englishmen in slavery'.

A letter in his own hand in 1842 was less sophisticated:

> I still helps Cooke at the General Hospital and I have plenty of every thing you can mention ... Dear Father it his a Butefull Cuntry it his very Hot in Summertime and there hiss plenty of Black men and whimon and they are very fond of wite men. I have sum fin games with them. I give them maney a swag of meet and Bred my elth is very good. I Ham very fat I Ham Twelve Stone ...

Wages, food and what a fine place it was are the recurring themes. In July 1843 Taylor described the cost of food in this 'fine Wholesome Plentiful Country,' from which he confidently expected to depart on the expiry of his sentence. In February 1845 ('looking forward to a partial restoration to liberty'), he was still determined to return to England, but he was less optimistic about opportunities in the colony:

> I am sorry to say times although they are mending now are not so good for a working man or indeed anyone else as they were a few years ago, but those who are determined to do well can get a comfortable living, perseverance and sobriety are the main principles and employment can be ensured although not so profitably as when I first arrived in the Colony.

Later in the year he was about to get his ticket of leave and looked forward, through good conduct, to embracing once more 'the Wings of Liberty' and to his return home. But by late December 1850, now a free man, Taylor had changed his mind, and wrote from Narellan near Camden to say he had decided to stay in New South Wales because he thought he could do 'a great deal better' there: trade was flourishing again and 'Everything is Cheap'. He encouraged his relatives to come to the colony where they too could do a great deal better than at home. By this stage the ex-convict, who was now in the boot and shoe trade making a comfortable living, had a 'good and faithfull Wife' and three children, the eldest seven.

Other letters give more information, much of which he had (seemingly) not thought of telling before: that when he arrived and was assigned to the General Hospital his duties were so light that he taught himself the boot trade from a mate. His wife had been a fellow servant and had come from near Cork in Ireland; one daughter would soon be 'a good scholar for her age'. Taylor at this time owned a little half-acre property on the road to the diggings, down which passed the weekly gold coach escorted by dragoons.

The pattern of letter-writing has the effect of constructing a certain narrative, to which in some ways Richard Taylor's letters conform. Some more literate and contrite convicts wrote early. Others wrote as soon as they arrived in the colony to encourage other members of the family to join them; some waited until they could afford a scribe or until they had established themselves. While a death may have caused a letter to be written, marriage seems to have been less often the subject of correspondence. This may have reflected an unwillingness to talk about a spouse's convict background or sensitivity about past relationships and familial obligations. Significant rites of passage are often commemorated retrospectively. Letters tend to be optimistic, either about the possibilities of return to Britain or about the opportunities in the colonies. They imply also that prosperity is conditional, and that a less pleasant fate awaits those who are neither sober nor hard-working.

Endings require another hand. Taylor's story would end (for the historian) on a cheerful note were it not for a letter written in 1856, this time to ex-convict Simon Brown, from someone quite unknown to Brown but well acquainted with his stepbrother Richard Taylor. Mrs Taylor was not 'scollar' enough to write to tell of her husband's death and so the letter came from Isabella Risley of Camden who, with her husband, had known the Taylors well in more prosperous times. She reported that Richard had died and his widow and her two remaining children were struggling to survive: the funeral had taken 'all the old Woman had'. With her cart and horse she was making what living she could selling fruit around Camden.

Mrs Risley was to have a more substantial inheritance. In 1873 on the death of her husband she became, albeit briefly, the proprietor of the Woolpack—Risley's Inn—in Argyle Street in Camden.[2]

The recipient of Mrs Risley's letter, Simon Brown, was also a convict, but he had been sent to Van Diemen's Land. Keeping in touch with family who moved in Britain and locating those who had been transported became increasingly difficult. This was especially so after the Home Department, confronted with large numbers of convicts dispersed across extensive and remote territories, relinquished their role in forwarding information and passed the responsibility on to the colonial authorities. A letter from Simon Brown in 1855 to his uncle, a smelter in Yorkshire, illustrates all these difficulties. Although he had written to his father (George Taylor of Burnley) several times at different places, he could not find out where he was and asked for his uncle's help in locating both him and his brother Richard. Had Richard been transported? He had heard nothing of him. He asked if his sisters could get in touch with his wife Margaret's father in Manchester.

The story is one of a gradual gathering together again of disrupted relationships. When he eventually wrote to his father,

Brown made it very clear that he had 'no intentions of ever going home'. He was married and doing better than he believed he could do in England. Although he had travelled widely in the colonies (in what he called his 'rambling wild state') 'all over Port Phillip side' and the diggings, and had gone to Sydney to seek intelligence about his stepbrother, he was now settled, working as he had done for many years on the estate of Edward Bisdee, member of the Legislative Council. Lovely Banks, on the main road between Hobart and Launceston, was a large sheep property, and by 1856 Brown was its overseer. In England he had been a weaver, but when he arrived in Van Diemen's Land he found that there was nothing but farm work, assuring his father, 'I am a much better hand among sheep and cattle than I was at the weaving loom'. Brown began working as a ploughman and wagoner and then overseer, becoming free while in the service of Mr Bisdee. Uninterested in returning home but at first unwilling to offer too much encouragement to others to emigrate in case they were disappointed, he gives in his letters a glimpse of what has frequently been seen as the stabilising influence of marriage and family life:

> Now I am settled I mean to look out for a bitt of ground where there is watter and begin fellmongering ... there is good living to be got. Before I was married I was just as wild as I was used to be at home. I had a good deal of money but wasted it all foolishly but now it is the reverse for I am saving all I can to get a place of my own and it will not be long first for my wife is very steady industrious woman and we get on very well. I get 50 pound a year with rations for myself and wife our rations is 20 lb of flour, 20 lb of beef or mutton: 1/2 lb of tea, 4 lb of sugar a week with as much fruit and vegetables and fruit when it is in season; and at present I have a 1/2 acres of ground to grow potatoes ... if I had been steady I could been independent long before now but at present I am doing very well and I will soon with the help of God and his blessing have a place of my own ... My wife has sent

her parents 6 pounds what she has been able to gather
from rearing poultry and selling the produce.[3]

Brown's letter is eloquent not merely for the picture it gives
of a productive economic unit, to which both husband and
wife contribute, but because his concerns are not confined only
to the material and the domestic. Mentioning that there is
'great talk of war out here', Brown asks if he can be sent a
paper as often as possible so that he can keep in touch with
what is happening at home.

Brown's letters give some information about his wife and
her family. A letter written in 1838 by Richard Dillingham
from Hobart Town to his parents in Bedfordshire told them
that he had two children—a 'weakly' son and a 'fine strong
girl' in her third year—but tells nothing of their mother. He
added that although it would be twelve months before he could
get married 'it is my intention to get married to a black woman
one of the natives of this country and a pretty woman she is
I never knew one who pleased me so well'. The creative
additions of the scribe were not always restricted to piety and
politics, as Dillingham later informed his parents:

I almost forgot to tell you that I was not married yet as
to my being married to a black woman I never thought
of such a thing it was only my nonsense and my fellow
servant who wrote the Letter for me had no business to
put it in. my Little girl is named Mary Anne. she is between four and five years of age.[4]

Dillingham—who wrote that he could not feel sorry for the
death of a sister's child because there is 'nothing but poverty
greif and sorrow for the liveing'—describes how it is possible
to do well in Van Diemen's Land: 'I am doing much better
than many Laboring men in England, If a man behaves well
in this country is sober honest and industrious tho he be a
prisoner he is respected by all who know him.'[5]

In the State Paper Office in Dublin among the hundreds
of applications from Irish convicts seeking assistance with
passage for their families, Patrick O'Farrell found letters from

sixteen male convicts to their wives. All, he suggests, agreed on one thing: how much better off they were in this 'best country under the sun' than they could have been in Ireland. Like the letters above, most spoke of the wages for men and what a fine place it was 'for ateing and drinking' but Thomas Fallon also wrote in 1835 from Goulburn plains to his wife in Athlone: 'Der mary if you wore in this country you cud be worth pound per week but by owne labour and if it be possible that you can come out bring your sister; there is fine girl comeing out as nemigrans.' James Halloran (in 1840) told his wife to bring her sister, as a servant maid could get twenty pounds a year in Sydney.[6]

While these are men's letters and women are marginal figures within them, they convey a sense of women who contribute to family income, who are valued for their steadiness and 'industriousness' and whose labour as 'family women' is recognised in all its dimensions—in Richard Dillingham's telling phrase (responding to the news of a young sister's marriage and pregnancy): 'it made tears come into my eyes to think my poor sister should have begun the work at such a tender age.'[7]

The Irish letters in particular are written to encourage others to come to the colonies and so contain optimistic assessments of their prospects. A letter from Sarah Thornton, a London needlewoman transported for life for stealing lace from a shop in Oxford Street, gives a different picture. Mrs Thornton arrived in Sydney in 1814 and was joined in the same year by her husband, a tailor. The mother of five children, she only lived for two years after the pardon she received in 1825. The family was moderately successful by then and one son went on to be the mayor of Sydney and a member of Parliament. A letter written to relatives at home in 1820 shows how hard-won success could be and was a warning to those who might think of Botany Bay as a place of easy opportunity:

> Myself and my husband have had many hard struggles to gain the means of an honest livelihood. To accomplish it we have worked night and day. I thank God that he has crowned our endeavours with success. I rose early in the

morning and went to market bringing home my articles
on my head, to furnish my shop to the best advantage.
With the greatest care of our little profits, and the greatest
frugality in housekeeping, we collected together a small
sum sufficient to buy a little house. I then applied to the
Gentleman of the Colony, for a [liquor] Licence; which
they not only granted, but said they would assist me and
my husband in any way in their power, as they noticed
our industry and that we associated with none but persons
of good character ...

I often wish my dear friend, you could see my little
family and they playing around me, while I am milking
my cows, or making my bread. O that my voice could be
heard by the young people in England, to deter them
from evil ways ... that they might not come to this
wretched country where so much evil abounds. For
though I have by a regular line of good conduct, and
great privations arrived at a state of comfort, not one in
twenty who is sent here, obtains even the necessaries of
life, by their own industry, independant of support from
the government.[8]

Sarah Thornton's letter suggests the heavy double burden
women with large families bore as well as the difficulties many
faced in maintaining themselves without government assistance.

Babette Smith has published in her book *A Cargo of Women*
some letters of Susannah Watson, who was transported in 1829
at the age of 34 on the *Princess Royal*. In old age, after an
undoubtedly hard life and a succession of relationships, she was
looked after by her two sons, who had been born in the
colony. In 1874 (three years before she died) she wrote that
she was living with her son John at Gundaroo and 'as far as
he can supply my wants, he lets me want for nothing'.[9] Over
the previous twenty years contact had been re-established with
the family she had left in England, including two of her
daughters who had been aged six and ten when she was forced
to leave them. This correspondence illustrates the difficulties
that could arise in sustaining communication at such a distance,
particularly when all parties had established other domestic
relationships. Smith says that while Susannah Watson wrote to

her family, she is not sure that they replied to her before 1857 when she received a letter from her elder daughter. In response she said that she was

> very sorry that there should be any uneasyness between your Father and Sister and I am also sorry that they did not wish to hear From me your Father always was a kind husband to me the only fault I [had] to Find was Following that Cursed poaching which was the Cause of my being sent away but only for [you] Children it was the Best thing Befell me. it would have been well for him to have followed me.[10]

Like Brown's, Watson's family worked in a declining industrial trade (they were framework knitters in Nottinghamshire) and she kept herself abreast of conditions by reading the papers ('we see accounts how bad of they are in England', she told her daughter in 1857). The comparison she made with Britain was thus in part informed by her own recollections of hardship and in part by contemporary press accounts. Like Simon Brown she too promised to send money ('we cannot send le[s]s than Five pounds') and described how much better off they were in New South Wales:

> things are plentifull plenty of work but short of people to do it. Wages is very high a Labouring Man wont star les than 10s a day your Brothers Gives 10s a day to their Man or 1.10 a week and find them Board and Lodging a woman to wash Gets 5 shillings a dozen and needlework is very high i Earns a Good deal myself a Making Sun Bonnets your brothers don't wont me to do it but it amuses me and keeps me in pocket Money the Reason work is so high in this part— its the Market Town for the Southern Diggins the Araluen diggins is only 14 miles from me ...[11]

The references to women's earnings in a number of these letters indicate a concern with women's economic contribution to the household income. Mrs Brown's personal earnings are acknowledged as significant. Mrs Thornton's letter shows how great that contribution could be. Hers is the earliest letter quoted—letters from Brown, Taylor and Mrs Watson are not only later but all refer to the diggings, suggesting a more prosperous time, and in Taylor's case a labour market affected through the 1840s by changes in the economy and in the pattern of immigration.

The impression gained from these letters is of convict men and women whose common experience at home was one of poverty and very limited opportunity. They believed (as Babette Smith says so clearly of Susannah Watson and her companions on the *Princess Royal*) that they had been given 'a second chance'. Some became religious. All became industrious. One could conclude from this handful of letters that the penal settlements did indeed succeed as places of reformation, in that they allowed many people to reconstruct their lives and relationships and achieve a degree a material comfort beyond what they might have hoped for in Britain.

Portia Robinson and John Hirst have argued that the conditions of the colonies, in contrast to Britain, allowed the opportunity for self-advancement and greater freedom, with Robinson in particular proposing that convict women attained upward mobility and respect through employment and marriage. In rejecting the critical views of convictism conveyed by the 'enemies of convict society' Hirst and Robinson echo the views of their nineteenth-century opponents, who saw transportation (and especially assignment) as reformatory. As John Hirst has pointed out, the defenders of convict society had seen 'the outcasts of one society transform themselves and take on new roles and characters not through the ministrations of religion or of the state, but because of the different social circumstances in which they were placed'.[12]

While in Britain social conditions created criminals, in the penal settlements, it is suggested, character not circumstance determined who would succeed and who would fail. An essential element in this construction is the new (colonial) outcast, the 'incorrigible', whose activities were the result of choice and disposition and who failed to take advantage of these opportunities. In their determination to reclaim all women from the condemnation of being 'whores', this history recreates the nineteenth-century moral category of the 'incorrigible', to which all the deviant and 'unreformed' are consigned. It is not an exclusively female category, although contemporaries were more inclined to place women within it.[13] Within this history, which reflects a determination to show the convict colonies as 'normal' and not depraved, the structural inequalities and vulnerability of convict women are invisible.

Were the circumstances in which convict women found themselves so benign that only choice and weakness of character led to social casualty? Sarah Thornton, who was most certainly a model 'family woman', described early New South Wales as 'this wretched country where so much evil abounds'. It might be useful to explore more fully the idea that while convict women were advantaged through sharing some of the benefits which flowed to those men who had secured a privileged position in the labour market, they were particularly vulnerable in other ways in the penal settlements because of the pattern of employment for women and the inequities of the family relationship. While the experiences of convict women differed, they shared a common vulnerability derived from their dependence (on men and on the state).

What economic opportunities were available to women? It has been argued that we have underestimated not only the skills of convict women (Oxley) but the value and range of their work (Robinson) and their success in performing it (Perrott). Successful women can certainly be found in a range of occupations from the earliest times. Among the most successful was Mary Haydock, whose belief that 'no one will do well' in New South Wales 'that is not thrifty Correct and Sober' was close to that of Sarah Thornton.[14] Transported to Sydney in 1790 at the age of thirteen for horse-stealing, four years later Mary Haydock married a young free settler who became a property-owner and a well-known trader. When he died in 1811, leaving her with seven children, Mary Reibey took over the business, building new warehouses, buying trading ships and extending her investments and property. Among the emancipists she gained considerable prominence as a businesswoman. On a visit to England with her daughters she was happy to be taken as a symbol of all that it was possible for a convict to achieve in New South Wales. Whether her story encouraged rather than deterred potential criminals, or demonstrated the reformatory power of the transportation system, her success was neither unique nor typical. Maria Lord was as successful as Mary Reibey before Edward left her, and had she been widowed rather than abandoned she may have become more prominent.

Few female convicts had experience of business before being transported, although some had run brothels and others, like Mrs Solomon, had played an entrepreneurial part in their husbands' illicit activities. One who was unusual in this regard was Eleanor Kirwan, described by John Nicol in his memoir of the journey on the *Lady Juliana* as 'a female of daring habits'.[15] Transported at 29 for forging a will, she had run a business providing loans, entertainment, berths and accommodation for seafarers as well as arranging crews for departing ships. As soon as her sentence expired in 1793 she left the colony. Women like Mrs Lord and Mrs Reibey achieved success because marriage gave them an arena in which they could first develop and then use their skills. Capital and support for their enterprise was more accessible. Widowhood allowed prosperity to be maintained. These opportunities had in the early period been extended to women in de facto relationships. They had, for instance, been allowed to administer intestate estates, a situation Macquarie prohibited in 1810 as a practice which encouraged 'illicit connexions'.

Arrangements of this kind and the government assistance which was given to individual women at the beginning of settlement enabled some to live independently, but these opportunities, always meagre, contracted with later settlement. How possible was it for women to support themselves? Some, like Margaret Catchpole, established themselves independently without the assistance of husbands or patrons. Transported like Mary Reibey for stealing a horse, Catchpole was, in 1806, living in the country outside Sydney trying to support herself by keeping a few animals and nursing local women through their confinements. As she said, she might have 'gon to Lived with maney of the saillrs that is to a Binn thear wife' and she would have 'Lived very well'. But for this she had 'no inklanashun'.[16] Hannah Pleasant Jones (who had abducted a child and sold her frock) was transported in 1789 on the *Lady Juliana* and then sent to Norfolk Island, where she was reported as living independently, supporting herself by washing and sewing. Although she lived briefly with a male convict after she returned to Sydney, she purchased a house in 1804 and thereafter was described as unattached (with children). Hannah Jones, having achieved both independence and a degree of upward mobility, returned home after nearly thirty years, sailing for England on the *Kangaroo* in 1817.[17]

Women sent to Norfolk Island in the early period were among the convicts encouraged by the granting of land and other assistance to support themselves. Catherine Heyland was one of the Second Fleet women who was granted land and time to tend it in 1791. By the following year she was living with a marine turned settler; they worked a small holding and produced grain and raised pigs and cattle, until 1807 when they, their two children and two assigned servants were transferred to Van Diemen's Land. Elizabeth Douglas received land, cleared it and had become partly self-supporting by mid–1792. She too established a relationship, this time with a convict; on their return to Sydney they were granted land and farmed in the Hawkesbury district. Mary Tuck was issued with a sow which she shared with a couple and cared for her own land. Later she married a convict and was transferred to Van Diemen's Land where they worked a larger land grant until house and piggery were destroyed in a bushfire and (like many of the early small landowners in New South Wales) they became dependent again on the government. Sarah Jones was issued with a pig and lived with a male convict twenty years her junior on a small farm until they (childless) were transferred to Van Diemen's Land and given a land grant there. None of these women remained independent but most continued to work the land with their husbands. With the help of what was in effect a state dowry they quickly established small farming households, a number of which survived with moderate success. Rachel Watkins, who was also allowed a government sow which she shared with two male convicts, bore four children to a former marine who stayed on Norfolk Island. They did not stay together and in 1828, aged 69, she was still working—employed (along with other family members) by Simeon Lord at Botany.[18]

While land grants as 'dowries' for free women became formalised as an encouragement to marriage, initiatives that encouraged unmarried women to become self-supporting seem to have been temporary measures. Macquarie, for instance, believed that land which had been granted to single women had not been sufficiently improved and declined to grant additional land to one woman in 1822 (although she already owned a farm valued at £1000 and had access to capital) because he believed that it was 'inexpedient to grant land to single women'.[19]

Many women shared the farm work with their husbands and children, but seldom did they become landowners or obtain land grants. Small enterprises were sometimes headed by women. Ex-convict women ran small shops and some became butchers and bakers. Some inherited businesses when their husbands died; others used cash cleverly acquired through dealing in goods bought on the voyage out or through hard work and careful saving, like Sarah Thornton. Mary Reibey had been among other things a hotelkeeper, an occupation in which, in the early colonial period, ex-convict women like Sarah Bird became quite conspicuous. Another innkeeper was Molly Morgan, who as well as keeping a wine shanty in the Hunter region and building the Angel Inn in what became Maitland, established a prosperous farming enterprise.[20] Morgan was transported twice (having escaped the first time and returned to Britain) and on her second journey was one of Maria Lord's shipboard companions on the *Experiment*. Other women in the early period, like Maria Lord, set up businesses for husbands who were barred from trade. Mary Hook, who was sentenced to death for theft but reprieved because she was so 'young and ignorant', became not only the mother of a large family (her husband was a private in the New South Wales Corps) but established a business in her own name selling tea, sugar and prints.[21] In fact few ex-convict women became employers, though a number helped husbands to run small businesses. Some became self-employed, among them women who sewed or washed clothes or who worked as milliners, seamstresses, bonnet and staymakers or nurses and midwives.

The range of employment for women was limited, regardless of the number of individuals who in various ways became successful. John Price, commenting on the employment of ticket-of-leave women in Hobart in the early 1840s, said that few of them worked as tradeswomen; most were employed as servants.[22] Domestic service and work that related to domestic tasks (such as laundry work and dairy-making) dominated. The descriptions in convict records of women's skills, such as whether they could cook or make butter, reflected the labour required in the colonies and that was largely domestic. Applicants requiring female convict workers from the *Buffalo* when it arrived in Sydney in 1833, for instance, wanted domestic servants, cooks, laundresses and dairy workers. At the 1828 muster in New South Wales 58 per cent of adult women employed were domestic servants, 15 per cent housekeepers and 4 per cent special servants, while another 6 per cent worked as laundresses.[23]

The great majority of women neither established businesses nor became independent but exchanged life as a government servant for life as a free servant. As the colonies grew the demand for domestic servants increased, as did competition in the labour market from free and immigrant women. The occupations for women did not expand significantly until factory work and clerical positions opened up new opportunities for women much later. Few women could hope to improve their lives through work or support themselves easily.

Nor was it possible in many occupations for women to combine working for wages with care of children. Domestic service (usually live-in work), made these dual responsibilities almost impossible to pursue. The records of orphanages and industrial schools reveal how women assigned to or seeking domestic work reverted to single status by the expedient of having their children placed in these institutions, thus reinforcing the illusion that underlies much public policy-making in this period, that wage work for women was mainly a temporary activity undertaken before establishing a family. Institutions took over the family role to enable women to conform better to the stereotype. Such a view did not underestimate the contribution women made within the family unit, especially in families on the land, but it did serve to conceal what was in actuality an employment problem for women.

With or without the 'inklanashun', marriage appeared to be a better option for women seeking freedom, security or greater material comfort. For convict women marriage provided the best chance of resuming a 'normal' life, and the lives of those who were assigned to their husbands most closely resembled those of free women. How many, like Penelope Burke, 'only married to be free', can only be guessed.[24]

If women wanted to find husbands or companions, the demographic balance of the convict colonies gave them ample opportunity to do so. In 1820 among the European population there were nine men for every woman in New South Wales and ten in Van Diemen's Land.[25] The records, particularly in the early period, show that differences of age and class were not barriers to matrimony. Women found much younger husbands (and much older), and officers lived with and sometimes married convict women.

The fragment of the family which was most likely to survive transportation was mother and infant or mother and child. Without fathers, brothers, husbands or grown sons to speak for them, deprived of the shelter afforded by established communities, women in the settlements lived lives that replicated the conditions which had led many convict women (already immigrants to towns and cities at home) into criminal activities in the first place. Relationships had to be reconstructed, and while in such an environment shipboard companions and friendships made in the female factories were of considerable significance, most important were relationships with men and the possibility of marriage. As we have seen, many women formed such relationships with the utmost haste soon after their arrival. The chance to do this depended to a great extent on the assignment system, which provided the opportunity but punished those who grasped it too avidly.

The advantages of marriage were understood by convict women once they arrived in the colonies; as one woman explained in a letter home: until she married she would be 'kept in bondage', after which 'I shall then be enabled to become in a manner of speaking a free subject, by being allowed to live of course with my husband'.[26] The convict records cannot disclose how many of the marriages made by convict women while still in servitude were happy ones, but they do provide some glimpses of married life. Mary Scales, for instance, was one of many convict women who married fellow convicts while they were still serving their sentences. Assigned to her husband, Scales absconded from him three times in the first three years of their marriage and in 1828 was sentenced to serve out the remainder of her sentence in the George Town Female Factory after being found leading 'a disorderly life'.[27] Regardless of the belief of some colonial administrators in the reformatory power of marriage, it failed to offer all who chose it a secure alternative to the factory. Some women sought refuge in the factories from violent husbands. Scales abandoned her husband and found herself returned to the factory.

Nor did marriage save Susannah Leake from incarceration. Married to a convict soon after her arrival in Hobart, within four years he had left her and she set up house with another man. In 1850, twenty-eight years after she was first sentenced to transportation for life to Van Diemen's Land, she was given a second life sentence, this time for sheep-stealing. For a minority marriage was an episode which did little to change a pattern of convictions for drunkenness, petty crime, assault and prostitution. For most it was a chance to recreate a family life and extricate themselves from the intrusions of the law. Leake's shipmate on the *Lord Sidmouth*, Ann Moore, arrived in the settlement, married, and disappeared from the records except for entries documenting her progression through the system from convicted felon to free person. In Moore's case her file reveals her acquisition of a conditional pardon and a free pardon, and, in the only other entry, records her application ten years after her conviction in Glasgow to have her children, still living in Scotland, brought out to her.[28]

The number of women for whom unsuccessful applications to marry different men followed in quick succession suggests pragmatism rather than affection. Alan Atkinson has drawn attention to the number of marriages between convicts which did not proceed from application to altar, suggesting that among the poor many who married were not driven as much by feelings of romantic attachment as by prudence.[29] On the other hand, women were not always put off their chosen partner by unenthusiastic officialdom; some applied to marry the same man a second and third time.

Some convict women were, however, deprived of a chance to marry at the time when they needed it most, that is when it would have allowed them to keep their children or keep themselves from incarceration. There are many women in the convict records who ask more than once to marry, are refused (because of behaviour or because their marital status is unclear) and drift into drunkenness and vagrancy.

Babette Smith's reconstruction of Susannah Watson's life and the histories of the other women who were transported with her on the *Princess Royal* in 1829 gives a clear picture of the consequences of transportation for a cluster of women. For most, what security they had came from family rather than from work. Smith concluded that marriage provided the best chance a convict had of living the life of a free woman; that inability to marry could be a tragedy, although marriage to a brutal husband or one who died, was retransported or left could also plunge a woman into complete destitution.

Susannah Watson was deprived of the chance to marry because of her declaration that she had a husband in England. Consequently, while she could conceive a child in servitude (as she did while she was first assigned) she was prevented from either establishing a marital relationship or from retaining control of her children. Some convict women who described themselves as married on arrival did so because they confused marital status with the benefits a husband conferred—as Mary Hughes wrote while on board ship: 'I was informed that the mareed weemen got their liberty for to do the best they could for themselves and the single weman was kept in confinement'.[30] From the 1830s in New South Wales legal marriage was necessary if convict women wished to be assigned with or to male companions, and marital status was closely scrutinised. Aware that being married was quite different from having a husband in the colonies, convicts—Susannah Watson among them—devised various strategies (including fabricated evidence of death) to allow them to remarry. Some time in the mid–1830s Watson convinced the authorities that an acquaintance from Nottingham, now transported, was her husband, and eventually she became assigned to him. In 1837, two years after their son was born, her 'husband' was reconvicted and she returned to the Parramatta Female Factory, where she gave birth to a daughter who did not survive childhood. She moved in and out of the factory, sometimes assigned to a master, sometimes to her 'husband'. It is her 'husband' who petitions the Governor for the release of 'his son' from the Orphan School when he approaches the age of apprenticeship, constructing for the purposes of the official document a convincing (though imaginary) image of stable and respectable family life. His second reconviction seems to have ended the relationship, and Susannah, once in possession of a ticket of leave, sought work for herself and the release of her younger son. Employment was short-lived (and probably difficult with children to care for).

With the death of her 'husband' in 1842 she assumed the status of a widow and married again twice.

Watson's life was punctuated by a series of attempts to re-establish a household and extricate herself and her children from the institutional care of the government. She had brought only one of her children with her and had three children in the colony. Her first pregnancy resulted in her return to the factory. The child who had accompanied her to Sydney was placed in the Orphan School, where he died. Smith suggests that Watson committed a series of thefts from shops to secure her return to the factory so that she could be near her son before his death. Work (apart from assignment) plays a minor and intermittent part in her story. Although she established a series of relationships with men, the relationship which sustained her into her old age was with her children. The need for support through marriage receded as the role of male provider passed to her sons.[31]

Continuing though partial dependence on the state became the experience of many women after they were freed. Like Susannah Watson, convict Mary Long, who lived first with a settler on Norfolk Island, bore four children in two subsequent relationships. In 1814 she was single, living in Windsor and the mother of five children. Within five years all of her children had been admitted to the Male Orphan School, where they were to remain until they were apprenticed at thirteen. In 1828 she was recorded as a laundress living with Thomas Bristow and three of her sons. She had not stayed in one domestic relationship and needed to work to support herself. Unable to keep her children all the time, she had reclaimed at least some of them and reconstructed her family.[32] The family, in these cases, was composed of a woman and those of her children the government allowed her to have, with a man or a series of men (sometimes the father of one or more of the children) moving in and out of the household.

Women sought security primarily through the support of family rather than through their own employment, through marriage or cohabitation, by trying to rebuild other family ties (sometimes with siblings) or through children old enough to work. While they could and did contribute to family income, their ability to do so was restricted by family responsibilities and the nature of the work available. Consequently many women, on their own or with children to support because of the death, desertion, illness or unemployment of a husband, lived in or on the edge of poverty, like the ex-convict Mrs Taylor whose husband died and left her to hawk fruit about Camden in an old cart.

It has been estimated that throughout the nineteenth century at least 10 per cent of Australians lived in permanent poverty. At the time Richard Taylor was first writing home, not only had wages declined but a tent city on Sydney's domain housed 2000 immigrant families and nearly 200 single women without work. While the mainland economies revived after the economic downturn in the early 1840s, Tasmania remained depressed and as Stephen Garton has pointed out, even massive emigration to the other colonies did not relieve the pressure of poverty, so that by the 1860s the island colony had a much higher number of people dependent on government than other areas, including many who were ex-prisoners.[33] While men left for the mainland, women were stranded on the island colony, which had by the end of transportation absorbed half the convict women sent to Australia. The institutions which took in some of this population and their children reveal in their records some of the problems of poor ex-convict women and how a group of transported women continued to be dependent on government support or returned to dependence as they grew old and infirm.

Orphan schools were from the early period of settlement an important element in the institutional arrangements created for the management of convict women. The significance of these institutions in the lives of convict women after they attained their freedom indicates the continuing relationship many had with the state and the difficulty they faced in trying to establish independent and self-sustaining households.

Orphan schools were established early. King set up institutions for female children who had lost or been deserted by their parents on Norfolk Island in 1796 and later in 1801 in Sydney, where girls thought to be in danger of prostitution were prepared for marriage or apprenticeship. Within the convict system children aged above three were removed from their mothers at the Parramatta factory and placed in the orphan schools. In Van Diemen's Land orphan schools established for both male and female children (in 1827 and 1828) took children who were destitute, in 'moral danger' or from families who were unable to support them, as well as the children of convict mothers, who remained in the schools until they were apprenticed. Accommodated in new Gothic buildings at New Town in 1832–33, by 1848 the vast majority were the children of convicts, with new inmates coming with each of the ships which arrived with convict women until 1851. Attempts were made during that time to control numbers by admitting only the children of convicts. The schools became an arm of the convict administration run by the Convict Department, their superintendent, Captain Charles O'Hara Booth, the ex-commandant of Port Arthur. Institutions which had initially taken the children of non-convict parents and in the 1830s Aboriginal children, in this period as the convict population swelled became places to house the children of convicts (although in 1847 a small group of Aboriginal children from Oyster Cove were admitted, among them Mathinna, the Aboriginal child temporarily adopted by the Franklins).[34]

The schools also took in many children of convict parents who after they had gained their freedom were not able to provide for them, usually because of death or desertion or the inability of the mother to support her children through work. During the gold rushes desertion increased. Female applicants who had been working to keep their children at home frequently mentioned their attempts to earn a living through washing and needlework, trades which were low-paid and overcrowded but had the advantage that they could be combined with care of children. The records also disclose the attempts women made to support at least some of their children while relinquishing others.[35]

While the factories operated as both a lying-in hospital and a refuge, the orphan schools were more unambiguously threatening, yet women still asked to put their children there. The belief that the child should not be contaminated by its parents could work against the idea that reformation could best be attained through the family. Isolation from parents became a key institutional strategy, essential if children were to imbibe habits of industriousness and regularity. Orphan schools and industrial schools, like the Female School of Industry set up by Lady Darling in Sydney in 1826 (which lasted as a separate institution for a hundred years) provided girls for general domestic work, as the female factories had done. Instruments of policy that had been developed initially to deal with convict women and their children (factories and assignment; orphan schools and apprenticeship) had quite rapidly extended beyond the convict population. By the 1820s, for instance, men were said to go to the Aboriginal Institution at Black Town seeking Aboriginal girls as indentured servants and placing applications 'to marry Native girls belonging to the School'.[36]

Should we assume that the growth of institutions to care for children was the result of maternal (and paternal) neglect by 'incorrigible' parents? Historians have written eloquently of the strength and brightness of the first generation of Australians, with Oxley arguing that convict women 'did not establish a cold and barren criminal subculture, but one based on families, intimacy and warmth'.[37] They were 'good mothers'. Yet the orphan schools played a significant part in the colonial settlements, suggesting that the predicament that faced Susannah Watson was common. The substantial presence of the children of ex-convicts in orphan schools and of ex-convicts in institutions established for the insane, infirm and destitute indicates continuing or recurring dependence on the state, although there were many who preferred a hard life outside or were not sufficiently deserving to be acceptable recipients of charitable or government assistance. The 'old lags' and 'Derwenters' who were in the goldfields in the 1850s, often the worse for drink, did not find a life of comfort and security in a new land. Among the aged were ex-convicts who had been self-reliant until financial collapse, natural disaster or illness intervened. Destitute and infirm couples also sought help, like Ann Harmsdem (who had come out on the Second Fleet) and her husband who in the 1830s were admitted to the Sydney Benevolent Asylum. She had made two attempts to return to Britain, the first thwarted by war and the refusal of the ship's captain to take a woman on board, the second (nearly twenty years later) because missing records prevented her from proving that she was free.[38]

While the fracturing of the family unit often reduced women to poverty and could lead to the institutionalisation of children, a prudent marriage which remained intact and economically viable could also be hazardous. Violence between women (visible in the factory environment) should not be disregarded, nor should the hidden abuse of children, but it is the pervasiveness of violence by men towards women that is most apparent. Whether or not a relationship began as one of affection rather than convenience (as in the case of Mary Sample), convict records show that many women assigned to their husbands were beaten by them. Drunkenness and physical assault are frequently linked. Lepailleur observed both—the drunken brutalisation of women and the night resounding with their cries.[39]

Not all convict women stayed in Australia. Some went home, like Jane Torr, whose return was a simple affair, a matter of buying a ticket on the *Prince Regent*. Other departures were more spectacular. Mary Bryant escaped in the Governor's stolen six-oar boat with her husband, their two children and seven other convicts. A treacherous voyage led eventually to Timor, then to England where (the only survivor from her family) she was reimprisoned. A pardon and an allowance of £10 a year from James Boswell, Johnson's biographer, allowed her, like Jane Torr, to go home to the West Country and disappear from our view. Returning home was difficult, and only a small minority were able to do so. Among the hardships of transportation for women (and one of the reasons they were said to dread it more than men) was the lifelong exile that transportation meant for most.

Most convict women who were sent to Australia built themselves a new life in the colonies. The fact that many could be 'better off' in a number of ways is not at variance with the conclusions drawn by feminist historians about the other disadvantages women suffered in colonial society: constrained economic opportunities, sexual exploitation, domestic violence, dependence, legal inequality. Maria Lord's experience suggests the extent to which individual circumstances and structural restraints coalesced to determine personal fortunes. Her story supports all of the contentions of those who suggest how much better off convict women were in Australia. She became prosperous both through marriage and through her own entrepreneurial endeavours. Mother of a large family, she brought up her children to be dutiful and respectable. Few female convicts enjoyed either her wealth, power, social position or personal business success. Vulnerability she shared with other convict women. Her material fortune derived from a decision to leave the factory to become the servant and mistress of a man she did not know. Her first two children were illegitimate. While her marriage lasted for a long time, it ended in desertion, the removal of some of her children and a breaking up of the family. Protection as she grew older came from her children rather than from her husband. The legal inequality of her relationship with Edward, even after marriage, was evident from the rights he held over her person, the proceeds of their enterprise and the children of their marriage. Her behaviour was circumscribed more than her husband's by the economy, the law and public morality. Disapproval relating to sexual morality attached itself disproportionately to her behaviour, and this had consequences for her economic position and her relationships with her children. Wealth greatly softened the impact of these inequalities, which for poorer women could be disastrous.

These are simply glimpses of a much larger story. A benign view of the fate of ex-convict women in Australia needs to be tempered by reflection on the underlying realities that determined women's experience in the colonies. Central to that experience was their vulnerability: economic, sexual, legal, domestic. Moreover, protections that the authorities provided convict women were not replicated for the free. The convict system had given women shelter and basic sustenance, work when it was available, assistance when sick or pregnant, a refuge from male assault and violence, a place to go for confinement, support and training for their children. Through their obligations in relation to the management of convict women, the colonial authorities were drawn into constructing what was in effect an interlocking set of policies and programs for women and children which looked forward in comprehensiveness if not in delivery to the 'welfare' of a much later period.

Freed women were less well served. Those without adequate resources of their own had to seek help from a variety of sources (some government-run, others organised by church or charitable groups), without the entitlement that the absence of freedom had conferred. Assistance was conditional on the willingness to conform to acceptable standards of behaviour. Often it was directed at children rather than their mothers, so that the pattern of relinquishing children to obtain support, established as a practice among convict women, continued to be part of the experience of the poor. Nor was the state always as willing to intervene on behalf of free women as it had for female convicts—in the privacy of the home, against a violent husband, women had little protection. On the other hand, the activities of women in public places were more restricted and they were likely to be apprehended for public behaviour that flouted morality and for displays of drunkenness and vagrancy. At the same time, women sought to use the law as they had done as convicts to assert their rights.[40] Moreover, the expectation that government would provide assistance either through support for women or for their children was part of the early experience of convict women, and when freed, as the records of orphan institutions show, they continued to try to use the state in the ways they had learned to do as convicts. The ambivalent relationship between women and the state, learned through their experience as convicts, continued to be acted out in a variety of encounters.

10

HERITAGE

O n 3 January 1827, the day the *Sir Charles Forbes* arrived in the Derwent Estuary with a cargo of convict women, the Hobart police magistrate charged a man with removing a page from the Indent lists of female convicts.[1] Attempts to destroy evidence of the shame and the pain of the convict inheritance took many forms, began early and continued well into the twentieth century. In Tasmania, from the time of Collins' death in 1810 when Edward Lord (temporarily in charge) destroyed many of the records of the colony, archives and convict buildings have been in danger of both individual and civic assault. The burning of convict buildings at Port Arthur and on Sarah Island were said to be deliberate, while at the end of the nineteenth century the Chief Justice publicly advocated the destruction of convict relics and structures to obliterate the memory of the island's 'convict stain'.[2]

This book draws on some of the textual records that survive, few of which were written by convict women themselves. Material remains are rare. The most extensive collections of convict artefacts are associated with major prison sites, and many of those, such as Port Arthur, were places of confinement for men alone. While surviving artefacts include objects relating to punishment from these establishments (whips and chains) and articles of male convict clothing, it is possible that as a result of archaeological work at some of the female factory sites (such as Ross, George Town and Cascades) artefacts relating to female convicts may be added.[3] One artefact of major significance to convict women's history presently held in a public collection is a quilt made by convict women during their voyage to Van Diemen's Land on the transport *Rajah*.

The *Rajah* embarked from Woolwich with 190 female convicts, arriving in Hobart on 19 July 1841.[4] Elizabeth Fry's ladies' committee often provided departing convict women with needles, thread and scraps of fabric to enable them to be employed in useful work during the voyage. By the time of the *Rajah* convict women were more effectively supervised (matrons sometimes accompanied them), and greater efforts were taken to ensure that their time was occupied. Efforts were also made to sell their work on arrival; the *Rajah* quilt may have survived because of this. Whether it was sent to Britain as a gift intended for Elizabeth Fry or whether it found its way back among private possessions is not known, but the quilt was privately owned by a family in Scotland before its acquisition by the Australian National Gallery in 1987.

The central panel of the quilt is surrounded by border strips of printed cloth, appliquéd flowers and flower shapes. The work shows varying degrees of skill and considerable variation in technique, evidence that many women worked on it. This and the wording of its embroidered dedication suggests that it was a group enterprise carried out under supervision:

> To the Ladies
> of the
> Convict ship Committee
> This quilt worked by the Convicts
> of the ship Rajah during their voyage
> to Van Diemens Land is presented as a
> testimony of the gratitude with which
> they remember their exertions for their
> welfare while in England and during
> their passage and also as a proof that

they have not neglected the Ladies
kind admonitions of being industrious
June 1841

With exceptions like this quilt, convict women cannot be remembered through remnants of attire, tools and utensils or through the paraphernalia of punishment, because few of these remain. Major historic places of significance to convict women's history do survive, however, even if the historical landscape as conserved tends to obscure women's narratives rather than disclose them.

Successful convict women are commemorated, like men, through their property. Two of Maria Lord's houses remain in Tasmania—which is of particular importance to the story told here. The Georgian townhouse Ingle Hall, on the corner of Macquarie and Argyle Streets looking down to the Hobart docks, is where she lived with Edward Lord. It is one of the oldest buildings in Hobart.[5] In her old age Mrs Lord owned Clifton Priory, a large two-storey Gothic house built of stone in the 1840s on the outskirts of Bothwell, and its substance is the best evidence we have that she remained well off after she left Hobart. Heritage studies of Bothwell fail to refer to Maria Lord but invariably mention among the prominant early settlers of the area her friend Charles Rowcroft.[6]

Aspects of convicts' lives can be imagined only with difficulty through the remains of places in which they worked or lived, and here also those aspects of the colonial landscape which have the closest association with convict labour have often been obliterated or obscured by an interpretation that gives pre-eminence to the lives of masters rather than servants. Often preserved in isolation from their surrounding environment, with little sense of the economy on which they depended, these houses suggest peace and harmony rather than work and conflict. Imagining the life of the owners of colonial houses is easier than imagining the lives of the convict servants on whose work their functioning depended, although houses like the Macarthurs' Elizabeth Farm have increasingly come to present the working areas (kitchen and servants' quarters) to view. Convict men worked on major public works, and the remains of roads, buildings and cuttings commemorate convict labour. Because of its domestic nature convict women's labour is more elusive, even when attempts have been made to reassert the convict role (as at Lanyon, a property outside Canberra).[7]

The most tangible surviving evidence of female convict history exists in the remains of institutional buildings which housed female convicts and their children, although little survives of the female factories. Women tend to be marginal within the construct of heritage except where it conserves the domestic, and as incarcerated convicts they are almost invisible. With the recent exception of the Cascades Female Factory site in Hobart (where a remnant of the factory walls has been maintained and a memorial erected), no site of major or specific significance in the history of convict women has been conserved and commemorated. Consequently Australia's convict heritage is for the most part the heritage of male convictism.

Lack of interest in female convict history is only a partial explanation for this. What survives and what is incorporated into heritage is often the result of the twin accidents of geography and development. Buildings disappear when, with continuous use, the remains of one activity are absorbed into another. Sites are cleared or buildings fall into disrepair and their materials are reused for other activities. Port Arthur, which is remote from urban development but accessible, early in its post-convict history came to see a future in tourism, and although many wished to see the convict story forgotten, its heritage (like that of Norfolk Island) was too important to the local economy. No female factory was of such significance. Some (like Launceston and the first female factory in Queensland on the site of the present Brisbane GPO) were in the central business areas of expanding towns. Others (like the female factory at Eagle Farm in Brisbane, which was situated near the runway of the old Brisbane Airport) were in the path of encroaching development.[8] Other female convict establishments continued their institutional existence as one form of care supplanted another and old institutions sought and found new inmates.

Macquarie's Female Factory at Parramatta was designed by Francis Greenway, who was also architect for the Hyde Park Barracks which housed male convicts (now conserved). The history of the Parramatta factory site shows how one institution was over time incorporated into or adapted to make way for later institutions, so that while little of the 1821 structure is now distinguishable, successive buildings map the history of incarceration and institutional care from convict times. In the 1840s a three-storey stone building was built to house a Catholic orphanage. Additions were made between then and the 1880s, when the orphanage became a girls' training school. The present 'Girls' Training School Precinct', as it is described in the register of the National Estate, includes a wall of the Female Factory. Adjoining this historic area is a second, the Parramatta Psychiatric Centre Precinct. This area contains a group of buildings contructed between 1840 and 1914 for the treatment of psychiatric patients. Surviving sandstone walls include the southern walls of the Female Factory compound. Nearby and better able to be distinguished (although substantially altered) is another building closely associated with the history of female convicts: the Female Orphan School, built between 1813 and 1818 and now part of Rydalmere Psychiatric Hospital.[9]

Images of these two Parramatta institutions are to be found in the work of early colonial artists and in that form have also become part of the national heritage. While architectural drawings and plans for institutions suggest machines for punishment and confinement, in artistic works female factories and orphan schools more often suggest progress and civilisation. In a landscape without ancient monuments the institution could imply the triumph of both domestic and public order. Joan Kerr has written that the Parramatta Orphan Asylum came to be presented visually 'as a British country house with charming vistas to the river across its park-like lawns'.[10] Its landscaping and architecture (influenced by Elizabeth Macquarie) made it ideal for this role, and both Joseph Lycett and later Augustus Earle represented the asylum in this manner.[11] Female factories lent themselves less easily to the domestic analogy but were similarly portrayed as elements in a tamed environment, as in Earle's watercolour of the Parramatta Factory.

The Female Factory Historic Site at Cascades was acquired in 1975 as part of the National Estate and consists of one of the yards, where the chapel stood.[12] Truganini, considered at the time to be the last of the original Tasmanians, was buried secretly in this yard in 1876, and her body remained there briefly (hidden, imprisoned, but also protected) before being exhumed and given to the museum. While Port Arthur, set in a picturesque rural landscape, was transformed by fire and neglect into a romantic neo-Gothic ruin, at Cascades the buildings were reused, then demolished and the materials taken for other dwellings. Like Parramatta, the Cascades Female Factory had a number of post-convict institutional functions. It served as a gaol, a reformatory for boys, an invalid and pauper depot, an asylum for 'Imperial lunatics', a lock hospital in which women thought to be common prostitutes were incarcerated under the Contagious Diseases Act, and a lying-in hospital. Charitable organisations including the Salvation Army used the buildings, and in the 1890s a Home of Mercy was established in one of the cottages.

By 1975 that part of the site which still retained some original fabric was used for semi-industrial purposes. Both the government-owned site and an area that is privately owned now commemorate convict women. Except for some masonry walls and some outlying cottages associated with the institution, the site is bereft of buildings and surrounded by nondescript suburban development, but its physical location, in the cleft of the gully, is still as distinct as it was in the early Prout lithograph and is identifiable from it.

The Cascades Female Factory survived long enough to be extensively photographed from the late 1860s. The whole site and its surrounds, including the five yards, the exterior of the chapel and the separate apartments in the third yard were photographed in the 1870s (the cells were removed in the 1880s), and progressive changes to the buildings are evident from the pictorial record.

In contrast to Cascades, the Orphan School at New Town designed by John Lee Archer is well preserved. It too attracted the eye of a colonial artist, but unlike the domesticated images Lycett and Earle made of the Parramatta school, John Glover represented this institution in 1837 as a solitary building set small and distant on a heavily wooded mountain, making invisible the signs of settlement which in actuality surrounded it. 'Mount Wellington with Orphan Asylum'—the 'asylum within a wilderness', as Tim Bonyhady has called it—presents a powerful image not of order and harmony but of civilisation dwarfed by nature.[13] If the picture with its overarching rainbow is an overt allegory of redemption (the children saved), it also suggests the uncertain fate of outcasts doubly banished, from homeland and from society, and entrapped in a wild landscape.

The other female convict site which has received some attention is the Female Factory at Ross in the Tasmanian midlands. This housed female convicts from 1847 to 1854 in an area which had been used from the 1830s for the male convict gangs employed on public works.[14] In 1841 a probation station for male convicts was established there, and six years later the site was extended to take in female convicts. The structures built there reflect the range of functions most of the factories came to perform: a hospital for the women which included a lying-in ward; a large nursery area adjacent to the work room; wards and yards, separated into areas for the crime class; punishment cells and separate apartments (a later addition). Other areas housed the factory's various institutional functions: receiving room, laundry, wash house, cook houses, rooms for stores, a 'dead house' with mortuary table, privies, a clergyman's room and a chapel in the far corner of the grounds close to the separate apartments. The assistant superintendent lived on the premises but other staff quarters were in a cottage outside the walls on higher ground.

Accommodation (including an office) for constables was situated in the street opposite the main gate.

In 1854, following the end of transportation, the factory closed, and while the chapel was used by residents, plans to extend the site's institutional life by making it a reformatory for boys came to nothing. Nor were attempts to subdivide the land and sell it any more successful. In the 1890s the Police Department installed the superintendent in the cottage, now extended using stone from the factory. Not long afterwards the remaining factory buildings were demolished. For thirty-five years from the 1930s the cottage became the residence of a local farmer whose sheep grazed in the paddocks where convict women had earlier been confined. Apart from the (now) 'picturesque stone cottage', the buildings which made up the factory in the 1850s are visible only as grassy mounds of earth. Stripped of its institutional buildings the aspect is rural and benign.

The management of the Ross Female Factory site was taken over by the Tasmanian National Parks and Wildlife Service in 1980 and recently became the subject of an archaeological survey and an interpretive study which is unusual in that it attempts to demonstrate the meaning of the place by examining the least substantial of its remains rather than its most intact fabric: the mounds which mark out what the guide calls the 'circle of transformation'. Just as the probation system was designed to convert the convict into citizen, the architecture of the Ross establishment allowed for the progression from punishment (in the crime class) through to release.

Although it was the last institution of any importance established to house female convicts, the architecture of the Ross factory reflects an earlier philosophy than the clinical zeal that lay behind the model prison at Port Arthur and Gipps' plans for the Parramatta factory. The emphasis was on separation of classes rather than separation of individuals, although at first even this was difficult and additional fences had to be erected to create separate yards after the first women arrived.[15] Work rooms and yards allowed opportunity for mingling and social interaction. Cells were designed for special punishment, not for routine isolation. Six solitary cells had been built just before the end of male occupation of the establishment, but the provision of a block of 24 separate apartments, although sought, was not completed (probably because of expense) until 1851.[16] The constables' office was placed outside the walls and the clergyman's room, though central and described as sitting like a 'toll both' between the wards and yards, 'controlling passage within the factory and the exit out', did not allow complete surveillance of inmates.

For all the importance of female convicts to the broader history of convictism in Australia, their story has for the most part been slow to emerge in the recreation of the convict narrative through heritage. Preliminary studies for a possible nomination of Australian convict transportation sites for World Heritage Listing suggest that convict women will continue to be marginal figures. Proposed for inclusion are major sites of confinement and incarceration of male convicts (Hyde Park Barracks, Port Arthur, Kingston on Norfolk Island, the Fremantle Prison, Cockatoo Island), a probation station (at Ross or on the Tasman Peninsula), and a building of administrative importance (First Government House).[17]

Narrating the story of female convicts through historic sites would require a different map—one in which major places of confinement for women such as Cascades and Parramatta (as well as less significant institutions of the probation period such as Ross) are linked with institutions which held their children (the substantial remains of orphan schools at Parramatta and New Town) and houses where they worked as assigned domestic servants. If the institutional transformations of buildings used for female convicts have deprived us of intact historical fabric, these adaptations also serve to remind us that the long history of institutionalisation in this country had its origins in the management of convict women and their children and extended to prisoners, newly arrived immigrants, the destitute, pregnant women, orphans, European and Aboriginal children who had been taken away from their parents, the destitute, 'wayward' women, people suffering from infectious diseases, the sick, the insane. Houses of correction, female factories, orphanages, destitute and insane asylums, prisons, industrial schools, penitentiaries, reformatories, lock hospitals—all were designed to house and, increasingly, to hide these groups.

While documentary records tend to locate convict women precisely within their historic period, the great contribution made by 'heritage', as manifested in place and surviving fabric, is its fresh reminder that theirs is part of a longer story. Enough remains to suggest the central relationships that made up the female convict experience—between women and the penal administrators, government, men, masters, their children, each other—relationships that continue to make their experience relevant to modern (not merely early) Australian history.

ENDNOTES

Abbreviations

AONSW	Archives Office of New South Wales
AOT	Archives Office of Tasmania
LTL	La Trobe Library, State Library of Victoria
ML	Mitchell Library, State Library of New South Wales
ADB	*Australian Dictionary of Biography, 1788–1850*, 2 vols, Melbourne University Press, Melbourne, 1966
AHS	*Australian Historical Studies*
HRA	*Historical Records of Australia*
HRNSW	*Historical Records of New South Wales*
Knopwood	Mary Nicholls (ed.), *The Diary of the Reverend Robert Knopwood 1803–1838, First Chaplain of Van Diemen's Land*, Tasmanian Historical Research Association, Hobart, 1977
Tardif	Phillip Tardif, *Notorious Strumpets and Dangerous Girls, Convict Women in Van Diemen's Land 1803–1829*, Angus & Robertson, Sydney, 1990
THRA *P & P*	Tasmanian Historical Research Association *Papers and Proceedings*

1 Maria Lord

1 'Mary Reibey' *ADB* 2, pp. 373–4; Diane Snowden refers to Maria Lord's entrepreneurial role in Women and Work in Van Diemen's Land, BA Hons, University of Tasmania, 1982.

2 Bligh to Castlereagh, 10 June 1809, *HRA*, 1, vii, p. 129; Greg Dening, *Mr Bligh's Bad Language: Passion, Power and Theatre on the Bounty*, Cambridge University Press, Cambridge, 1994, pp. 55–61.

3 'Edward Lord', *ADB* 2, p. 128; see Mrs Lord to Hull, 7 September 1820, *HRA* 111, iii, p. 680–1; Hull to Bigge, 8 August 1820, ibid. pp. 669–70.

4 Hull to Sorell, 6 September 1820, 7 September 1820, ibid. pp. 678–80.
5 Sorell to Bigge, 22 September 1820, ibid. p. 684.
6 Maria Lord, 15 January 1820, James and Maria Lord Letterbook, copies of outgoing correspondence, A1399, ML; see also Knopwood, 21 February 1820, p. 325.
7 See *ADB*, 2, 'Edward Lord', pp. 127–8; E. R. Henry, 'Edward Lord: The John Macarthur of Van Diemen's Land', THRA *P & P*, vol. 20, no 2, June 1973, pp. 98–108.
8 John Currey (ed.), *A. W. H. Humphrey, Narrative of a voyage to Port Philip and Van Diemen's Land with Lieut. Governor Collins 1803–4*, The Colony Press, Melbourne, 1984, p. 115.
9 John West, *The History of Tasmania*, Angus & Robertson, Sydney, 1981; see also Henry, 'Edward Lord', p. 100.
10 West, *The History of Tasmania*, p. 36; Currey, *A. W. H Humphrey*, p. 114.
11 Knopwood, p. 78, p. 96.
12 'Edward Lord', *ADB*, 2, p. 127; Henry, 'Edward Lord', p. 101.
13 John Pascoe Fawkner, 'The Reminiscences of John Pascoe Fawkner containing the attempt to settle Port Phillip in 1803, the formation of the settlement at Hobart Town, River Derwent in 1804', Book 1, p. 35, p. 45, Box 3659/Folder 1, Fawkner Papers, LTL. Fawkner does not give their names here, but elsewhere, listing officers in Collins' party to Port Phillip, he refers to Edward Lord's later marriage to the 'notorious Maria Risley of Sydney' ('Reminiscences', Fawkner Papers, MS 3337, National Library of Australia).
14 Knopwood, 30 November 1807, p. 147.
15 Mrs Lord's notice in the *Hobart Town Gazette*, 18 August 1829. For the spelling of her name see note 37.
16 'Edward Lord', *ADB*, 2 , p. 127.
17 Calder Papers, LTL.
18 Ibid.
19 Knopwood, 28 March 1814, p. 171; Rev. R. Knopwood Papers, 1791–1832, B293, ML.
20 Details are from Henry, 'Edward Lord', shipping news in the *Hobart Town Gazette*, and Knopwood.
21 Mabel Hookey, 23 February 1948, in Hudspeth Files, NS 690/29, AOT.
22 See Mrs Lord's notice in the *Hobart Town Gazette*, 18 August 1829; Letterbook, A1399, ML. Within a year she was looking forward to having in place a new 'regular and fixed system both in the store and office'.
23 D. R. Hainsworth, *The Sydney Traders, Simeon Lord and his Contemporaries 1788–1821*, Melbourne University Press, Melbourne, p. 16.
24 Maria Lord to W. Walker, Calcutta, 30 October 1819, Letterbook, A1399, ML.
25 Undated, incomplete letter, *c.* December 1810, Letterbook, A1399, ML.
26 Ibid.
27 Fawkner, 'Reminiscences', Book 1, pp. 35–6, LTL.
28 Maria Lord to Messrs Jones & Riley, Sydney, 28 August 1819, Letterbook, A1399, ML.
29 See 13 November 1825, 11 February 1826, 22 September 1827, *Hobart Town Gazette*; 13 September 1828, *Hobart Town Courier*; 18 August 1829, *Hobart Town Gazette*; 11 May 1849, *Colonial Times*.

30 Henry, 'Edward Lord', pp. 100–5.
31 Currey, *A. W. H. Humphrey*, p. 114.
32 Lloyd Robson, *A History of Tasmania, vol. 1*, Oxford University Press, Melbourne, 1983, p. 131.
33 Ibid. p. 196.
34 Henry, 'Edward Lord', p. 107.
35 Robson, *A History of Tasmania*, p. 75.
36 Snowden, 'Women and Work'.
37 Her name appears as Risley in the eary period (in convict records and as she signed the marriage register). She used Riseley later (which is the way her brother spelt his name); see Tardif, pp. 65, 68; Knopwood, pp. 76, 97, 99. Sometimes also spelt Risely.
38 Fawkner, 'Reminiscences', Book 1, p. 35, LTL; *HRA*, 111, iii, p. 346; St David's Church Records, NS 282–8–1–3, AOT; Maria Lord's application for a special marriage licence for 'my daughter Caroline Maria Riseley', 20 May 1823, CSO 1/6/100, AOT.
39 Birth recorded of Carolina Mary Risley, 1805, vol. 4/888, AONSW.
40 Fawkner, 'Reminiscences', Book 1, p. 35, LTL.
41 8 October 1808, St David's Church Records, NS 282–8–1–2, AOT; Knopwood, p. 152–3.
42 Ann Allen: Tardif, p. 65; Jane Willmot: Tardif, p. 69.
43 This story originated with James Belbin, who had himself been flogged and gaoled by Collins for supporting Bligh and was, therefore, no friend of Edward Lord (on Belbin see Robson, *A History of Tasmania*, p. 107), Hudspeth Files, NS 690/29, AOT.
44 Knopwood, pp. 308, 341, 343; *Hobart Town Gazette*, 2 December 1820.
45 Knopwood, pp. 358–9.
46 Ibid. pp. 362–3, 367, 371; *ADB*, p. 128.
47 17 January 1823, Knopwood, p. 382.
48 Knopwood, pp. 390–1; St David's Church Records, NS 282–8–1–2, AOT.
49 Rowcroft (1798–1856) left Van Diemen's Land in 1825 and on the voyage to England met and married a widow with nine children. He wrote a number of novels, including *Tales of the Colony; or the Adventures of an Emigrant*, published in 1845, described as 'the first Australian novel of the emigrant genre of any stature' ('Charles Rowcroft' *ADB*, 2, p. 402).
50 Knopwood, pp. 435–8. *Lord v Rowcroft*, December 1824, VDL Chief Justices Reports of Persons tried at the Supreme Court Sessions at Hobart and Launceston, 1823–39, Dixson Library.
51 Thomson to Arthur, 16 December 1824, transcribed in Eustace Fitzsymonds, *A Looking-Glass for Tasmania*, Sullivan's Cove, Hobart, 1980, pp. 46–8.
52 Ibid., transcribed pp. 22–4.
53 9 August 1823, 11 October 1823, 30 July 1824, *Hobart Town Gazette*.
54 *HRA* 111, iv, pp. 340–3. Edward Lord's 1857 will made provision for an annuity of 200 pounds to his wife 'in lieu of any dower and of any estate title or interest whatsoever to which by common law custom or otherwise she would be entitled' (Probate, 10 April 1860, Hobart, Supreme Court Registry, no. 829).
55 The Priory was advertised for sale in the *Hobart Town Gazette*, 18 May 1858, as Mrs Lord's property and again on 6 December 1859 by the

executors of her estate, but on 19 November 1861 it was described as part of the estate of the late Edward Lord.

56 Tardif, pp. 162–3.

57 R. L. Murray to D'Arcy Wentworth, 5 January 1825, Wentworth Papers, A754, ML.

58 23 June 1828, CSO 1/288/6893, AOT. The woman was Ann Fry, transported on the *Brothers*, 1824. Edward Fry was born 5 May 1828 while his mother was in the Female Factory, and was baptised 11 June 1828 (NS 282–3, AOT). Colonial authorities had no power to enforce maintenance payments in the absence of a Poor Law.

59 *Hobart Town Gazette*, 30 July 1824.

60 See Kay Daniels, 'Maria Lord', in Heather Radi (ed.), *200 Australian Women, A Redress Anthology*, Women's Redress Press, Sydney, n.d., pp. 3–4; Alison Alexander, *Governors' Ladies The Wives and Mistresses of Van Diemen's Land Governors*, THRA, Hobart, 1987.

61 St David's Church Records, NS 282–8–1–2, AOT.

62 Robson, *A History of Tasmania*, pp. 180–2.

63 Departures are recorded in the *Hobart Town Gazette* and in Knopwood. Edward Lord's will makes provision for three of his children by Maria (Edward Robert, Eliza and Corbetta) and his four children by Elizabeth Storer, including William Lord and Emma Lord (who may actually have been Maria's).

64 *Colonial Times*, 13 November 1829.

65 23 December 1824, Knopwood, p. 438.

66 Maria Lord to Eyre Coote Lord, 1 July 1820, Letterbook, A1399, ML.

67 Eliza Lord to T. Hassall, 4 April 1821, Hassall Correspondence, vol. 3, pp. 1119–21, A1677, ML.

68 Lord arrived on 14 February 1827, and on both 9 and 13 February 1828 Knopwood recorded that he was 'very ill at Maria Lds' (pp. 504, 514, 517). On February 12, referring to himself as an 'Asthmatic Patient' and writing from 'Morris' Inn Newtown road', Lord asked to be 'lent' the services of a convict woman who he said had nursed him well when she was assigned to the managers of his estates, but who he had been obliged to return to the government (see transcribed correspondence in Fitzsymonds, *A Looking-Glass for Tasmania*, pp. 130–2). She possessed, he said, 'the rare qualities of honesty and sobriety'. The woman, Ann Fry, was by that time pregnant with his child and gave birth a fortnight after he returned to England on April 1 (see note 58 above).

69 13 November 1829, *Colonial Times*.

70 Joy Damousi describes the inquiry in *Depraved and Disorderly, Female Convicts, Sexuality and Gender in Australia*, Cambridge University Press, Cambridge, 1997, pp. 142–3.

2 *Writing about Convict Women*

1 Miriam Dixson, *The Real Matilda, Woman and Identity in Australia, 1788 to 1975*, Penguin, Melbourne, 1976; Anne Summers, *Damned Whores and God's Police, The Colonization of Women in Australia*, Penguin, Melbourne, 1975.

2 J. B. Hirst, *Convict Society and its Enemies*, Allen & Unwin, Sydney, 1983.

3 Lloyd Robson, 'The convict cargo re-inspected', in *Bulletin of the Centre*

for Tasmanian Historical Studies, vol. 2, no 1, 1988; see also A. G. L. Shaw, *Convicts and the Colonies*, Melbourne University Press, Melbourne, 1978 (first published 1966); L. L. Robson, 'The origin of the women convicts sent to Australia 1787–1852', *Historical Studies*, 41, 1963; L. L. Robson, *The Convict Settlers of Australia*, Melbourne University Press, Melbourne, 1976 (first published 1965); C. M. H. Clark, *A History of Australia*, vol. 1, Melbourne University Press, Melbourne, 1963.

4   Portia Robinson, 'The first forty years', in Judy Mackinolty and Heather Radi (eds), *In Pursuit of Justice*, Hale & Iremonger, Sydney, 1979; Portia Robinson, *The Hatch and Brood of Time*, vol. 1, Oxford University Press, Melbourne, 1985; Portia Robinson, *The Women of Botany Bay*, The Macquarie Library, Sydney, 1988.

5   Kay Daniels, 'Prostitution in Tasmania during the transition from penal settlement to "civilised society"', in Kay Daniels (ed.), *So Much Hard Work: Women and Prostitution in Australian History*, Fontana/Collins, Sydney, 1984, pp. 22–3.

6   Marilyn Lake, 'Convict Women as Objects of Male Vision', *Bulletin of the Centre for Tasmanian Historical Studies*, vol. 2, no. 1, 1988; see also Joy Damousi, 'Beyond the "Origins Debate": theorising sexuality and gender disorder in convict women's history', *AHS*, vol. 27, no. 106, 1996.

7   Stephen Nicholas (ed.), *Convict Workers. Reinterpreting Australia's Past*, Cambridge University Press, Cambridge, 1988, pp. 3, 7.

8   Deborah Oxley, 'Female Convicts', in Nicholas (ed.), *Convict Workers*, p. 94.

9   Ibid. p. 95.

10 Deborah Oxley, *Convict Maids: The Forced Migration of Women to Australia*, Cambridge University Press, Cambridge, 1996.

11 Katrina Alford, *Production or Reproduction? An Economic History of Women in Australia, 1788–1850*, Oxford University Press, Melbourne, 1984.

12 Robert Hughes, *The Fatal Shore, A History of the Transportation of Convicts to Australia, 1788–1868*, Collins Harvill, London, 1987.

13 Hirst, *Convict Society*, pp. 32–3.

14 Ibid. p. 57.

15 Ibid. p. 214.

16 Robinson, *The Hatch and Brood of Time*, pp. 68, 95.

17 See Dixson, *The Real Matilda*, pp. 89–94, pp. 126–8.

18 Michael Sturma, 'Eye of the Beholder: the stereotype of female convicts 1788–1852, *Labour History*, vol. 34, May 1978.

19 Jan Kociumbas, *The Oxford History of Australia*, vol. 2, Oxford University Press, Melbourne, 1992, p. 14.

20 Ibid.

21 Ibid. pp. 19, 23.

22 See Alan Frost, *Botany Bay Mirages*, Melbourne University Press, Melbourne, 1994, pp. 214–23.

23 Patricia Grimshaw, Marilyn Lake, Ann McGrath, Marion Quartly, *Creating a Nation*, McPhee Gribble, Melbourne, 1994; Patricia Grimshaw, Susan Janson, Marion Quartly (eds), *Freedom Bound*, vol. 1, Allen & Unwin, Sydney, 1995; Marilyn Lake and Katie Holmes, *Freedom Bound*, vol. 11, Allen & Unwin, Sydney, 1995.

24 Marian Aveling, 'Bending the Bars. Convict Women and the State', in Kay

Saunders and Raymond Evans (eds), *Gender Relations in Australia*, Harcourt Brace Jovanovich, Sydney, 1992.

25 Ibid. p. 149.
26 Ibid. p. 156.
27 Miriam Dixson, 'The "Born-Modern" Self: Revisiting The Real Matilda: An Exploration of Women and Identity in Australia', *AHS*, vol. 27, no. 106, April 1996.
28 Grimshaw, Lake et al., *Creating a Nation*, p. 49.
29 Joy Damousi, *Depraved and Disorderly*.
30 See Quartly cited above and Alan Atkinson and Marion Aveling (eds), *Australians 1838*, Fairfax, Syme & Weldon, Sydney, 1987; Paula J. Byrne, *Criminal Law and Colonial Subject: New South Wales 1810–1830*, Cambridge University Press, Cambridge, 1993; Kay Daniels, cited above and 'The Flash Mob: Rebellion, Rough Culture and Sexuality in the Female Factories of Van Diemen's Land', in *Australian Feminist Studies*, no. 18, 1993.
31 Babette Smith, *A Cargo of Women, Susannah Watson and the Convicts of the Princess Royal*, New South Wales University Press, Sydney, 1988.

3 Transportation and its Management

1 Lyndall Ryan, 'From Stridency to Silence: The Policing of Convict Women 1803–1853', in Diane Kirkby (ed.), *Sex, Power and Justice*, Oxford University Press, Melbourne, 1995; Lyndall Ryan, 'The Governed: Convict Women in Tasmania, 1803–1853', *Bulletin of the Centre for Tasmanian Historical Studies*, vol. 3, 1990–1.
2 CSO 22/50, AOT.
3 Tardif, pp. 1–2.
4 Figures from Robson, *The Convict Settlers*, pp. 74–5.
5 Oxley, *Convict Maids*, p. 135.
6 Robson, *The Convict Settlers*, pp. 75–6.
7 This information and the following figures are from Oxley, *Convict Maids*, pp. 109–111.
8 Tardif, pp. 1369–70.
9 Oxley, *Convict Maids*, p. 111.
10 Ibid. p. 256.
11 Figures are from Robson, *The Convict Settlers*, p. 75; Oxley, *Convict Maids*, pp. 55, 125.
12 Tardif, p. 23.
13 Tardif lists these women from the *Harmony* pp. 1507–70, 1762–3; Macdowell's family was described as 'a notorious family of thieves known as the Rob Roys of the East Riding'.
14 This and following comments from Robson, *The Convict Settlers*, p. 84.
15 1843, cited in Ivy Pinchbeck, *Women Workers and the Industrial Revolution, 1750–1850*, Frank Cass, London, 1969, p. 275.
16 For this discussion see Oxley, *Convict Maids*, pp. 161–9, 248–51, 269–72.
17 Robson, *The Convict Settlers*, pp. 77–80.
18 See also Robson, 'The Origin of the Women Convicts', pp. 47–8, 53.
19 For this and subsequent discussion see Oxley, *Convict Maids*, pp. 72–94, 265.

20 Tim Flannery (ed.), *John Nicol, Mariner: Life and Adventures, 1776–1801*, Text Publishing, Melbourne, p. 121.

21 See West, *The History of Tasmania*, p. 346; Charles Bateson, *The Convict Ships 1787–1868*, Reed, Sydney, 1974, pp. 208–9; Damousi, *Depraved and Disorderly*, pp. 9–12.

22 Tasmanian Papers 112 (A1141), ML.

23 Mrs Fry mentioned seeking approval for her scheme to send out matrons on board transports in a letter to Jane Franklin, 29 August 1842, reprinted in George Mackaness, *Some Private Correspondence of Sir John and Lady Jane Franklin*, Ford, Sydney, 1947, pt 2, p. 52.

24 Evidence given on 1 January 1851, Tasmanian Papers 112 (A1141), ML. Mary Anne Downing was by this time employed as a catechist at Brickfields.

25 On shipwrecks, see West, *The History of Tasmania*, pp. 350–1; Bateson, *The Convict Ships*, pp. 246–52.

26 For figures and details of convict women in this period see Tardif, pp. 1–2, 49–79.

27 West, *The History of Tasmania*, p. 47.

28 See the discussion of chronology in Ryan, 'From Stridency to Silence', pp. 70–4; Tardif suggests that from around 1818 regulations established the 'ground rules' for master and servant and a 'system of order began to emerge' (p. 19).

29 Ann McDermott, convicted in Dublin 1812, aged 34 (1814), Tardif, p. 130.

30 Knopwood, pp. 187–9.

31 Laurel Heath, The Female Convict Factories of New South Wales and Van Diemen's Land, MA, Australian National University, 1978, p. 275.

32 Paul Ashton with Sue Rosen, *Eagle Farm Agricultural Establishment and Female Factory and Prison*, History Report, February 1990, pp. 8, 11.

33 Transcribed in Eustace Fitzsymonds, *A Looking-Glass for Tasmania*, pp. 68, 109–10.

34 Ian Brand, *Sarah Island Penal Settlements*, Regal Publications, Launceston, 1990, pp. 42–3.

35 See Ryan, 'The Governed', 'From Stridency to Silence'.

36 For a comparison of Ross and Phillip, see Alan Atkinson, *The Europeans in Australia*, vol. 1, Oxford University Press, Melbourne, 1997, pp. 72–8.

37 Glenelg to Bourke, 26 May 1837; Glenelg to Franklin, 30 May 1837, Shaw, *Convicts and the Colonies*, p. 268; see also pp. 267–72; reference to improvements in Glenelg to Bourke, 10 December 1836, *HRA*, 1, xviii, p. 612.

38 Cited in Ruth Teale (ed.), *Colonial Eve, Sources on Women in Australia 1788–1914*, Oxford University Press, Melbourne, 1978, p. 23.

39 Hilary Weatherburn, 'The Female Factory', in Mackinolty and Radi, *In Pursuit of Justice*, p. 25; Annette Salt, *These Outcast Women: The Parramatta Female Factory 1821–1848*, Hale & Iremonger, Sydney, pp. 83, 121.

40 25 November 1842; see Ian Brand, *The Probation System: Van Diemen's Land 1839–1854*, Blubber Head Press, Hobart, 1990, pp. 21–2; G. R. Lennox, 'A Private and Confidential Despatch of Eardley-Wilmot', in THRA *P & P*, vol. 29, no. 2, June 1982, pp. 83–4.

41 See Martin J. Wiener, *Reconstructing the Criminal: Culture, Law, and Policy in England, 1830–1914*, Cambridge University Press, Cambridge, 1994, pp. 92–108.

4 Assignment

1 For a discussion of the report and attempts to institute greater control see Shaw, *Convicts and the Colonies*, pp. 100–1.

2 Helen Proudfoot, Anne Bickford, Brian Egloff, Robyn Stocks, *Australia's First Government House*, Allen & Unwin, Sydney, 1991, pp. 39, 45; Tim Flannery (ed.), *Watkin Tench 1788*, Text Publishing, Melbourne, 1996, p. 77.

3 Flannery, *Watkin Tench*, p. 77.

4 Hunter to the Duke of Portland, 18 November 1796, adding 'and they are generally found to be worse characters than the men', *HRNSW*, iii, p. 182. For a discussion of the official view of female convict labour see Robinson, *The Women of Botany Bay*, pp. 177–9.

5 Robinson, *The Women of Botany Bay*, pp. 178–9.

6 12 August 1806, King, 'Present State of His Majesty's Settlements of the East Coast of New Holland, called New South Wales', *HRNSW*, vi, pp. 150–1.

7 Proudfoot et al., *Australia's First Government House*, p. 67.

8 Bayly to Sir H. E. Bunbury, 13 March 1816, *HRA* 1, ix, p. 199.

9 Flannery, *Watkin Tench*, p. 156.

10 J. F. Nagle, *Collins, the Convicts and the Colony, Law and Society in Colonial New South Wales 1788–1796*, University of New South Wales Press, Sydney, 1996, pp. 196–7. Nagle describes a burglary at one of the huts in October 1792.

11 Henry Cowper's evidence, 16 November 1819, John Ritchie (ed.), *The Evidence to the Bigge Reports*, vol. 1, Heinemann, Melbourne, 1971, p. 129.

12 Sorell to Macquarie, 6 December 1820, *HRA*, 111, iii, p. 1; Sorell proposed a building to house 50 or 60 women both on arrival and when 'quitting their places' in service; see also *HRA* 111, iv, p. 165.

13 Tardif, pp. 381, 386, 395–6, 405.

14 Samuel Marsden, 'Essays: a Few Observations on the Situation of Female Convicts in New South Wales', Marsden Papers, MSS 18, ML; see Kay Daniels and Mary Murnane (eds), *Uphill All the Way: A Documentary History of Women in Australia*, University of Queensland Press, Brisbane, 1980, p. 8.

15 Shaw, *Convicts and the Colonies*, pp. 92–3.

16 Tardif, pp. 19–20.

17 Byrne, *Criminal Law and Colonial Subject*, p. 42.

18 Tardif, pp. 1494–5.

19 Hirst, *Convict Society and its Enemies*, p. 57.

20 CSO 22/50, AOT.

21 Byrne, *Criminal Law and Colonial Subject*, p. 44; Weatherburn, 'The Female Factory', p. 25.

22 LC 251/2 (27 June 1851), AOT; CON 15/7, AOT; CON 41/30, AOT; Daniels, 'Prostitution in Tasmania', pp. 34–5.

23 LC 251/2 (5–10 August 1850), AOT; CON 15/4, AOT; CON 41/17, AOT; Daniels, 'Prostitution in Tasmania', p. 36.

24 July 1852, Tasmanian Papers, 112 (A1141), ML.

25 CSO 22/50, AOT.

26 Ibid.

27 Cited in A. G. L. Shaw, *Sir George Arthur, Bart 1784–1854*, Melbourne University Press, Melbourne, 1980, p. 90.
28 Tardif, pp. 1495–7, 1675; Clifford was later reassigned to this 'unfit' master in 1833–34.
29 Tardif, pp. 1565–6, 1758–9.
30 CSO 22/50, AOT; see also p. 217.
31 CSO 22/50, AOT. Heinbury arrived on the *Atwick* in 1838 (CON 18/23, AOT; CON 40/6, AOT).
32 LC 251/2, AOT.
33 CSO 22/50, AOT.
34 LC 251/2, AOT; individual records throughout the period disclose the same experiences as do court records in New South Wales, see Court of General Sessions at Parramatta 1826, CSD 4/1917.2, AONSW.
35 CSO 22/50, AOT. Haigh was sentenced to fourteen years for theft in 1835 (CON 40/6, AOT).
36 Hirst, *Convict Society and its Enemies*, p. 49.
37 Monica Perrott, *A Tolerable Good Success: Economic Opportunities for Women in New South Wales 1788–1830*, Hale & Iremonger, Sydney, 1983, p. 56.
38 For the *Duke of Cornwall* (arrived 1850) see Tasmanian Papers 112 (A1141), ML; Heinbury, CSO 22/50, AOT; McLauchlan, Tardif, p. 1566.
39 Jane Elliott, 'Was there a convict dandy? Convict consumer interests in Sydney, 1788–1815', *AHS*, vol. 26, no 104, April 1995, p. 373.
40 Jane Miller, 2 November 1848, forwarded to Comptroller General of Convicts, Tasmanian Papers, 93/f.11028, ML; file includes extract from the Police Office Records at New Norfolk and a letter from J. S. Hampton to Denison. That Hampton wrote to the governor about this suggests its importance. Josiah Spode arrived in Van Diemen's Land in 1821 and retired from public service in 1845 after holding a number of senior positions in convict administration. He left in 1854 (*ADB* 2, p. 466).
41 21 January 1826, Tardif, p. 669.
42 Tardif, pp. 1351–2. Mrs Solomon was not immune from punishment. She was sent back to the factory once following a quarrel with the Newmans (in 1828) and once in 1835, after threatening her husband and as a result of disturbances that were said to have arisen 'from a combination between the mother and the children against the father'.
43 Robert Hughes, *The Fatal Shore*, pp. 586–7.
44 See Nicholas (ed.), *Convict Workers*, p. 53.
45 Tardif, p. 1460, p. 1528.
46 Byrne, *Criminal Law and Colonial Subject*, pp. 48–51.
47 Tardif, pp. 1238–9.
48 Tardif, pp. 507–8.
49 CSO 22/50, AOT.
50 Lady Franklin to Mrs Fry, 3 August 1841, in Mackaness, *Some Private Correspondence*, pt. 2, p. 22.
51 Ibid. p. 58, 5 September 1842. She added that though she had waited for their conclusions and remedies before writing to Mrs Fry, 'I cannot adopt them'. Nor had Sir John time to contemplate the report.
52 GO 33/74, AOT.
53 GO 33/71, AOT.
54 CSD 1/56/1192, AOT.

55 Proceedings of an Enquiry held by the Visiting Magistrate at the House of Correction for Females, 12 May 1855, Tasmanian Papers, 112 (A1141), ML.

5 The Female Factories: The Failure of Reform

1   On Pentonville, which was opened in 1842, see Michael Ignatieff, *A Just Measure of Pain: The Penitentiary in the Industrial Revolution, 1750–1850*, Macmillan, London, 1978, pp. 3–14. Other relevant studies of prisons and prison policy in this period include Michael Ignatieff, 'State, Civil Society and Total Institutions: a Critique of Recent Social Histories of Punishment', in Stanley Cohen and Andrew Scull (eds), *Social Control and the State, Historical and Comparative essays*, Martin Robertson, Oxford, 1983; Michel Foucault, *Discipline and Punish: The Birth of the Prison*, Allen Lane, London, 1977; Russell P. Dobash, R. Emerson Dobash and Sue Gutteridge, *The Imprisonment of Women*, Basil Blackwell, Oxford, 1986; Wiener, *Reconstructing the Criminal.*

2   Ignatieff, *A Just Measure of Pain*, pp. 89–90.

3   Alex C. Castles, *An Australian Legal History*, The Law Book Company, Sydney, 1982, p. 62.

4   Flannery, *John Nicol*, pp. 123–4; Paul Fidlon and R. J. Ryan (eds), *The Journal and Letters of Lt. Ralph Clark, 1787–1792*, Australian Documents Library, Sydney, pp. 181–212.

5   Tardif, pp. 84–5.

6   Ibid. pp. 82–3.

7   Nagle, *Collins, the Courts and the Colony*, p. 74.

8   Ibid. pp. 74–5.

9   Tardif, pp. 62–3.

10 Tardif, pp. 146–7; Miriam Dixson (*The Real Matilda*, pp. 140–1) discusses the investigation of this case in 1820, where evidence was given that Alice Blackstone's husband kicked her, jumped on her and beat her using a stick two and a half inches thick.

11 King to Hobart, 14 August 1804, *HRA*, series 1, vol. 5, p. 12. Damousi (*Depraved and Disorderly*, p. 99) calls the establishment of the first female factory 'an experiment', quoting in support King's comment that he had completed the upper floor 'for all female convicts who came by the experiment'. King was referring to the women of the *Experiment*, the ship carrying female convicts (including Maria Lord) that had arrived in Sydney six weeks earlier.

12 Samuel Marsden, 'Essays', MSS 18, ML; quoted in Daniels and Murnane, *Uphill All the Way*, p. 8.

13 J. Oxley, 'Account of the Settlement at Port Dalrymple', 1810, *HRA*, III, i, pp. 766–7.

14 Salt, *These Outcast Women*, p. 69.

15 See Miriam Dixson's discussion of Macquarie's tardiness and his responses to Sorell in *The Real Matilda*, pp. 129–30; Tardif, p. 29.

16 Tardif, pp. 29, 1775; Mary Ryan was convicted on 19 February 1820 and sent to Newcastle (Tardif, p. 245).

17 10 January 1818, Tardif, p. 211.

18 Fitzsymonds, *A Looking-Glass for Tasmania*, pp. 17–8. Fitzsymonds identifies five of the women.

19 See Ignatieff, *A Just Measure of Pain*, pp. 99–109, for a discussion of the Gloucester regime.

20 30 August 1823, Elizabeth Fry to Horton, in Bathurst to Brisbane, *HRA*, 1, x, pp. 689–90.

21 See Dobash et al., *The Imprisonment of Women*, pp. 49–55.

22 CSO 22/50, AOT; Lady Franklin to Mrs Fry, 3 August 1841, in Mackaness, *Some Private Correspondence*, pt 2, p. 24.

23 Alexander Harris, An Emigrant Mechanic, *Settlers and Convicts*, Melbourne University Press, Melbourne, 1995, p. 138.

24 Damousi, *Depraved and Disorderly*, p. 89.

25 Salt, *These Outcast Women*, p. 87.

26 Tardif, p. 1619. Black was eighteen at the time (24 July 1832). She had been convicted in 1828 for 'stealing cloathes from a bleach field'.

27 Lady Franklin to Mrs Fry, 3 August 1841, in Mackaness, *Some Private Correspondence*, pt 2, p. 24.

28 Fitzpatrick, 19 April 1830, Tardif, p. 1525; Wood, 31 March 1830, Tardif, p. 1614.

29 Dobash et al., *The Imprisonment of Women*, p. 54.

30 Salt, *These Outcast Women*, p. 77. At morning inspections attention was paid to cleanliness, especially of heads.

31 Rules and Regulations for the Management of the House of Correction for Females, 1 January 1829 (reproduced in Tardif, pp. 1747–54).

32 12 May 1855, Tasmanian Papers 112 (A1141), ML.

33 Mrs Fry to Lady Franklin, 29 August 1842, Mackaness, *Some Private Correspondence*, pt 2, p. 51.

34 CSO 22/50, AOT.

35 Great Britain, House of Commons, *Select Committee on Transportation*, London, 1838, pp. 23, 42.

36 Salt, *These Outcast Women*, p. 70.

37 CSO 4/6177G, AONSW, Return relating to the female inmates, 1836. At Parramatta in 1834 the Board of Management recommended that the third class be further subdivided into two divisions to 'obviate the necessity of Building Cells' (Minutes, 1 April 1834, CSO 4/2234.5, AONSW).

38 Rules and Regulations for the Management of the House of Correction for Females, 1 January 1829, Tardif, p. 1751.

39 Charlotte Anley, *The Prisoners of Australia*, Hatchard, London, 1841, p. 40.

40 Excerpts from Gipps' letters to Glenelg (19 September 1837, 9 October 1837) prior to his departure, discussing appointments and the need for separate cells are transcribed in Daniels and Murnane, *Uphill All the Way*, p. 18; see also Inspectors of Prisons to Phillipps, 17 August 1840, *HRA*, 1, xx, pp. 784–5 criticising the dimensions, ventilation and purpose of Gipps' cells, commenting: 'Imprisonment in a dark cell is a punishment which loses even its detering effects by continuance or repetition; while it produces no moral benefit but is generally found to harden and degrade.'

41 Gipps to Russell, 1 October 1840, *HRA* 1, xxi, p. 2.

42 Cited in Tony Rayner, *Historical Survey of the Female Factory Historic Site, Cascades, Hobart*, National Parks & Wildlife Service, Tasmania, Occasional Paper, no. 3, 1981, pp. 13–14.

43 Ibid.; R. C. Hutchinson, 'Mrs Hutchinson and the Female Factories of Early Australia', THRA *P & P*, vol. 11, no. 2, 1963; Lindy Scripps and Audrey Hudspeth, *The Female Factory Historic Site, Cascades*, Department of Parks, Wildlife & Heritage, Hobart, 1992.

44 CSD Special Bundles 4/7199, AONSW.

45 Rayner, *Historical Survey of the Female Factory Historic Site*, p. 17.

46 See Joan C. Brown, *'Poverty is not a Crime', Social Services in Tasmania 1803–1900*, THRA, Hobart, 1972, p. 65.

47 Salt, *These Outcast Women*, pp. 64–5; Weatherburn, 'The Female Factory', p. 26.

48 Mamie O'Keefe, *A Brief Account of the Moreton Bay Penal Settlement, 1824–1839*, Oxley Memorial Library, Brisbane, 1974, pp. 6–7; J. G. Steele, *Brisbane Town in Convict Days, 1824–1842*, University of Queensland Press, Brisbane, 1975, pp. 192–3.

49 Godfrey Charles Mundy, *Our Antipodes*, 3 vols, Bentley, London, 1852, vol. 1, pp. 136–8.

50 See Salt, *These Outcast Women*, pp. 53–6; Hutchinson, 'Mrs Hutchinson', pp. 51–2.

51 Daniels and Murnane, *Uphill All the Way*, p. 17; Salt, *These Outcast Women*, pp. 57–9; Glenelg to Bourke, 10 December 1836, *HRA*, 1, xviii, pp. 613–4.

52 Salt, *These Outcast Women*, pp. 60–1.

53 Steele, *Brisbane Town*, pp. 165–6.

54 Rayner, *Historical Survey of the Female Factory Historic Site*, p. 9.

55 Thomas Bell to the Colonial Secretary, 20 September 1836, CSD4/2317.2, AONSW.

56 See Hutchinson, 'Mrs Hutchinson'; R. C. Hutchinson, 'The Reverend John Hutchinson', THRA *P & P*, vol. 9, no. 3, 1961; Rayner, *Historical Survey of the Female Factory Historic Site*; GO 33/73, AOT, relates to Mrs Hutchinson's appointment to Launceston (1851); Mundy, *Our Antipodes*, vol. 3, p. 189; Tasmanian Papers 112 (A1141), ML.

57 Lady Franklin to Mrs Fry, 3 August 1841, in Mackaness, *Some Private Correspondence*, pt 2, p. 28.

58 Anley, *The Prisoners of Australia*, pp. 46–50.

59 West, *The History of Tasmania*, p. 510.

60 Brand, *The Probation System*, p. 23; on Mrs Bowden, the *Anson* and plans for a penitentiary, see Lennox, 'A Private and Confidential Despatch'; Brand, *The Probation System*; GO 33/59, AOT.

61 Regulations of the Probationary Establishment for Female Convicts in Van Diemen's Land, 1 July 1845, reproduced in Brand, *The Probation System*, pp. 242–9.

62 Foucault, *Discipline and Punish*, pp. 269–70.

63 Brand, *The Probation System*, p. 84.

64 E. S. Hall, 22 October 1852, Tasmanian Papers 112 (A1141), ML.

65 Brand, *The Probation System*, pp. 104, 93.

66 West, *The History of Tasmania*, p. 511.

67 Cited in Dixson, *The Real Matilda*, p. 127.

68 West, *The History of Tasmania*, p. 511.

69 Mundy, *Our Antipodes*, pp. 190–1.

70 Ibid. p. 193.

71 Mrs Fry to Lady Franklin, 29 August 1842, Mackaness, *Some Private Correspondence*, pt 2, p. 51.
72 Cited in Ignatieff, *A Just Measure of Pain*, p. 179.
73 CSO 22/50, AOT.
74 Ibid.

6 *Rough Culture and Rebellion*

1 Jane New to James New, 3 April 1829, enclosed in correspondence from the Committee of Management, Parramatta Female Factory to Colonial Secretary Macleay, 6 April 1829, *HRA*, 1, xv, p. 48.
2 Letters and testimony, unless otherwise stated, come from the Inquiry into Female Convict Discipline in Van Diemen's Land, 1841–43, CSO 22/50, AOT; Franklin (to Stanley, 4 June 1843) refers to selecting women to give evidence, GO 25/9, AOT.
3 CON 40/6, AOT.
4 CON 18/23, AOT.
5 Tardif, p. 398.
6 Tardif, p. 1429.
7 9 July 1852, Tasmanian Papers 112 (A1141), ML.
8 Miriam Dixson, *The Real Matilda*, p. 128.
9 See Fidlon and Ryan, *The Journal and Letters of Lt. Ralph Clark*, pp. 21–8.
10 *Select Committee on Transportation, Report*, p. 118.
11 Tardif, pp. 358–9.
12 Ibid. p. 1634.
13 Tasmanian Papers 112 (A1141), ML.
14 Tardif, pp. 468–71; J. E. Drabble to J. Lakeland (Principal Superintendent of Convicts), 1 May 1827, transcribed in Fitzsymonds, *A Looking-Glass for Tasmania*, pp. 102–4; see also Hughes, *The Fatal Shore*, pp. 257–8; Damousi, *Depraved and Disorderly*, p. 88.
15 Statement of Jesse Pullen, overseer, Cascades Female Factory, 9 February 1829, transcribed in Fitzsymonds, *A Looking-Glass for Tasmania*, pp. 165–6.
16 2 October 1823 (Catherine Grady, Tardif, p. 352; Eleanor Butler, Tardif, p. 345; Ann Dickins, Tardif, p. 347). When smuggling was apprehended punishments could be severe, as in the case of Charlotte Phillips who had her sentence extended by six months for bringing in one and a half ounces of tobacco (4 November 1830, Tardif p. 1031).
17 Mundy (*Our Antipodes*, vol. 3, p. 137) describes the riot as having been caused by the 'periodical close-cropping of the women's hair'; Smith, *A Cargo of Women*, pp. 54–5 describes the involvement of Marsden; for reference to Mrs Gordon's hair see Damousi, *Depraved and Disorderly*, p. 89; for the reaction to Mrs Gordon's replacement see Daniels and Murnane, *Uphill All the Way*, p. 17; CSD correspondence relating to the Female Factory, 1836, 4/2317.2, AONSW.
18 Josiah Spode to Principal Superintendent's Office, 5 April 1832; note from Arthur, 10 April 1832, transcribed in Fitzsymonds, *A Looking-Glass for Tasmania*, p. 214.
19 Lindy Scripps and Julia Clark, *The Ross Female Factory, Tasmania*, Department of Parks, Wildlife and Heritage, Hobart, April 1991, p. 10.
20 CSO 22/50, AOT.

21 Summers describes this incident (*Damned Whores and God's Police*, p. 284), emphasising in contrast to many later historians how the riot demonstrated the women's solidarity with each other.

22 For the origins of the popular version see Teale, *Colonial Eve*, p. 18.

23 Ignatieff, *A Just Measure of Pain*, p. 40.

24 Henry Mayhew and John Binney, *The Criminal Prisons of London and Scenes of Prison Life*, Griffin, London, 1862, p. 272.

25 On occasions women were punished for singing obscene songs in the factory, as in the case of Mary Ann Lucas and Grace McKenzie (7 September 1827) who had both arrived on the *Sir Charles Forbes* (Tardif, pp. 1024, 1027). The form of record-keeping disguises rather than discloses group offences.

26 Damousi, 'Beyond the "Origins Debate": Theorising Sexuality and Gender Disorder in Convict Women's History', p. 64.

27 *ADB* 2, pp. 351–2; see also Robert Hughes' discussion of Price, *The Fatal Shore*, p. 543–8; Flannery, *Watkin Tench*, p. 270.

28 Joy Damousi, 'Chaos and Order: Gender, Space and Sexuality on Female Convict Ships', *AHS*, no. 104, April 1995, pp. 355, 363; Damousi, *Depraved and Disorderly*, pp. 62–6.

29 The *Colonial Times* alleged that the Flash Mob existed at the Cascades Factory and was beyond control (18 February 1840).

30 CON 78/2, AOT; CSO 22/50, AOT; Tardif, pp. 1684–8; see also Daniels, 'The Flash Mob'.

31 CON 78/3, AOT; CSO 22/50, AOT; CSO 22/8/1742, AOT.

7 Sexuality

Unless otherwise stated testimony is from the Inquiry into Female Convict Discipline, Van Diemen's Land, 1841–43, CSO 22/50, AOT.

1 Hughes, *The Fatal Shore*, pp. 244–64.

2 For a discussion of the historiography of prostitution see Daniels, *So Much Hard Work*.

3 See Hughes, *The Fatal Shore*, pp. 248–50; Marian Aveling, 'Convict Women and the State', in Kay Saunders and Raymond Evans (eds), *Gender Relations in Australia*, Harcourt Brace Jovanovich, Sydney, 1992, p. 147.

4 Leonore Davidoff and Catherine Hall, *Family Fortunes: Men and Women of the English Middle Class 1780–1850*, Hutchinson, London, 1987, pp. 150–5, 401–2.

5 Michael Mason, *The Making of Victorian Sexuality*, Oxford University Press, Oxford, 1995, pp. 44–5, 284–5.

6 Lawrence Stone, *The Family, Sex and Marriage in England 1500–1800*, Penguin, Melbourne, 1979, p. 392, 395.

7 Mason, *The Making of Victorian Sexuality*, pp. 153–6, pp. 170–1.

8 Françoise Barret-Ducrocq, *Love in the Time of Victoria: Sexuality and Desire Among Working-Class Men and Women in Nineteenth-Century London*, Penguin, New York, 1991, pp. 176–81.

9 See Mason, *The Making of Victorian Sexuality*, pp. 146–9; E. P. Thompson and Eileen Yeo (eds), *The Unknown Mayhew: Selections from the Morning Chronicle 1849–50*, Penguin, Melbourne, 1973.

10 Michael Sturma, *Vice in a Vicious Society: Crime and Convicts in Mid-*

Nineteenth Century New South Wales, University of Queensland Press, Brisbane, 1983, p. 7.

11 Davidoff and Hall, *Family Fortunes*, p. 400.

12 Hughes, *The Fatal Shore*, p. 530.

13 Tasmanian Papers, 107/f.13859 (FM4/8515), ML.

14 Tasmanian Papers, 93/f.11037 (FM4/8508), ML.

15 See Thompson and Yeo, *The Unknown Mayhew*, p. 77.

16 For biographical details see Bateson, *The Convict Ships*, pp. 364–5; CSO 50/16, CSO 50/17, CSO 50/21, CSO 50/22, CSO 50/24, CSO 50/25, AOT; Scripps and Clark, *The Ross Female Factory*, pp. 47–9; *Hobart Town Courier*, 23 June 1843; *Hobart Town Courier*, 22 November 1845.

17 Tasmanian Papers 111/f.15163 (FM4/8517), ML.

18 This incident is described in Daniels, 'The Flash Mob', p. 144; Damousi refers to their marriages in 1854 and 1856 in *Depraved and Disorderly*, p. 49.

19 CSO 22/50, AOT, cited in Daniels and Murnane, *Uphill All the Way*, p. 23.

20 Irvine to Pringle Stuart, 1850, Tasmanian Papers 107/f.13859 (FM4/8515), ML.

21 Ignatieff, 'State, Civil Society and Total Institutions', p. 80.

22 Eardley-Wilmot to Lord Stanley, 2 November 1843, GO 25/11, AOT; see Lennox, 'A Private and Confidential Despatch', p. 80.

23 Hughes, *The Fatal Shore*, p. 263.

24 Kociumbas, *The Oxford History of Australia*, vol. 2, pp. 285–92.

25 Robson, *A History of Tasmania*, pp. 162, 441, 527, 529; Bateson, *The Convict Ships*, pp. 365, 367, 369, 373; Scripps and Clark, *The Ross Female Factory*, pp. 47, 49–50, 53.

26 See Dobash et al., *Imprisonment of Women*, p. 115; Phyllis Grosskurth, *Havelock Ellis: A Biography*, Alfred Knopf, New York, 1980, p. 116.

27 C. H. J. Jawewardene, 'The English Precursors of Lombroso', *British Journal of Criminology*, vol. 4, 1963, pp. 164–6.

28 James Semple Kerr, *Out of Sight, Out of Mind, Australia's Places of Confinement, 1788–1988*, S. H. Ervin Gallery, Sydney, 1988, p. 44.

29 *Launceston Advertiser*, 27 March 1834, p. 3; see also CSO 22/50, AOT; PWD 266/892, PWD 266/894, PWD 266/898, PWD 266/907, AOT.

30 John Walton, 'The treatment of Pauper Lunatics in Victorian England', in Andrew Scull (ed.), *Madhouses, Mad-doctors, and Madmen: The Social History of Psychiatry in the Victorian Era*, Athlone Press, London, 1981, pp. 166–8, 177–9; William F. Bynum, 'Rationales for Therapy in British Psychiatry, 1780–1835', in Scull , pp. 51–2.

31 Mason, *The Making of Victorian Sexuality*, pp. 194–205, 221–6.

32 Elaine Showalter, 'Victorian Women and Insanity', in Scull, *Madhouses, Mad-doctors, and Madmen*, pp. 324–29.

33 Cited in Dobash et al., *Imprisonment of Women*, p. 109.

34 Wiener, *Reconstructing the Criminal*, p. 230.

35 See Lennox, 'A Private and Confidential Despatch', pp. 87–8.

36 Ibid. See also Brand, *The Probation System*, p. 156.

8 Prostitution

1 Clark, *A History of Australia*, vol. 1, p. 95; Robinson, 'The First Forty Years', pp. 6–7, 10, 16.

2   Robson, *The Convict Settlers of Australia*, p. 3; Robson, 'The Origin of the Women Convicts', pp. 47–8, 53; H. S. Payne, 'A Statistical Study of Female Convicts in Tasmania', 1843–53, THRA *P & P*, vol. 9, no. 2, 1961, p. 59.

3   Records of women transported on the *Sovereign* are transcribed in Tardif, pp. 1125–1220 and all references unless otherwise stated are to this source.

4   See Frances Finnegan, *Poverty and Prostitution: A Study of Victorian Prostitutes in York*, Cambridge University Press, Cambridge, 1979, p. 24.

5   Davidoff and Hall, *Family Fortunes*, pp. 388, 394.

6   See Kay Daniels, 'Prostitution in Tasmania'. Contagious Diseases Acts were passed in Queensland in 1868 and Tasmania in 1879. Part of both the Cascades and Launceston Female Factories became lock hospitals for 'diseased' women apprehended as 'common prostitutes' (p. 59).

7   See also Daniels, 'Prostitution in Tasmania'; GO 33/8, AOT; CON 40/9, AOT; Inquest of Margaret Torr, SC 195/5/272, AOT; *Launceston Advertiser Supplement*, 6 February 1840; 'Ronald Campbell Gunn', *ADB* 1, pp. 492–3; G. H. Crawford, 'The Scotts: Thomas, George and James', THRA *P & P*, vol. 14, no. 1, 1966.

8   CON 40/9, CON 31/27, AOT. The Sample-Laverty marriage is recorded in the parish records of St John's, Launceston, 16 February 1831; see also Tardif, pp. 827–8.

9   Robson, *The Convict Settlers*, p. 142; Miriam Dixson, *The Real Matilda*, pp. 123, 128.

10 Flannery, *John Nichol*, p. 114.

11 Byrne, *Criminal Law and Colonial Subject*, p. 116.

12 Marian Aveling in Patricia Grimshaw et al., *Creating a Nation*, p. 36.

13 See Nagle, *Collins, the Courts and the Colony*, pp. 83–4, 117–8.

14 *Mercury*, 20 January 1860, 20 April 1860; EC 4/9/132, EC 4/9/154, AOT; SC 41/6, AOT; Court of Petty Sessions, Hamilton, LC 208/4, AOT; CON 41/25, CON 33/00, CON 14/41, AOT; see also Daniels, 'Prostitution in Tasmania, pp. 42–5.

15 Nagle, *Collins, the Courts and the Colony*, pp. 153–4.

16 See Michael Flynn, *The Second Fleet: Britain's Grim Convict Armada of 1790*, Library of Australian History, Sydney, 1993, pp. 346–8.

17 Tardif, pp. 508–9.

18 Frances Finnegan, *Poverty and Prostitution*, pp. 85–96.

19 CSO 22/50, AOT.

20 Portia Robinson 'The First Forty Years', p. 7.

21 Henry Mayhew, 'The Slop-Workers and Needlewomen', from the *Morning Chronicle* 1849–1850, in Thompson and Yeo, *The Unknown Mayhew*, pp. 201, 211, 216.

22 Michael Sturma, 'Eye of the Beholder. The stereotype of women convicts 1788–1852', *Labour History*, vol. 34, May 1978.

23 See Daniels, 'Prostitution in Tasmania', p. 29.

24 Ibid. pp. 27–30; George Hull, 30 August 1824, described his female convict servant as 'living in a state of prostitution' and as 'being in the factory at George Town a few Hours of the day—and living with Serjt Kirwin of the Buffs—who keeps the canteen' (transcribed in Fitzsymonds, *A Looking-Glass for Tasmania*, pp. 40–1); *Fifth Annual Report of the Hobart Town City Mission*, 1857.

25 GO 33/17, AOT.
26 *Select Committee on Transportation*, p. 109.

9 Freedom

1 Manuscript letters of Richard Taylor, Simon Brown, Richard Dillingham and their associates are in the Lancashire Record Office (LRO).
2 Alan Atkinson, *Camden, Farm and Village Life in Early New South Wales*, Oxford University Press, Melbourne, pp. 110, 146.
3 Simon Brown to his father George Taylor, 2 February 1856, DDX 505 LPRO.
4 Richard Dillingham, 27 November 1839, DDX 505 LPRO.
5 Richard Dillingham, 4 October 1838, DDX 505 LPRO.
6 Patrick O'Farrell, *Letters from Irish Australia 1825–1929*, New South Wales University Press, Sydney, 1984, p. 9; Thomas Fallon to his wife Mary, 13 March 1835, p. 14; James Halloran to his wife Catherine, p. 18.
7 Richard Dillingham, 4 October 1838, DDX 505 LPRO.
8 Transcribed in Teale, *Colonial Eve*, p. 34.
9 Smith, *A Cargo of Women*, p. 161.
10 28 June 1857, ibid. p. 152.
11 Ibid. pp. 151–2.
12 Hirst, *Convict Society and its Enemies*, p. 210.
13 See Hirst's reference to Nathaniel Kentish, editor of the *Sydney Times*, ibid. p. 206.
14 'Mary Reibey', *ADB* 2, pp. 373–4; Heather Radi (ed.), *200 Australian Women*, Women's Redress Press, Sydney, n.d., pp 1–3; Alford, *Production or Reproduction?*, pp. 7, 171, 212.
15 Flannery, *John Nicol*, p. 120; see also Flynn, *The Second Fleet*, pp. 386–7 (Eleanor Kirvein).
16 Daniels and Murnane, *Uphill All the Way*, p. 164.
17 Flynn, *The Second Fleet*, pp. 368–9.
18 Ibid. pp. 328–9, 249, 578–9, 373–4, 596. Stephen Garton refers to 47 landowners in 1802 who were forced to give up their land to creditors (Stephen Garton, *Out of Luck*, Allen & Unwin, Sydney, 1990, p. 17).
19 CSD Memorials, 1822, f/397, AONSW.
20 Flynn, *The Second Fleet*, p. 442; see Perrott, *A Tolerable Good Success*, pp. 56–9 for other women publicans.
21 Flynn, *The Second Fleet*, p. 339.
22 CSO 22/50, AOT.
23 *Buffalo*, 1833, CSD 4/21803.3, AONSW; Garton, *Out of Luck*, p. 27. Monica Perrott discusses the work of ex-convict women in *A Tolerable Good Success*, pp. 48–65.
24 Penelope Burke married in 1832. See Atkinson, 'Convicts and Courtship', in Patricia Grimshaw, Chris McConville and Ellen McEwen (eds), *Families in Colonial Australia*, Allen & Unwin, Sydney, 1985, p. 23.
25 Garton, *Out of Luck*, p. 26.
26 Mary Furner to T. E. Williams, 16 February 1830, cited in Atkinson, 'Convicts and Courtship' p. 22.
27 Tardif, p. 655.
28 Ibid. pp. 585–6, 589.

29 Atkinson, 'Convicts and Courtship', pp. 25–7.
30 Mary Hughes to J. E. Keane, 5 June 1832, cited ibid. p. 21. See Atkinson's discussion of these ideas.
31 For discussion of these aspects of Watson's life see Smith, *A Cargo of Women*, particularly pp. 52, 85–91.
32 Flynn, *The Second Fleet*, pp. 407–8.
33 Garton, *Out of Luck*, pp. 3, 30–4.
34 See Kociumbas, *The Oxford History of Australia*, vol. 2, pp. 28–31; Brown, *'Poverty is not a Crime'*, pp. 26–32, 55–73; Dora Heard (ed.), *The Journal of Charles O'Hara Booth, Commandant of the Port Arthur Penal Settlement*, THRA, Hobart, 1981, pp. 66–79; CSO 1/122/3073, AOT.
35 CSD 1/105/3233, CSD 1/106/3270, AOT.
36 Letters relating to the Aboriginal Institution at Black Town, 1826–29, are in the AONSW.
37 Oxley, *Convict Maids*, p. 108.
38 Flynn, *The Second Fleet*, pp. 316–7.
39 Cited in Aveling, 'Bending the Bars', p. 152. Francois-Maurice Lepaillieur was a French-Canadian political prisoner who arrived in 1840. His journal covers the period 1839–45. See also Hughes, *The Fatal Shore*, pp. 261–2.
40 On controlling the public behaviour of women see Daniels, 'Prostitution in Tasmania', pp. 58–80; Bryne, *Criminal Law and Colonial Subject*, pp. 161–2, 171.

10 Heritage

1 Knopwood, p. 501.
2 Kay Daniels, 'Cults of Nature, Cults of History', *Island*, no. 16, Spring 1983, p. 3; Tom Griffiths, *Hunters and Collectors: The Antiquarian Imagination in Australia*, Cambridge University Press, Cambridge, 1996, p. 116; Peter Bolger, *Hobart Town*, Australian National University Press, Canberra, 1973, p. 2.
3 Recent archaeological work in Tasmania has included excavations by Cathie Searle at the privately owned sections of the Cascades Female Factory; at Ross by Eleanor Casella, and at George Town by Campbell MacKnight and Diane Phillips. See also John Thompson, 'Brutal Life of our Women Convicts Unearthed', *Mercury*, 4 January 1997.
4 Information provided by Australian National Gallery.
5 *The Heritage of Australia: The Illustrated History of the National Estate*, Macmillan, Melbourne, 1981, 7/46.
6 Ibid. 7/10–11; K. R. von Stieglitz in *The History of Bothwell and its Early Settlers at the Clyde*, Telegraph Printery, Launceston, 1958, refers to the early presence of Edward Lord's cattle in the area and the role of Charles Rowcroft as a pioneer settler. He also mentions that Mrs Lord was living at the Priory at the time of her death 'during her husband's absence in England' (p. 79).
7 *The Heritage of Australia*, 8/49.
8 See Ashton and Rosen, *Eagle Farm*.
9 *The Heritage of Australia*, 2/52, 2/51, 2/56–7.
10 Joan Kerr, introduction to Kerr, *Out of Sight, Out of Mind*, p. 3; see also

Tim Bonyhady, *Images in Opposition, Australian Landscape Painting 1891–1890*, Oxford University Press, Melbourne, pp. 42–5.

11   Proudfoot et al., *Australia's First Government House*, pp. 95–6.

12   *The Heritage of Australia*, 7/56; Rayner, *Historical Survey of the Female Factory Historic Site, Cascades*; Scripps and Hudspeth, *The Female Factory Historic Site*.

13   Bonyhady, *Images in Opposition*, p. 74.

14   National Parks and Widlife Service, Tasmania, *Ross Female Factory*, Hobart, n.d.; Scripps and Clark, *The Ross Female Factory*.

15   Scripps and Clark, p. 10.

16   Ibid. pp. 11–12.

17   Michael Pearson and Duncan Marshall, *Study of World Heritage Values: Convict Places*, for the Department of the Environment, Sport and Territories, 20 December 1995; Australia ICOMOS, *Report on an Expert Workshop: Australia's Convict Places and World Heritage Values*, October 1996.

INDEX

Aborigines, 43, 45, 101–2, 202, 215, 219, 235–6, 246, 249
abortion, 86, 136
Alford, Katrina, 36, 42, 45
Anley, Charlotte, 117, 125
Archer, John Lee, 247
Arthur, Lieutenant-Governor Sir George, 19–20, 27–8, 64, 69, 85, 98, 114, 118–19, 123, 146
assignment, viii–xi, 15, 50, 59, 63, 65–102, 115, 117, 125, 127, 132, 134–8, 142–3, 162, 164, 213, 230, 233, 236; manipulation of, viii, 54, 83–9, 93, 96, 101, 143, 175, 233; see also employment of women; masters
Atkinson, Alan, 231
Ayton, John, 201–4

Balmain, Dr William, 207
Barracks, Hyde Park (Sydney), 78, 245, 249
Barret-Ducrocq, Françoise, 161
Bathurst, Lord Henry, 3, 12
Batman, John, 123
Bedford, Revd, 140, 149, 190
behaviour: colonial offences, 79–83, 90, 101, 233; contemporary opinion, x, 34, 37, 39–41, 58–61, 72–4, 81–2, 108, 141–3, 157–8, 163, 204–5, 210–12; historians' views, x, 33–4, 37–41, 58, 81,

141–2, 157–8, 163, 184–5, 204, 209–11; see also convict women; prostitution; resistance; sexuality
Bentham, Jeremy, 110
Benthamite influence, 179
Bigge, Commissioner J. T., 3
Bigge Report, 10, 50, 66, 75
Bisdee, Edward, 218
Bligh, Governor William, 1, 6, 13–14, 77
Bonyhady, Tim, 247
Boswell, James, 237
Bourke, Governor Sir Richard, 66–7, 79, 117
Bowen, Lieutenant John, 4, 61
Bowman, James, 21
Brice, Constable, 149–51
Brown, Margaret, 217–19, 222
Brown, Simon, 217–19, 222
Browne, Revd, 204
Byrne, Paula, 47, 80, 82, 95–6, 205

Cascades (Hobart), see female factories
Chadwick, Edwin, 56
child bearing, 7, 10, 14–16, 220, 236; 'good mothers', 42, 236; reproduction, 41–4, 94–5; see also abortion; pregnancy
children, ix, 24–8, 43–4, 53–4, 73, 199, 212; and institutions, 118–19, 124, 135–6; maintenance of, 2, 10, 22, 28, 77, 229, 232–3, 239–40;

INDEX

Risley, Isabella, 217
Risley, Maria; *see* Lord, Maria
Robinson, Francis, 181
Robinson, Portia, 33, 39–40, 45–6, 74,
   184, 209, 223, 224
Robson, L. L. (Lloyd), 12, 23–5, 32–3,
   35, 41, 52–4, 57, 185–6, 204, 209
Ross, Lieutenant-Governor Robert, 66
Rowcroft, Charles, 17–22, 243
Rowcroft, Horatio, 20
Ryan, Lyndall, 50, 64–5, 69

Salt, Annette, 116
Saunders, Kay, 45
Scott, Thomas, 200, 203
Select Committee on Transportation
   (1812), 4, 72
self-esteem, 40, 89, 115–16
sexual: codes, 161–3, 210; exploitation,
   29, 33, 40–1, 43–4, 59–60, 76–8,
   80, 83–6, 102, 123, 184, 203, 238;
   restraint, 159–64, 180
sexuality, 47, 58, 96, 142, 152, 157–83
   passim, 205; asexuality, 158, 163;
   male sexuality, 42–3, 157, 162; and
   medical opinion, 180–1; observation
   of, 165–6; suspicion of, 174–9, 205;
   see also lesbian behaviour
Shaw, A. G. L., 32–3, 35, 41, 50
Shaw, Francis, 202
ships, *see* convict ships
Showalter, Elaine, 181
silence, 65, 68–9, 103–4, 110, 117,
   125, 128–31
Sladden, Lieutenant William, 5
Small, Rebecca, 123
Smith, Babette, 48, 136, 221, 223,
   231–2, 233
Snowden, Diane, 13
Sorell, Lieutenant-Governor William,
   75–6, 109
Spence, Dr James, 200–3
Spode, Josiah, 90–2, 98, 113, 146–7
Spode, Mrs, 90–2

statistics, 35, 49, 51–3, 56–7, 62,
   185–6; age, 52–3; country of origin,
   52; criminal background, 56–8;
   marital status, 53; skills, 52, 54–6
Stanley, Lord Edward, 67, 99, 125, 175
Stone, Lawrence, 160
Stuart, Robert Pringle, 147, 165
Sturma, Michael, 41, 162, 210
Summers, Anne, 31, 33, 40, 42, 45,
   211
surveillance, 59, 71, 85, 103, 111, 153,
   164, 167, 174–80, 205, 212, 249

Tardif, Phillip, 53
Taylor, Richard, 214–17, 222–4
Taylor, Mrs, 217, 234
Tench, Watkin, 72, 75, 153
Thompson, John, 15
Thompson, James Bruce, 178
Thomson, James, 19–20
trafficking, 87, 134–9, 145, 171, 175
Turnbull, Dr Adam, 98, 177

Vestal, 212
violence, ix, 25, 46, 64, 84–5, 97–8,
   106, 155–6, 195–7, 204–8, 212,
   230, 232, 237–9; between women,
   143–4, 155, 169–74; rape, 205–8
voyages, 51, 58–63, 151–2, 242–3;
   matrons, 58–60, 151, 242, surgeon
   superintendents, 58–60, 167–8, 177,
   187

Wallace, Hamilton, 202
welfare, 102, 209; women and the
   state, viii–ix, 43–5, 47, 54, 61,
   96–8, 101–2, 234, 236–40, 249–50
Wentworth, D'Arcy, 21
West, Revd John, 5, 62, 76, 125, 128,
   179
Wiener, Martin, 182
women, *see* convict women
Wright, Henry, 207